C-1785   CAREER EXAMINATION SERIES

This is your
PASSBOOK for...

Human Resources Aide

Test Preparation Study Guide
Questions & Answers

COPYRIGHT NOTICE

This book is SOLELY intended for, is sold ONLY to, and its use is RESTRICTED to individual, bona fide applicants or candidates who qualify by virtue of having seriously filed applications for appropriate license, certificate, professional and/or promotional advancement, higher school matriculation, scholarship, or other legitimate requirements of education and/or governmental authorities.

This book is NOT intended for use, class instruction, tutoring, training, duplication, copying, reprinting, excerption, or adaptation, etc., by:

1) Other publishers
2) Proprietors and/or Instructors of "Coaching" and/or Preparatory Courses
3) Personnel and/or Training Divisions of commercial, industrial, and governmental organizations
4) Schools, colleges, or universities and/or their departments and staffs, including teachers and other personnel
5) Testing Agencies or Bureaus
6) Study groups which seek by the purchase of a single volume to copy and/or duplicate and/or adapt this material for use by the group as a whole without having purchased individual volumes for each of the members of the group
7) Et al.

Such persons would be in violation of appropriate Federal and State statutes.

PROVISION OF LICENSING AGREEMENTS – Recognized educational, commercial, industrial, and governmental institutions and organizations, and others legitimately engaged in educational pursuits, including training, testing, and measurement activities, may address request for a licensing agreement to the copyright owners, who will determine whether, and under what conditions, including fees and charges, the materials in this book may be used them. In other words, a licensing facility exists for the legitimate use of the material in this book on other than an individual basis. However, it is asseverated and affirmed here that the material in this book CANNOT be used without the receipt of the express permission of such a licensing agreement from the Publishers. Inquiries re licensing should be addressed to the company, attention rights and permissions department.

All rights reserved, including the right of reproduction in whole or in part, in any form or by any means, electronic or mechanical, including photocopying, recording, or by any information storage and retrieval system, without permission in writing from the Publisher.

Copyright © 2025 by
National Learning Corporation

212 Michael Drive, Syosset, NY 11791
(516) 921-8888 • www.passbooks.com
E-mail: info@passbooks.com

PASSBOOK® SERIES

THE *PASSBOOK® SERIES* has been created to prepare applicants and candidates for the ultimate academic battlefield – the examination room.

At some time in our lives, each and every one of us may be required to take an examination – for validation, matriculation, admission, qualification, registration, certification, or licensure.

Based on the assumption that every applicant or candidate has met the basic formal educational standards, has taken the required number of courses, and read the necessary texts, the *PASSBOOK® SERIES* furnishes the one special preparation which may assure passing with confidence, instead of failing with insecurity. Examination questions – together with answers – are furnished as the basic vehicle for study so that the mysteries of the examination and its compounding difficulties may be eliminated or diminished by a sure method.

This book is meant to help you pass your examination provided that you qualify and are serious in your objective.

The entire field is reviewed through the huge store of content information which is succinctly presented through a provocative and challenging approach – the question-and-answer method.

A climate of success is established by furnishing the correct answers at the end of each test.

You soon learn to recognize types of questions, forms of questions, and patterns of questioning. You may even begin to anticipate expected outcomes.

You perceive that many questions are repeated or adapted so that you can gain acute insights, which may enable you to score many sure points.

You learn how to confront new questions, or types of questions, and to attack them confidently and work out the correct answers.

You note objectives and emphases, and recognize pitfalls and dangers, so that you may make positive educational adjustments.

Moreover, you are kept fully informed in relation to new concepts, methods, practices, and directions in the field.

You discover that you are actually taking the examination all the time: you are preparing for the examination by "taking" an examination, not by reading extraneous and/or supererogatory textbooks.

In short, this PASSBOOK®, used directedly, should be an important factor in helping you to pass your test.

HUMAN RESOURCES AIDE

DUTIES
Performs clerical and assists paraprofessionals in entering payroll and personnel data into the computer; reviews and verifies information on time entry forms prior to entry; verifies changes in hours and hourly rates, leave balances, vacation advances and adjustments to base salaries; reviews for accuracy and completeness information contained on personnel change forms and payroll change forms submitted by county departments; consults with departmental payroll clerks to assure the proper submission of personnel and payroll data; researches and resolves problems resulting from inaccurate and/or incomplete information on time entry forms and relate documents and reviews the outcomes with the Human Resources Coordinator; files and distributes all payroll and personnel documents received from county departments; queries system to produce routine and special request management reports; assists benefits representative in data management; and performs related duties.

SCOPE OF THE EXAMINATION
The <u>written test</u> will cover knowledge, skills and/or abilities in such areas as:

1. Arithmetic computation;
2. Coding/decoding information;
3. Office record keeping;
4. Preparing written material; and
5. Understanding and interpreting written material.

HOW TO TAKE A TEST

I. YOU MUST PASS AN EXAMINATION

A. *WHAT EVERY CANDIDATE SHOULD KNOW*

Examination applicants often ask us for help in preparing for the written test. What can I study in advance? What kinds of questions will be asked? How will the test be given? How will the papers be graded?

As an applicant for a civil service examination, you may be wondering about some of these things. Our purpose here is to suggest effective methods of advance study and to describe civil service examinations.

Your chances for success on this examination can be increased if you know how to prepare. Those "pre-examination jitters" can be reduced if you know what to expect. You can even experience an adventure in good citizenship if you know why civil service exams are given.

B. *WHY ARE CIVIL SERVICE EXAMINATIONS GIVEN?*

Civil service examinations are important to you in two ways. As a citizen, you want public jobs filled by employees who know how to do their work. As a job seeker, you want a fair chance to compete for that job on an equal footing with other candidates. The best-known means of accomplishing this two-fold goal is the competitive examination.

Exams are widely publicized throughout the nation. They may be administered for jobs in federal, state, city, municipal, town or village governments or agencies.

Any citizen may apply, with some limitations, such as the age or residence of applicants. Your experience and education may be reviewed to see whether you meet the requirements for the particular examination. When these requirements exist, they are reasonable and applied consistently to all applicants. Thus, a competitive examination may cause you some uneasiness now, but it is your privilege and safeguard.

C. *HOW ARE CIVIL SERVICE EXAMS DEVELOPED?*

Examinations are carefully written by trained technicians who are specialists in the field known as "psychological measurement," in consultation with recognized authorities in the field of work that the test will cover. These experts recommend the subject matter areas or skills to be tested; only those knowledges or skills important to your success on the job are included. The most reliable books and source materials available are used as references. Together, the experts and technicians judge the difficulty level of the questions.

Test technicians know how to phrase questions so that the problem is clearly stated. Their ethics do not permit "trick" or "catch" questions. Questions may have been tried out on sample groups, or subjected to statistical analysis, to determine their usefulness.

Written tests are often used in combination with performance tests, ratings of training and experience, and oral interviews. All of these measures combine to form the best-known means of finding the right person for the right job.

II. HOW TO PASS THE WRITTEN TEST

A. NATURE OF THE EXAMINATION

To prepare intelligently for civil service examinations, you should know how they differ from school examinations you have taken. In school you were assigned certain definite pages to read or subjects to cover. The examination questions were quite detailed and usually emphasized memory. Civil service exams, on the other hand, try to discover your present ability to perform the duties of a position, plus your potentiality to learn these duties. In other words, a civil service exam attempts to predict how successful you will be. Questions cover such a broad area that they cannot be as minute and detailed as school exam questions.

In the public service similar kinds of work, or positions, are grouped together in one "class." This process is known as *position-classification*. All the positions in a class are paid according to the salary range for that class. One class title covers all of these positions, and they are all tested by the same examination.

B. FOUR BASIC STEPS

1) Study the announcement

How, then, can you know what subjects to study? Our best answer is: "Learn as much as possible about the class of positions for which you've applied." The exam will test the knowledge, skills and abilities needed to do the work.

Your most valuable source of information about the position you want is the official exam announcement. This announcement lists the training and experience qualifications. Check these standards and apply only if you come reasonably close to meeting them.

The brief description of the position in the examination announcement offers some clues to the subjects which will be tested. Think about the job itself. Review the duties in your mind. Can you perform them, or are there some in which you are rusty? Fill in the blank spots in your preparation.

Many jurisdictions preview the written test in the exam announcement by including a section called "Knowledge and Abilities Required," "Scope of the Examination," or some similar heading. Here you will find out specifically what fields will be tested.

2) Review your own background

Once you learn in general what the position is all about, and what you need to know to do the work, ask yourself which subjects you already know fairly well and which need improvement. You may wonder whether to concentrate on improving your strong areas or on building some background in your fields of weakness. When the announcement has specified "some knowledge" or "considerable knowledge," or has used adjectives like "beginning principles of…" or "advanced … methods," you can get a clue as to the number and difficulty of questions to be asked in any given field. More questions, and hence broader coverage, would be included for those subjects which are more important in the work. Now weigh your strengths and weaknesses against the job requirements and prepare accordingly.

3) Determine the level of the position

Another way to tell how intensively you should prepare is to understand the level of the job for which you are applying. Is it the entering level? In other words, is this the position in which beginners in a field of work are hired? Or is it an intermediate or advanced level? Sometimes this is indicated by such words as "Junior" or "Senior" in the class title. Other jurisdictions use Roman numerals to designate the level – Clerk I, Clerk II, for example. The word "Supervisor" sometimes appears in the title. If the level is not indicated by the title, check the description of duties. Will you be working under very close supervision, or will you have responsibility for independent decisions in this work?

4) Choose appropriate study materials

Now that you know the subjects to be examined and the relative amount of each subject to be covered, you can choose suitable study materials. For beginning level jobs, or even advanced ones, if you have a pronounced weakness in some aspect of your training, read a modern, standard textbook in that field. Be sure it is up to date and has general coverage. Such books are normally available at your library, and the librarian will be glad to help you locate one. For entry-level positions, questions of appropriate difficulty are chosen – neither highly advanced questions, nor those too simple. Such questions require careful thought but not advanced training.

If the position for which you are applying is technical or advanced, you will read more advanced, specialized material. If you are already familiar with the basic principles of your field, elementary textbooks would waste your time. Concentrate on advanced textbooks and technical periodicals. Think through the concepts and review difficult problems in your field.

These are all general sources. You can get more ideas on your own initiative, following these leads. For example, training manuals and publications of the government agency which employs workers in your field can be useful, particularly for technical and professional positions. A letter or visit to the government department involved may result in more specific study suggestions, and certainly will provide you with a more definite idea of the exact nature of the position you are seeking.

III. KINDS OF TESTS

Tests are used for purposes other than measuring knowledge and ability to perform specified duties. For some positions, it is equally important to test ability to make adjustments to new situations or to profit from training. In others, basic mental abilities not dependent on information are essential. Questions which test these things may not appear as pertinent to the duties of the position as those which test for knowledge and information. Yet they are often highly important parts of a fair examination. For very general questions, it is almost impossible to help you direct your study efforts. What we can do is to point out some of the more common of these general abilities needed in public service positions and describe some typical questions.

1) General information

Broad, general information has been found useful for predicting job success in some kinds of work. This is tested in a variety of ways, from vocabulary lists to questions about current events. Basic background in some field of work, such as sociology or economics, may be sampled in a group of questions. Often these are principles which have become familiar to most persons through exposure rather than through formal training. It is difficult to advise you how to study for these questions; being alert to the world around you is our best suggestion.

2) Verbal ability

An example of an ability needed in many positions is verbal or language ability. Verbal ability is, in brief, the ability to use and understand words. Vocabulary and grammar tests are typical measures of this ability. Reading comprehension or paragraph interpretation questions are common in many kinds of civil service tests. You are given a paragraph of written material and asked to find its central meaning.

3) Numerical ability

Number skills can be tested by the familiar arithmetic problem, by checking paired lists of numbers to see which are alike and which are different, or by interpreting charts and graphs. In the latter test, a graph may be printed in the test booklet which you are asked to use as the basis for answering questions.

4) Observation

A popular test for law-enforcement positions is the observation test. A picture is shown to you for several minutes, then taken away. Questions about the picture test your ability to observe both details and larger elements.

5) Following directions

In many positions in the public service, the employee must be able to carry out written instructions dependably and accurately. You may be given a chart with several columns, each column listing a variety of information. The questions require you to carry out directions involving the information given in the chart.

6) Skills and aptitudes

Performance tests effectively measure some manual skills and aptitudes. When the skill is one in which you are trained, such as typing or shorthand, you can practice. These tests are often very much like those given in business school or high school courses. For many of the other skills and aptitudes, however, no short-time preparation can be made. Skills and abilities natural to you or that you have developed throughout your lifetime are being tested.

Many of the general questions just described provide all the data needed to answer the questions and ask you to use your reasoning ability to find the answers. Your best preparation for these tests, as well as for tests of facts and ideas, is to be at your physical and mental best. You, no doubt, have your own methods of getting into an exam-taking mood and keeping "in shape." The next section lists some ideas on this subject.

IV. KINDS OF QUESTIONS

Only rarely is the "essay" question, which you answer in narrative form, used in civil service tests. Civil service tests are usually of the short-answer type. Full instructions for answering these questions will be given to you at the examination. But in case this is your first experience with short-answer questions and separate answer sheets, here is what you need to know:

1) Multiple-choice Questions

Most popular of the short-answer questions is the "multiple choice" or "best answer" question. It can be used, for example, to test for factual knowledge, ability to solve problems or judgment in meeting situations found at work.

A multiple-choice question is normally one of three types—
- It can begin with an incomplete statement followed by several possible endings. You are to find the one ending which *best* completes the statement, although some of the others may not be entirely wrong.
- It can also be a complete statement in the form of a question which is answered by choosing one of the statements listed.

- It can be in the form of a problem – again you select the best answer.

Here is an example of a multiple-choice question with a discussion which should give you some clues as to the method for choosing the right answer:

When an employee has a complaint about his assignment, the action which will *best* help him overcome his difficulty is to
    A. discuss his difficulty with his coworkers
    B. take the problem to the head of the organization
    C. take the problem to the person who gave him the assignment
    D. say nothing to anyone about his complaint

In answering this question, you should study each of the choices to find which is best. Consider choice "A" – Certainly an employee may discuss his complaint with fellow employees, but no change or improvement can result, and the complaint remains unresolved. Choice "B" is a poor choice since the head of the organization probably does not know what assignment you have been given, and taking your problem to him is known as "going over the head" of the supervisor. The supervisor, or person who made the assignment, is the person who can clarify it or correct any injustice. Choice "C" is, therefore, correct. To say nothing, as in choice "D," is unwise. Supervisors have and interest in knowing the problems employees are facing, and the employee is seeking a solution to his problem.

2) True/False Questions

The "true/false" or "right/wrong" form of question is sometimes used. Here a complete statement is given. Your job is to decide whether the statement is right or wrong.

SAMPLE: A roaming cell-phone call to a nearby city costs less than a non-roaming call to a distant city.

This statement is wrong, or false, since roaming calls are more expensive.
This is not a complete list of all possible question forms, although most of the others are variations of these common types. You will always get complete directions for answering questions. Be sure you understand *how* to mark your answers – ask questions until you do.

V. RECORDING YOUR ANSWERS

Computer terminals are used more and more today for many different kinds of exams.
For an examination with very few applicants, you may be told to record your answers in the test booklet itself. Separate answer sheets are much more common. If this separate answer sheet is to be scored by machine – and this is often the case – it is highly important that you mark your answers correctly in order to get credit.
An electronic scoring machine is often used in civil service offices because of the speed with which papers can be scored. Machine-scored answer sheets must be marked with a pencil, which will be given to you. This pencil has a high graphite content which responds to the electronic scoring machine. As a matter of fact, stray dots may register as answers, so do not let your pencil rest on the answer sheet while you are pondering the correct answer. Also, if your pencil lead breaks or is otherwise defective, ask for another.

Since the answer sheet will be dropped in a slot in the scoring machine, be careful not to bend the corners or get the paper crumpled.

The answer sheet normally has five vertical columns of numbers, with 30 numbers to a column. These numbers correspond to the question numbers in your test booklet. After each number, going across the page are four or five pairs of dotted lines. These short dotted lines have small letters or numbers above them. The first two pairs may also have a "T" or "F" above the letters. This indicates that the first two pairs only are to be used if the questions are of the true-false type. If the questions are multiple choice, disregard the "T" and "F" and pay attention only to the small letters or numbers.

Answer your questions in the manner of the sample that follows:

32. The largest city in the United States is
    A. Washington, D.C.
    B. New York City
    C. Chicago
    D. Detroit
    E. San Francisco

1) Choose the answer you think is best. (New York City is the largest, so "B" is correct.)
2) Find the row of dotted lines numbered the same as the question you are answering. (Find row number 32)
3) Find the pair of dotted lines corresponding to the answer. (Find the pair of lines under the mark "B.")
4) Make a solid black mark between the dotted lines.

VI. BEFORE THE TEST

Common sense will help you find procedures to follow to get ready for an examination. Too many of us, however, overlook these sensible measures. Indeed, nervousness and fatigue have been found to be the most serious reasons why applicants fail to do their best on civil service tests. Here is a list of reminders:

- Begin your preparation early – Don't wait until the last minute to go scurrying around for books and materials or to find out what the position is all about.
- Prepare continuously – An hour a night for a week is better than an all-night cram session. This has been definitely established. What is more, a night a week for a month will return better dividends than crowding your study into a shorter period of time.
- Locate the place of the exam – You have been sent a notice telling you when and where to report for the examination. If the location is in a different town or otherwise unfamiliar to you, it would be well to inquire the best route and learn something about the building.
- Relax the night before the test – Allow your mind to rest. Do not study at all that night. Plan some mild recreation or diversion; then go to bed early and get a good night's sleep.
- Get up early enough to make a leisurely trip to the place for the test – This way unforeseen events, traffic snarls, unfamiliar buildings, etc. will not upset you.
- Dress comfortably – A written test is not a fashion show. You will be known by number and not by name, so wear something comfortable.

- Leave excess paraphernalia at home – Shopping bags and odd bundles will get in your way. You need bring only the items mentioned in the official notice you received; usually everything you need is provided. Do not bring reference books to the exam. They will only confuse those last minutes and be taken away from you when in the test room.
- Arrive somewhat ahead of time – If because of transportation schedules you must get there very early, bring a newspaper or magazine to take your mind off yourself while waiting.
- Locate the examination room – When you have found the proper room, you will be directed to the seat or part of the room where you will sit. Sometimes you are given a sheet of instructions to read while you are waiting. Do not fill out any forms until you are told to do so; just read them and be prepared.
- Relax and prepare to listen to the instructions
- If you have any physical problem that may keep you from doing your best, be sure to tell the test administrator. If you are sick or in poor health, you really cannot do your best on the exam. You can come back and take the test some other time.

VII. AT THE TEST

The day of the test is here and you have the test booklet in your hand. The temptation to get going is very strong. Caution! There is more to success than knowing the right answers. You must know how to identify your papers and understand variations in the type of short-answer question used in this particular examination. Follow these suggestions for maximum results from your efforts:

1) Cooperate with the monitor

The test administrator has a duty to create a situation in which you can be as much at ease as possible. He will give instructions, tell you when to begin, check to see that you are marking your answer sheet correctly, and so on. He is not there to guard you, although he will see that your competitors do not take unfair advantage. He wants to help you do your best.

2) Listen to all instructions

Don't jump the gun! Wait until you understand all directions. In most civil service tests you get more time than you need to answer the questions. So don't be in a hurry. Read each word of instructions until you clearly understand the meaning. Study the examples, listen to all announcements and follow directions. Ask questions if you do not understand what to do.

3) Identify your papers

Civil service exams are usually identified by number only. You will be assigned a number; you must not put your name on your test papers. Be sure to copy your number correctly. Since more than one exam may be given, copy your exact examination title.

4) Plan your time

Unless you are told that a test is a "speed" or "rate of work" test, speed itself is usually not important. Time enough to answer all the questions will be provided, but this does not mean that you have all day. An overall time limit has been set. Divide the total time (in minutes) by the number of questions to determine the approximate time you have for each question.

5) Do not linger over difficult questions

If you come across a difficult question, mark it with a paper clip (useful to have along) and come back to it when you have been through the booklet. One caution if you do this – be sure to skip a number on your answer sheet as well. Check often to be sure that you have not lost your place and that you are marking in the row numbered the same as the question you are answering.

6) Read the questions

Be sure you know what the question asks! Many capable people are unsuccessful because they failed to *read* the questions correctly.

7) Answer all questions

Unless you have been instructed that a penalty will be deducted for incorrect answers, it is better to guess than to omit a question.

8) Speed tests

It is often better NOT to guess on speed tests. It has been found that on timed tests people are tempted to spend the last few seconds before time is called in marking answers at random – without even reading them – in the hope of picking up a few extra points. To discourage this practice, the instructions may warn you that your score will be "corrected" for guessing. That is, a penalty will be applied. The incorrect answers will be deducted from the correct ones, or some other penalty formula will be used.

9) Review your answers

If you finish before time is called, go back to the questions you guessed or omitted to give them further thought. Review other answers if you have time.

10) Return your test materials

If you are ready to leave before others have finished or time is called, take ALL your materials to the monitor and leave quietly. Never take any test material with you. The monitor can discover whose papers are not complete, and taking a test booklet may be grounds for disqualification.

VIII. EXAMINATION TECHNIQUES

1) Read the general instructions carefully. These are usually printed on the first page of the exam booklet. As a rule, these instructions refer to the timing of the examination; the fact that you should not start work until the signal and must stop work at a signal, etc. If there are any *special* instructions, such as a choice of questions to be answered, make sure that you note this instruction carefully.

2) When you are ready to start work on the examination, that is as soon as the signal has been given, read the instructions to each question booklet, underline any key words or phrases, such as *least, best, outline, describe* and the like. In this way you will tend to answer as requested rather than discover on reviewing your paper that you *listed without describing*, that you selected the *worst* choice rather than the *best* choice, etc.

3) If the examination is of the objective or multiple-choice type – that is, each question will also give a series of possible answers: A, B, C or D, and you are called upon to select the best answer and write the letter next to that answer on your answer paper – it is advisable to start answering each question in turn. There may be anywhere from 50 to 100 such questions in the three or four hours allotted and you can see how much time would be taken if you read through all the questions before beginning to answer any. Furthermore, if you come across a question or group of questions which you know would be difficult to answer, it would undoubtedly affect your handling of all the other questions.

4) If the examination is of the essay type and contains but a few questions, it is a moot point as to whether you should read all the questions before starting to answer any one. Of course, if you are given a choice – say five out of seven and the like – then it is essential to read all the questions so you can eliminate the two that are most difficult. If, however, you are asked to answer all the questions, there may be danger in trying to answer the easiest one first because you may find that you will spend too much time on it. The best technique is to answer the first question, then proceed to the second, etc.

5) Time your answers. Before the exam begins, write down the time it started, then add the time allowed for the examination and write down the time it must be completed, then divide the time available somewhat as follows:
    - If 3-1/2 hours are allowed, that would be 210 minutes. If you have 80 objective-type questions, that would be an average of 2-1/2 minutes per question. Allow yourself no more than 2 minutes per question, or a total of 160 minutes, which will permit about 50 minutes to review.
    - If for the time allotment of 210 minutes there are 7 essay questions to answer, that would average about 30 minutes a question. Give yourself only 25 minutes per question so that you have about 35 minutes to review.

6) The most important instruction is to *read each question* and make sure you know what is wanted. The second most important instruction is to *time yourself properly* so that you answer every question. The third most important instruction is to *answer every question*. Guess if you have to but include something for each question. Remember that you will receive no credit for a blank and will probably receive some credit if you write something in answer to an essay question. If you guess a letter – say "B" for a multiple-choice question – you may have guessed right. If you leave a blank as an answer to a multiple-choice question, the examiners may respect your feelings but it will not add a point to your score. Some exams may penalize you for wrong answers, so in such cases *only*, you may not want to guess unless you have some basis for your answer.

7) Suggestions
    a. Objective-type questions
        1. Examine the question booklet for proper sequence of pages and questions
        2. Read all instructions carefully
        3. Skip any question which seems too difficult; return to it after all other questions have been answered
        4. Apportion your time properly; do not spend too much time on any single question or group of questions

5. Note and underline key words – *all, most, fewest, least, best, worst, same, opposite,* etc.
6. Pay particular attention to negatives
7. Note unusual option, e.g., unduly long, short, complex, different or similar in content to the body of the question
8. Observe the use of "hedging" words – *probably, may, most likely,* etc.
9. Make sure that your answer is put next to the same number as the question
10. Do not second-guess unless you have good reason to believe the second answer is definitely more correct
11. Cross out original answer if you decide another answer is more accurate; do not erase until you are ready to hand your paper in
12. Answer all questions; guess unless instructed otherwise
13. Leave time for review

b. Essay questions
1. Read each question carefully
2. Determine exactly what is wanted. Underline key words or phrases.
3. Decide on outline or paragraph answer
4. Include many different points and elements unless asked to develop any one or two points or elements
5. Show impartiality by giving pros and cons unless directed to select one side only
6. Make and write down any assumptions you find necessary to answer the questions
7. Watch your English, grammar, punctuation and choice of words
8. Time your answers; don't crowd material

8) Answering the essay question

Most essay questions can be answered by framing the specific response around several key words or ideas. Here are a few such key words or ideas:

M's: manpower, materials, methods, money, management
P's: purpose, program, policy, plan, procedure, practice, problems, pitfalls, personnel, public relations

a. Six basic steps in handling problems:
1. Preliminary plan and background development
2. Collect information, data and facts
3. Analyze and interpret information, data and facts
4. Analyze and develop solutions as well as make recommendations
5. Prepare report and sell recommendations
6. Install recommendations and follow up effectiveness

b. Pitfalls to avoid
1. *Taking things for granted* – A statement of the situation does not necessarily imply that each of the elements is necessarily true; for example, a complaint may be invalid and biased so that all that can be taken for granted is that a complaint has been registered

2. *Considering only one side of a situation* – Wherever possible, indicate several alternatives and then point out the reasons you selected the best one
3. *Failing to indicate follow up* – Whenever your answer indicates action on your part, make certain that you will take proper follow-up action to see how successful your recommendations, procedures or actions turn out to be
4. *Taking too long in answering any single question* – Remember to time your answers properly

IX. AFTER THE TEST

Scoring procedures differ in detail among civil service jurisdictions although the general principles are the same. Whether the papers are hand-scored or graded by machine we have described, they are nearly always graded by number. That is, the person who marks the paper knows only the number – never the name – of the applicant. Not until all the papers have been graded will they be matched with names. If other tests, such as training and experience or oral interview ratings have been given, scores will be combined. Different parts of the examination usually have different weights. For example, the written test might count 60 percent of the final grade, and a rating of training and experience 40 percent. In many jurisdictions, veterans will have a certain number of points added to their grades.

After the final grade has been determined, the names are placed in grade order and an eligible list is established. There are various methods for resolving ties between those who get the same final grade – probably the most common is to place first the name of the person whose application was received first. Job offers are made from the eligible list in the order the names appear on it. You will be notified of your grade and your rank as soon as all these computations have been made. This will be done as rapidly as possible.

People who are found to meet the requirements in the announcement are called "eligibles." Their names are put on a list of eligible candidates. An eligible's chances of getting a job depend on how high he stands on this list and how fast agencies are filling jobs from the list.

When a job is to be filled from a list of eligibles, the agency asks for the names of people on the list of eligibles for that job. When the civil service commission receives this request, it sends to the agency the names of the three people highest on this list. Or, if the job to be filled has specialized requirements, the office sends the agency the names of the top three persons who meet these requirements from the general list.

The appointing officer makes a choice from among the three people whose names were sent to him. If the selected person accepts the appointment, the names of the others are put back on the list to be considered for future openings.

That is the rule in hiring from all kinds of eligible lists, whether they are for typist, carpenter, chemist, or something else. For every vacancy, the appointing officer has his choice of any one of the top three eligibles on the list. This explains why the person whose name is on top of the list sometimes does not get an appointment when some of the persons lower on the list do. If the appointing officer chooses the second or third eligible, the No. 1 eligible does not get a job at once, but stays on the list until he is appointed or the list is terminated.

X. HOW TO PASS THE INTERVIEW TEST

The examination for which you applied requires an oral interview test. You have already taken the written test and you are now being called for the interview test – the final part of the formal examination.

You may think that it is not possible to prepare for an interview test and that there are no procedures to follow during an interview. Our purpose is to point out some things you can do in advance that will help you and some good rules to follow and pitfalls to avoid while you are being interviewed.

What is an interview supposed to test?

The written examination is designed to test the technical knowledge and competence of the candidate; the oral is designed to evaluate intangible qualities, not readily measured otherwise, and to establish a list showing the relative fitness of each candidate – as measured against his competitors – for the position sought. Scoring is not on the basis of "right" and "wrong," but on a sliding scale of values ranging from "not passable" to "outstanding." As a matter of fact, it is possible to achieve a relatively low score without a single "incorrect" answer because of evident weakness in the qualities being measured.

Occasionally, an examination may consist entirely of an oral test – either an individual or a group oral. In such cases, information is sought concerning the technical knowledges and abilities of the candidate, since there has been no written examination for this purpose. More commonly, however, an oral test is used to supplement a written examination.

Who conducts interviews?

The composition of oral boards varies among different jurisdictions. In nearly all, a representative of the personnel department serves as chairman. One of the members of the board may be a representative of the department in which the candidate would work. In some cases, "outside experts" are used, and, frequently, a businessman or some other representative of the general public is asked to serve. Labor and management or other special groups may be represented. The aim is to secure the services of experts in the appropriate field.

However the board is composed, it is a good idea (and not at all improper or unethical) to ascertain in advance of the interview who the members are and what groups they represent. When you are introduced to them, you will have some idea of their backgrounds and interests, and at least you will not stutter and stammer over their names.

What should be done before the interview?

While knowledge about the board members is useful and takes some of the surprise element out of the interview, there is other preparation which is more substantive. It *is* possible to prepare for an oral interview – in several ways:

1) Keep a copy of your application and review it carefully before the interview

This may be the only document before the oral board, and the starting point of the interview. Know what education and experience you have listed there, and the sequence and dates of all of it. Sometimes the board will ask you to review the highlights of your experience for them; you should not have to hem and haw doing it.

2) Study the class specification and the examination announcement

Usually, the oral board has one or both of these to guide them. The qualities, characteristics or knowledges required by the position sought are stated in these documents. They offer valuable clues as to the nature of the oral interview. For example, if the job involves supervisory responsibilities, the announcement will usually indicate that knowledge of modern supervisory methods and the qualifications of the candidate as a supervisor will be tested. If so, you can expect such questions, frequently in the form of a hypothetical situation which you are expected to solve. NEVER go into an oral without knowledge of the duties and responsibilities of the job you seek.

3) Think through each qualification required

Try to visualize the kind of questions you would ask if you were a board member. How well could you answer them? Try especially to appraise your own knowledge and background in each area, *measured against the job sought*, and identify any areas in which you are weak. Be critical and realistic – do not flatter yourself.

4) Do some general reading in areas in which you feel you may be weak

For example, if the job involves supervision and your past experience has NOT, some general reading in supervisory methods and practices, particularly in the field of human relations, might be useful. Do NOT study agency procedures or detailed manuals. The oral board will be testing your understanding and capacity, not your memory.

5) Get a good night's sleep and watch your general health and mental attitude

You will want a clear head at the interview. Take care of a cold or any other minor ailment, and of course, no hangovers.

What should be done on the day of the interview?

Now comes the day of the interview itself. Give yourself plenty of time to get there. Plan to arrive somewhat ahead of the scheduled time, particularly if your appointment is in the fore part of the day. If a previous candidate fails to appear, the board might be ready for you a bit early. By early afternoon an oral board is almost invariably behind schedule if there are many candidates, and you may have to wait. Take along a book or magazine to read, or your application to review, but leave any extraneous material in the waiting room when you go in for your interview. In any event, relax and compose yourself.

The matter of dress is important. The board is forming impressions about you – from your experience, your manners, your attitude, and your appearance. Give your personal appearance careful attention. Dress your best, but not your flashiest. Choose conservative, appropriate clothing, and be sure it is immaculate. This is a business interview, and your appearance should indicate that you regard it as such. Besides, being well groomed and properly dressed will help boost your confidence.

Sooner or later, someone will call your name and escort you into the interview room. *This is it.* From here on you are on your own. It is too late for any more preparation. But remember, you asked for this opportunity to prove your fitness, and you are here because your request was granted.

What happens when you go in?

The usual sequence of events will be as follows: The clerk (who is often the board stenographer) will introduce you to the chairman of the oral board, who will introduce you to the other members of the board. Acknowledge the introductions before you sit down. Do not be surprised if you find a microphone facing you or a stenotypist sitting by. Oral interviews are usually recorded in the event of an appeal or other review.

Usually the chairman of the board will open the interview by reviewing the highlights of your education and work experience from your application – primarily for the benefit of the other members of the board, as well as to get the material into the record. Do not interrupt or comment unless there is an error or significant misinterpretation; if that is the case, do not hesitate. But do not quibble about insignificant matters. Also, he will usually ask you some question about your education, experience or your present job – partly to get you to start talking and to establish the interviewing "rapport." He may start the actual questioning, or turn it over to one of the other members. Frequently, each member undertakes the questioning on a particular area, one in which he is perhaps most competent, so you can expect each member to participate in the examination. Because time is limited, you may also expect some rather abrupt switches in the direction the questioning takes, so do not be upset by it. Normally, a board member will not pursue a single line of questioning unless he discovers a particular strength or weakness.

After each member has participated, the chairman will usually ask whether any member has any further questions, then will ask you if you have anything you wish to add. Unless you are expecting this question, it may floor you. Worse, it may start you off on an extended, extemporaneous speech. The board is not usually seeking more information. The question is principally to offer you a last opportunity to present further qualifications or to indicate that you have nothing to add. So, if you feel that a significant qualification or characteristic has been overlooked, it is proper to point it out in a sentence or so. Do not compliment the board on the thoroughness of their examination – they have been sketchy, and you know it. If you wish, merely say, "No thank you, I have nothing further to add." This is a point where you can "talk yourself out" of a good impression or fail to present an important bit of information. Remember, *you close the interview yourself.*

The chairman will then say, "That is all, Mr. _____, thank you." Do not be startled; the interview is over, and quicker than you think. Thank him, gather your belongings and take your leave. Save your sigh of relief for the other side of the door.

How to put your best foot forward

Throughout this entire process, you may feel that the board individually and collectively is trying to pierce your defenses, seek out your hidden weaknesses and embarrass and confuse you. Actually, this is not true. They are obliged to make an appraisal of your qualifications for the job you are seeking, and they want to see you in your best light. Remember, they must interview all candidates and a non-cooperative candidate may become a failure in spite of their best efforts to bring out his qualifications. Here are 15 suggestions that will help you:

1) Be natural – Keep your attitude confident, not cocky

If you are not confident that you can do the job, do not expect the board to be. Do not apologize for your weaknesses, try to bring out your strong points. The board is interested in a positive, not negative, presentation. Cockiness will antagonize any board member and make him wonder if you are covering up a weakness by a false show of strength.

2) Get comfortable, but don't lounge or sprawl

Sit erectly but not stiffly. A careless posture may lead the board to conclude that you are careless in other things, or at least that you are not impressed by the importance of the occasion. Either conclusion is natural, even if incorrect. Do not fuss with your clothing, a pencil or an ashtray. Your hands may occasionally be useful to emphasize a point; do not let them become a point of distraction.

3) Do not wisecrack or make small talk

This is a serious situation, and your attitude should show that you consider it as such. Further, the time of the board is limited – they do not want to waste it, and neither should you.

4) Do not exaggerate your experience or abilities

In the first place, from information in the application or other interviews and sources, the board may know more about you than you think. Secondly, you probably will not get away with it. An experienced board is rather adept at spotting such a situation, so do not take the chance.

5) If you know a board member, do not make a point of it, yet do not hide it

Certainly you are not fooling him, and probably not the other members of the board. Do not try to take advantage of your acquaintanceship – it will probably do you little good.

6) Do not dominate the interview

Let the board do that. They will give you the clues – do not assume that you have to do all the talking. Realize that the board has a number of questions to ask you, and do not try to take up all the interview time by showing off your extensive knowledge of the answer to the first one.

7) Be attentive

You only have 20 minutes or so, and you should keep your attention at its sharpest throughout. When a member is addressing a problem or question to you, give him your undivided attention. Address your reply principally to him, but do not exclude the other board members.

8) Do not interrupt

A board member may be stating a problem for you to analyze. He will ask you a question when the time comes. Let him state the problem, and wait for the question.

9) Make sure you understand the question

Do not try to answer until you are sure what the question is. If it is not clear, restate it in your own words or ask the board member to clarify it for you. However, do not haggle about minor elements.

10) Reply promptly but not hastily

A common entry on oral board rating sheets is "candidate responded readily," or "candidate hesitated in replies." Respond as promptly and quickly as you can, but do not jump to a hasty, ill-considered answer.

11) Do not be peremptory in your answers

A brief answer is proper – but do not fire your answer back. That is a losing game from your point of view. The board member can probably ask questions much faster than you can answer them.

12) Do not try to create the answer you think the board member wants

He is interested in what kind of mind you have and how it works – not in playing games. Furthermore, he can usually spot this practice and will actually grade you down on it.

13) Do not switch sides in your reply merely to agree with a board member

Frequently, a member will take a contrary position merely to draw you out and to see if you are willing and able to defend your point of view. Do not start a debate, yet do not surrender a good position. If a position is worth taking, it is worth defending.

14) Do not be afraid to admit an error in judgment if you are shown to be wrong

The board knows that you are forced to reply without any opportunity for careful consideration. Your answer may be demonstrably wrong. If so, admit it and get on with the interview.

15) Do not dwell at length on your present job

The opening question may relate to your present assignment. Answer the question but do not go into an extended discussion. You are being examined for a *new* job, not your present one. As a matter of fact, try to phrase ALL your answers in terms of the job for which you are being examined.

Basis of Rating

Probably you will forget most of these "do's" and "don'ts" when you walk into the oral interview room. Even remembering them all will not ensure you a passing grade. Perhaps you did not have the qualifications in the first place. But remembering them will help you to put your best foot forward, without treading on the toes of the board members.

Rumor and popular opinion to the contrary notwithstanding, an oral board wants you to make the best appearance possible. They know you are under pressure – but they also want to see how you respond to it as a guide to what your reaction would be under the pressures of the job you seek. They will be influenced by the degree of poise you display, the personal traits you show and the manner in which you respond.

ABOUT THIS BOOK

This book contains tests divided into Examination Sections. Go through each test, answering every question in the margin. We have also attached a sample answer sheet at the back of the book that can be removed and used. At the end of each test look at the answer key and check your answers. On the ones you got wrong, look at the right answer choice and learn. Do not fill in the answers first. Do not memorize the questions and answers, but understand the answer and principles involved. On your test, the questions will likely be different from the samples. Questions are changed and new ones added. If you understand these past questions you should have success with any changes that arise. Tests may consist of several types of questions. We have additional books on each subject should more study be advisable or necessary for you. Finally, the more you study, the better prepared you will be. This book is intended to be the last thing you study before you walk into the examination room. Prior study of relevant texts is also recommended. NLC publishes some of these in our Fundamental Series. Knowledge and good sense are important factors in passing your exam. Good luck also helps. So now study this Passbook, absorb the material contained within and take that knowledge into the examination. Then do your best to pass that exam.

EXAMINATION SECTION

EXAMINATION SECTION
TEST 1

DIRECTIONS: Each question or incomplete statement is followed by several suggested answers or completions. Select the one that BEST answers the question or completes the statement. *PRINT THE LETTER OF THE CORRECT ANSWER IN THE SPACE AT THE RIGHT.*

Questions 1-10.

DIRECTIONS: For each of the sentences given below, numbered 1 through 10, select from the following choices the MOST correct choice and print your choice in the space at the right. Select as your answer:
- A – if the statement contains an unnecessary word of expression
- B – if the statement contains a slang term or expression ordinarily not acceptable in government report writing
- C – if the statement contains an old-fashioned word or expression, where a concrete, plain term would be more useful
- D – if the statement contains no major faults

1. Every one of us should try harder.   1.____
2. Yours of the first instant has been received.   2.____
3. We will have to do a real snow job on him.   3.____
4. I shall contact him next Thursday.   4.____
5. None of us were invited to the meeting with the community.   5.____
6. We got this here job to do.   6.____
7. She could not help but see the mistake in the checkbook.   7.____
8. Don't bug the Director about the report.   8.____
9. I beg to inform you that your letter has been received.   9.____
10. This project is all screwed up.   10.____

Questions 11-15.

DIRECTIONS: Read the following Inter-office Memo. Then answer Questions 11 through 15 based ONLY on the memo.

INTER-OFFICE MEMORANDUM

To: Alma Robinson, Human Resources Aide
From: Frank Shields, Social Worker

I would like to have you help Mr. Edward Tunney who is trying to raise his two children by himself. He needs to learn to improve the physical care of his children and especially of his daughter Helen, age 9. She is avoided and ridiculed at school because her hair is uncombed, her teeth not properly cleaned, her clothing torn, wrinkled and dirty, as well as shabby and poorly fitted. The teachers and school officials have contacted the Department and the social worker for two years about Helen. She is not able to make friends because of these problems. I have talked to Mr. Tunney about improvements for the child's clothing, hair, and hygiene. He tends to deny these things are problems, but is cooperative, and a second person showing him the importance of better physical care for Helen would be helpful.

Perhaps you could teach Helen how to fix her own hair. She has all the materials. I would also like you to form your own opinion of the sanitary conditions in the home and how they could be improved.

Mr. Tunney is expecting your visit and is willing to talk with you about ways he can help with these problems.

11. In the above memorandum, the Human Resources Aide is being asked to help Mr. Tunney to

    A. improve the learning habits of his children
    B. enable his children to make friends at school
    C. take responsibility for the upbringing of his children
    D. give attention to the grooming and cleanliness of his children

12. This case was brought to the attention of the social worker by

    A. government officials
    B. teachers and school officials
    C. the Department
    D. Mr. Tunney

13. In general, Mr. Tunney's attitude with regard to his children could BEST be described as

    A. interested in correcting the obvious problems, but unable to do so alone
    B. unwilling to follow the advice of those who are trying to help
    C. concerned, but unaware of the seriousness of these problems
    D. interested in helping them, but afraid of taking the advice of the social worker

14. Which of the following actions has NOT been suggested as a possible step for the Human Resources Aide to take?

    A. Help Helen to learn to care for herself by teaching her grooming skills
    B. Determine ways of improvement through information gathered on a home visit
    C. Discuss her own views on Helen's problems with school officials
    D. Ask Mr. Tunney in what ways he believes the physical care may be improved

15. According to the memo, the Human Resources Aide is ESPECIALLY being asked to observe and form her own opinions about

    A. the relationship between Mr. Tunney and the school officials
    B. Helen's attitude toward her classmates and teacher
    C. the sanitary conditions in the home
    D. the reasons Mr. Tunney is not cooperative with the agency

16. In one day, an aide receives 18 inquiries by phone and 27 inquiries in person. What percentage of the inquiries received that day were by phone?

    A. 33%   B. 40%   C. 45%   D. 60%

17. If the weekly pay checks for 5 part-time employees are: $129.32, $162.74, $143.67, $135.75, and $156.56, then the combined weekly income for the 5 employees is

    A. $727.84   B. $728.04   C. $730.84   D. $737.04

18. Suppose that there are 17 aides working in an office where many community complaints are received by telephone. In one ten-day period, 4250 calls were received. If the same number of calls were received each day, and the aides divided the work load equally, about how many calls did each aide respond to daily?

    A. 25   B. 35   C. 75   D. 250

19. Suppose that an assignment was divided among 5 aides. If the first aide spent 67 hours on the assignment, the second aide spent 95 hours, the third aide spent 52 hours, the fourth aide spent 78 hours, and the fifth aide spent 103 hours, what was the AVERAGE amount of time spent by each aide on the assignment?
    _____ hours.

    A. 71   B. 75   C. 79   D. 83

20. If there are 240 employees in a center and 1/3 are absent on the day of a bad snowstorm, how many employees were at work in the center on that day?

    A. 80   B. 120   C. 160   D. 200

KEY (CORRECT ANSWERS)

1. D
2. C
3. B
4. D
5. D

6. B
7. D
8. B
9. C
10. B

11. D
12. B
13. C
14. C
15. C

16. B
17. B
18. A
19. C
20. C

TEST 2

DIRECTIONS: Each question or incomplete statement is followed by several suggested answers or completions. Select the one that BEST answers the question or completes the statement. *PRINT THE LETTER OF THE CORRECT ANSWER IN THE SPACE AT THE RIGHT.*

1. Suppose that an aide takes 25 minutes to prepare a letter to a client. 1.____
   If the aide is assigned to prepare 9 letters on a certain day, how much time should she set aside for this task? _____ hours.

   A. 3 3/4 B. 4 1/4 C. 4 3/4 D. 5 1/4

2. Suppose that a certain center uses both Form A and Form B in the course of its daily work, and that Form A is used 4 times as often as Form B. 2.____
   If the total number of both forms used in one week is 750, how many times was Form A used?

   A. 100 B. 200 C. 400 D. 600

3. Suppose a center has a budget of $1092.70 from which 8 desks costing $78.05 apiece must be bought? 3.____
   How many ADDITIONAL desks can be ordered from this budget after the 8 desks have been purchased?

   A. 4 B. 6 C. 9 D. 14

4. When researching a particular case, a team of 16 aides was asked to check through 234 folders to obtain the necessary information. 4.____
   If half the aides worked twice as fast as the other half, and the slow group checked through 12 folders each hour, about how long would it take to complete the assignment? _____ hours.

   A. $4\frac{1}{4}$ B. 5 C. 6 D. $6\frac{1}{2}$

5. The difference in the cost of two printers is $28.32. If the less expensive printer costs $153.61, what is the cost of the other printer? 5.____

   A. $171.93 B. $172.03 C. $181.93 D. $182.03

Questions 6-8.

DIRECTIONS: Questions 6 through 8 are to be answered on the basis of the following information contained on a sample page of a payroll book.

Emp. No.	Name of Employee	M	T	W	Th	F	Total Hours Worked	Pay PerHour	Total Wages
1	James Smith	8	8	8	8	8			$480.00
2	Gloria Jones	8	7 3/4	7		7 1/2		$16.00	$560.00
3	Robert Adams	6	6	7 1/2	7 1/2	8 3/4		$18.28	

6. The pay per hour of Employee No. 1 is 6.____
   A. $12.00   B. $13.72   C. $15.00   D. $19.20

7. The number of hours that Employee No. 2 worked on Friday is 7.____
   A. 4   B. 5 1/2   C. 4.63   D. 4 3/4

8. The total wages for Employee No. 3 is 8.____
   A. $636.92   B. $648.94   C. $661.04   D. $672.96

9. As a rule, the FIRST step in writing a check should be to 9.____
   A. number the check
   B. write in the payee's name
   C. tear out the check stub
   D. write the purpose of the check in the space provided at the bottom

10. If an error is made when writing a check, the MOST widely accepted procedure is to 10.____
    A. draw a line through the error and initial it
    B. destroy both the check and check stub by tearing into small pieces
    C. erase the error if it does not occur in the amount of the check
    D. write *Void* across both the check and check stub and save them

11. The check that is MOST easily cashed is one that is 11.____
    A. not signed   B. made payable to *Cash*
    C. post-dated   D. endorsed in part

12. 12.____

No. 103	$ 142. 77
May 14	
To Alan Jacobs	
For Wages (5/6-5/10)	
Bal. Bro't For'd	2340. 63
Amt. Deposited	205. 24
Total	
Amt. This Check	142. 77
Bal. Car'd For'd	

   The balance to be carried forward on the check stub above is
   A. $2,278.16   B. $1,992.62   C. $2,688.64   D. $2,403.10

13. The procedure for reconciling a bank statement consists of _____ the bank balance 13.____
    and _____ the checkbook balance.

    A. *adding* outstanding checks to; *subtracting* the service and check charges from
    B. *subtracting* the service charge from; *subtracting* outstanding checks from
    C. *subtracting* the service charge from; *adding* outstanding checks to
    D. *subtracting* outstanding checks from; *subtracting* the service and check charges from

14. An employee makes $15.70 an hour and receives time-and-a-half in overtime pay for every hour more than 40 in a given week. If the employee works 47 hours, the employee's total wages for that week would be

    A. $792.85 B. $837.90 C. $875.25 D. $1,106.85

15. A high-speed copier can make 25,000 copies before periodic service is required. Before this service is necessary, _____ copies of a 137-page document can be printed.

    A. 211 B. 204 C. 190 D. 178

16. An aide is typing a letter to the James Weldon Johnson Head Start Center. To be sure that a Mr. Joseph Maxwell reads it, an attention line is typed below the inside address. The salutation should, therefore, read:

    A. To Whom It May Concern: B. Dear Mr. Maxwell:
    C. Gentlemen: D. Dear Joseph:

17. When describing the advantages of the numeric filing system, it is NOT true that it

    A. is the most accurate of all methods
    B. allows for unlimited expansion according to the needs of the agency
    C. is a system useful for filing letters directly according to name or subject
    D. allows for cross-referencing

18. In writing a letter for your Center, the PURPOSE of the letter should usually be stated in

    A. the first paragraph. This assists the reader in making more sense of the letter.
    B. the second paragraph. The first paragraph should be used to confirm receipt of the letter being answered
    C. the last paragraph. The first paragraphs should be used to build up to the purpose of the letter.
    D. any paragraph. Each letter has a different purpose and the letter should conform to that purpose.

19. If you open a personal letter addressed to another aide by mistake, the one of the following actions which it would generally be BEST for you to take is to

    A. reseal the envelope or place the contents in another envelope and pass it on to the employee
    B. place the letter inside the envelope, indicate under your initials that it was opened in error and give it to the employee
    C. personally give the employee the letter without any explanation
    D. ignore your error, attach the envelope to the letter, and give it out in the usual manner

20. Of the following, the MAIN purpose of the head start program is to

    A. provide programs for pre-school development of children
    B. provide children between the ages of 6 and 12 with after-school activity
    C. establish a system for providing care for teenage youngsters with working parents
    D. supervise centers providing 24-hour child care

KEY (CORRECT ANSWERS)

1. A
2. D
3. B
4. D
5. C

6. A
7. D
8. B
9. A
10. D

11. B
12. D
13. D
14. A
15. D

16. C
17. C
18. A
19. B
20. A

EXAMINATION SECTION
TEST 1

DIRECTIONS: Each question or incomplete statement is followed by several suggested answers or completions. Select the one that BEST answers the question or completes the statement. *PRINT THE LETTER OF THE CORRECT ANSWER IN THE SPACE AT THE RIGHT.*

1. One day an elderly man asks you if he can apply for Social Security at the welfare office.
   Your response should be to
   A. tell him that it is foolish to think he can apply for Social Security at the welfare office
   B. take him back to his apartment because he is too old to be roaming the streets asking questions
   C. explain that Social Security is a federal program and direct him to the nearest Social Security office
   D. call his daughter and tell her that the family should take better care of their father

   1.____

2. One of your duties is to occasionally visit clients. On one occasion, you visit Mrs. B., who needs assistance in referral of her children for day care so that she may enter a job training program. She has postponed completing the referral.
   What should you do in this situation?
   A. Tell her that if she doesn't hurry there will be no room at the day care center and the training program will be closed
   B. Make the arrangements and tell Mrs. B. that she should do what you say
   C. Remember that all people who ask for help are not always ready to receive it and continue to allow Mrs. B. to complete the referral by herself
   D. The next time Mrs. B. asks for help, see that she gets it as slowly as possible

   2.____

3. Assume that you are trying to contact a community group to offer to meet with their representative to explain a new agency policy about intake procedures.
   In order to "get your message across," you should
   A. write a short concise letter explaining why you want to meet with them and when you will be available
   B. write a short letter stating only that it is important that they contact you in order to arrange a meeting
   C. ask a secretary to help you because you do not really like to write to groups
   D. call the agency rather than write since you know someone there

   3.____

2 (#1)

4. It is necessary for you to call the director of a head start center in order to discuss a training program for teaching aides. The operator asks who you are and what you wish to discuss with the director.
   Your response should be to
   A. tell her that you would rather explain to the director and you want to speak to her immediately
   B. identify yourself, your department, and the nature of your business with the director
   C. hang up and try to call again when another operator is on duty
   D. tell your supervisor that the operator at the head start center is rude and you would rather not be asked to call there again

4.____

5. Mr. A. wants her children to go to summer camp. She has receive the request forms, but does not understand all of the questions and you are asked to help her complete them. She comes to the office at the appointed time.
   Of the following, the action you should take is to
   A. tell her she has taken so long that maybe the children will not go to camp
   B. see her as quickly as possible, explain the questions to her, and help her in completing the forms
   C. help her, but tell her she will have to learn to read better and refer her to an evening school
   D. fill out the forms or her by yourself

5.____

6. Mrs. B. needs a referral to the cancer clinic. You contact the clinic and make arrangements for her visit. You go to her home to inform her about the time because she has no phone. She thanks you for your help and then offers you a piece of jewelry that appears to be rather expensive.
   Of the following, the action you should take is to
   A. take the gift because you don't want to hurt her feelings
   B. tell her that she is foolish and should spend her money on herself
   C. explain to her that you are pleased with her thoughtfulness, but you are unable to accept the gift
   D. refuse the gift and get someone else to make referrals in the future because she is trying to pay you for your help

6.____

7. Mrs. C., a seemingly healthy, intelligent woman whose husband is disabled, and who works part-time, asks for help in getting homemaker services.
   Of the following, the action you should take is to
   A. give Mrs. C. the necessary information and help her get the services
   B. tell Mrs. C. that you do not feel she needs these services since her husband is capable of helping
   C. make note of her request since you do not feel it is urgent
   D. refer her to a caseworker since she obviously needs help in defining her role as a woman

7.____

8. When you are interviewing clients, it is important to notice and record how they say what they say—angrily, nervously, or with "body English"—because these signs may

8.____

A. tell you that the client's words are the opposite of what the client feels and you may need to dig to find out what those feelings are
B. be the prelude to violent behavior which no aide is prepared to handle
C. show that the client does not really deserve serious consideration
D. be important later should you be asked to defend what you did for the client

9. You are recording a visit you have made with a client who was angry and abusive to you during the interview. At one point, you lost your temper and said some things that you immediately regretted. You are embarrassed to record that you lost your temper.
However, it would be desirable to record this MAINLY because
   A. you would feel guilty if you did not record it
   B. your supervisor might hear about it from the client, so it would be better to have it written down from your point of view
   C. your supervisor can use the information to help you to improve your skills
   D. it is agency policy to write down everything

10. Through one of your clients you learn that a day care program's hours have been extended. You confirm this information with the day care center.
It is then MOST important for you to
   A. make a note of this fact, since it will mean you have to change your schedule in working with the client
   B. add this information to your personal resource file so that you can refer other clients to the day dare program
   C. inform your supervisor of the new information so that it can be added to the central resource file
   D. ignore the information, since your client does not need to have her child in day care for any extra hours

11. You are sent to a meeting of day-care parents to explain the programs of your agency. One of the parents becomes very angry, saying that welfare departments treat people like animals.
You should remain as calm as possible and say to the parent that
   A. he is right, but you have no control over what your agency does
   B. he is disrupting the meeting and you have come to explain a program, not to listen to complaints
   C. you understand his feelings and that sometimes clients do not get the services they wish as quickly as possible; however, you will do whatever you can to assist him
   D. he should call your supervisor tomorrow and make an appointment to discuss his feelings

12. Assume that you receive a telephone call from a very angry father. His daughter took money from his wallet, and he wants the caseworker to control the daughter. He yells, screams, and swears at you.
What is the BEST way for you to respond?

A. Hang up because you are not responsible for his daughter's actions. He shouldn't scream and swear at you.
B. Remember to be courteous and polite at all times, never losing your temper
C. Transfer the call to the supervisor because you are concerned about the father's unreasonableness and do not want the responsibility of dealing with him
D. Tell him that behavior such as he is demonstrating is the reason his daughter steals from him

13. Mrs. D.'s son, aged 12, has been getting into difficulty in the neighborhood. At a community meeting, she asks your help in finding worthwhile activities for him. It is APPROPRIATE for you to respond to her because
    A. you should have knowledge of the social services available in the neighborhood and the activities they offer
    B. you have known Mrs. D. and her family for several years and know how much trouble she has had with her son
    C. it is your job to do what the caseworker assigns to you without question
    D. you are concerned about impressing Mrs. D with your knowledge

14. Several clients live in your neighborhood. They know that you work for the human resources administration. One day one of them tells you that there is a rumor that another client is pregnant and asks if this is true. You know from a past discussion with the caseworker that this client is pregnant.
    The BEST answer for you to give would be to
    A. tell her it is none of her business and if she wants to know, she should ask the caseworker
    B. ask her who told her that this client is pregnant
    C. explain that anything told to the agency is held in confidence and will not be shared with anyone else
    D. tell her you don't know, but will ask when you get back to the office and let her know later

15. The area senior citizens group asks for an agency representative to discuss old-age assistance and new SSI regulations. Your supervisor asks you to attend this meeting; however, you do not wish to go because you really do not feel that you work well with older people. In fact, you don't like them very much.
    What should be your response?
    A. Tell the supervisor that you cannot go because you have an appointment with the doctor that day
    B. Get another worker to go for you and assume his task while he is gone
    C. Explain to your supervisor what problems you have in working with old-age clients
    D. Go, because you should do the tasks that are assigned to you according to your job description

16. At a center where you are distributing literature about agency programs, a citizen comes up to you and begins to complain loudly about agency programs. What should be your response?
    A. Call the police and have the complainer removed from the center
    B. Tell him that you do not make policy; suggest that he go to the office and complain
    C. Remain as calm as possible and ask that he discuss the complaints with you calmly. If necessary, make an appointment with him
    D. Yell at him since this seems to be the way he relates to agency people

17. A community group is having a training program. You are sent to explain agency policy and answer questions.
    Providing this type of contact between the agency and community groups is PROPER because
    A. you like people and are a good public speaker
    B. it is the responsibility of the agency to cooperate with community groups in order to help the public to be well-informed about agency policy
    C. you were once in the same training program and understand the kind of people who are being trained
    D. once in a while everyone should have the opportunity to speak to a community group

18. While you are assisting in the intake area, a young man who is applying is cooperative but begins to ask you personal questions: your age, where you live, whether you have children, and other similar questions.
    You are disturbed by these questions, so you should
    A. tell him that agency policy does not allow you to answer personal questions and send him to another intake worker
    B. tell him it is your responsibility to ask questions, not his
    C. tell your supervisor that you do not want to work in intake because clients can get too nosy and you get nervous
    D. avoid answering personal questions and try to get him to return to the purpose of the interview

19. You are assigned to the reception area for the day. A mother arrives in the office with three small children. In a rage, she says that she does not have enough money to feed the children and demands that you find a home for them.
    The BEST action for you to take should be to
    A. call a security officer and have him remove her and the children from the office
    B. attempt to calm her down by listening to her, attend to the children's needs and call for a supervisor
    C. take the children from her and ask her to leave at once
    D. call the supervisor and security because it is their job to take care of abusive clients

20. Assume that you are interviewing a young unwed mother who has recently arrived in the city from Alabama. She is a likable girl and is very cooperative. However, it is difficult to understand the meaning of her conversation due to her accent and different use of words.
    You would like to establish a good relationship with her, so you should FIRST
    A. suggest that she go to evening school so that she can learn to speak like other people in the city
    B. tell her that you don't understand her sometimes and you would appreciate it if she would explain what she means
    C. take another worker with you on visits to help you in the interview
    D. try to find a worker in the agency who has a similar background and have the case handled by the worker

21. A man being interviewed is entitled to Medicaid, but he refuses to sign up for it because he says he cannot accept any form of welfare.
    Of the following, the BEST course of action for an aide to take FIRST is to
    A. try to discover the reason for his feeling this way
    B. tell him that he should be glad financial help is available
    C. explain that others cannot get help him if he will not help himself
    D. suggest that he speak to someone who is already on Medicaid

22. Of the following, the outcome of an interview by an aide depends MOS heavily on the
    A. personality of the interviewee
    B. personality of the aide
    C. subject matter of the questions asked
    D. interaction between aide and interviewee

23. Some patients being interviewed are PRIMARILY interested in making a favorable impression. The aide should be aware of the fact that such patients are more likely than other patients to
    A. try to anticipate the answers the interviewer is looking for
    B. answer all questions openly and frankly
    C. try to assume the role of interviewer
    D. be anxious to get the interview over as quickly as possible

24. The type of interview which an aide usually conducts is substantially different from most interviewing situations in all of the following aspects EXCEPT the
    A. setting   B. kinds of clients
    C. techniques employed   D. kinds of problems

25. During an interview, an aide uses a "leading question."
    This type of question is so-called because it generally
    A. starts a series of questions about one topic
    B. suggests the answer which the aide wants
    C. forms the basis for a following "trick" question
    D. sets, at the beginning, the tone of the interview

KEY (CORRECT ANSWERS)

1.	C	11.	C
2.	C	12.	B
3.	A	13.	A
4.	B	14.	C
5.	B	15.	C
6.	C	16.	C
7.	A	17.	B
8.	A	18.	D
9.	C	19.	B
10.	C	20.	B

21. A
22. D
23. A
24. C
25. B

TEST 2

DIRECTIONS: Each question or incomplete statement is followed by several suggested answers or completions. Select the one that BEST answers the question or completes the statement. *PRINT THE LETTER OF THE CORRECT ANSWER IN THE SPACE AT THE RIGHT.*

1. Miss Lally is an old-age assistance recipient. Her health is not good and it is important that she have three good meals each day. She follows these instructions except on Friday she refuses to eat meat because of her religious beliefs. She will not even substitute fish.
   You are very concerned about this, so you should
   A. tell your supervisor so that she will go to see Miss Lally and make her eat nourishing meals on Friday
   B. call her doctor and tell him so that he will see her and explain to her that fasting is not good for her health
   C. attempt to understand her value system and accept that it is possible that she is acting in good faith with her own values even though they may be harmful to her health
   D. explain to her how important it is that she eat meat each day in order to be in good health and enjoy the remaining years of her life

1.____

2. Theodore is a junkie. Every cent he can get his hands on legally or illegally is used to supply his habit. You are angry because the junkie is destroying himself and his family. You feel that the courts should punish him for his illegal acts.
   Of the following, the BEST action for you to take is to
   A. suggest to your supervisor that the income maintenance center reduce the family grant, taking out his portion
   B. help his wife to find another apartment for her and the children away from him
   C. call the local police to find out why they are doing nothing about this man's activities in the community
   D. reconsider your ideas about punishment, remembering that punishment alone will not help the man to change his behavior

2.____

3. You are regularly assigned to taking Sarah Jones and her young son to the clinic. She is a very warm, friendly woman and your relationship with her is good. However, she invited you to come for dinner on Sunday and to go to a school play with her. You would like to accept the invitations because you need weekend activities and you like her.
   What should be your PRIMARY consideration in coming to a decision?
   A. You need friends just as she does, so you should accept the invitations
   B. You are a worker and should not be seen with a client in public places
   C. Decide whether accepting the invitations will help to meet agency needs or will hamper the relationship you are expected to establish
   D. Tell her "no" because it is not a good policy to be on such friendly terms with clients

3.____

4. Martha's husband has been arrested in a drug raid and she is extremely anxious. Your supervisor asks that you visit her to determine ways in which the agency may help her. You visit and find her weeping; the house and the children have obviously been neglected.
   The BEST thing for you to do is to
   A. tell her to stop crying and help her to clean the apartment and the children
   B. remind her that her husband has been warned and now has to pay for not listening
   C. listen to her, allowing her to express her feelings of fear, loss, and grief, and reassure her of your concern
   D. listen to her but caution her that she is neglecting the home and children because of her anxiety and you may have to ask your supervisor to remove the children if she doesn't get any better

4.____

5. Mrs. Dwight's landlord is very slow in making repairs in her apartment. Each time you see her, she complains about this over and over again, calling her landlord names and threatening to report him to the city. She complains to any agency person she meets.
   Realizing that these complaints are not getting any action, you should
   A. avoid meeting with her because she is annoying
   B. suggest that she see a doctor because she is irrational and should get some help
   C. ask her what she would like to do about the problem and assist her in carrying out her plans
   D. ask the supervisor to see her because you do not have the skills to help her

5.____

6. In the day-to-day operations of the human resources administration, which of the following would you consider to be the PRIMARY function of the agency?
   A. Getting work done to meet city and federal deadlines
   B. Being sure that all of the clients who come to the agency are seen before closing time
   C. Delivering services to those persons who are eligible for assistance
   D. Making sure everyone gets his check on time

6.____

7. During the course of an interview you find it is necessary to arrange a special appointment for the client to return for a further interview. After checking your calendar, you tell the client the date she is to come back. The client, however, says she cannot see you on that date because she is to attend a rally at a community center in her neighborhood.
   Of the following, your BEST action should be to
   A. let her know that any other day is an inconvenience to you and remind her that the appointment is for her benefit
   B. forget about the special appointment and try to get along with the information you have
   C. explain to her the need for the appointment and ask when she can meet with you
   D. tell her that since the community center is not city-operated, she must keep her appointment with you

7.____

8. In working with community groups, it is important that you be able to define what a community is.
   Of the following definitions, which is the MOST appropriate?
   A community
   A. consists of a group of people living fairly close together in a more or less compact territory, who come together in their chief concerns
   B. is a particular section of a city designated on a census tract
   C. is that portion of a city which constitutes an election district
   D. is a section of a city or town in which a particular ethnic group conducts its social, business, and religious life

8.____

9. The agency has implemented a new policy regarding the intake procedure. You wish to explain and discuss this policy with as many community groups as possible. You make an initial contact by mail.
   In order to get your message across well, your letter should be
   A. short and as concise as possible explaining why you want to meet with them, and offer several possible times that you will be available
   B. short, explaining only that it is important that the groups contact you in order to arrange a meeting
   C. drafted by the center's secretary and sent to the usual groups
   D put in the usual announcement form in the center's newsletter

9.____

10. A group of young welfare mothers want to form an organization that will provide babysitting services for mothers of children who are too young to enroll in a day care center.
    What should be your answer to them?
    A. Tell them to try to get the center to change its policy to include young children
    B. Arrange the time to meet with them to offer as much advice and support as possible, since most communities do need this service
    C. Suggest that it may be better that they spend their time taking care of their own children
    D. Ask a social worker to survey the community to determine if such a service is really needed at this time

10.____

11. New regulations have removed the disabled, blind, and old-age assistance cases from the public assistance caseload. Assistance in these categories is given directly by the federal government. A former client has not received his check. The chairman of the senior citizens committee calls and angrily demands that your agency do something in this man's behalf.
    In response, you should
    A. answer politely, explaining that your agency is not concerned about OAA clients
    B. arrange to meet with him in order to discuss the new policy
    C. refer him to the Social Security office covering the area where the client lives
    D. ask that he call again when he is calmer so that you may discuss this matter with him

11.____

4 (#2)

12. A high school student from the community comes to see you about a homework assignment to write a report on your center.
    The BEST way to help him is to
    A. refer him to a social worker who has daily contact with clients in their homes
    B. contact the boy's teacher and find out why you were not warned of his coming
    C. explain your center's program and answer as many of his questions as you can
    D. give him literature about the welfare system in the city and state

12.____

13. Assume that the women's group of the Community Baptist Church has invited you to a Sunday afternoon service to celebrate the tenth anniversary of the pastor. The agency's relationship with the women is good in that they often offer their homes as emergency homes for adult clients.
    What should you do about the invitation?
    A. Do not attend but send them a note congratulating the pastor and explaining that agency personnel do not work on Sundays
    B. Ask a social worker who lives close to the church to go
    C. Accept the invitation if at all possible, attend the service and whatever social hour they may have afterwards
    D. Ignore the invitation since this function has little relationship to your job

13.____

14. Suppose that a person you are interviewing becomes angry at some of the questions you have asked, calls you meddlesome and nosy, and states that she will not answer those questions.
    Of the following, which is the BEST action for you to take
    A. Explain the reasons the questions are asked and the importance of the answers
    B. Inform the interviewee that you are only doing your job and advise her that she should answer your questions or leave your office
    C. Report to your supervisor what the interviewee called you and refuse to continue the interview
    D. End the interview and tell the interviewee she will not be serviced by your department

14.____

15. Suppose that during the course of an interview the interviewee demands in a very rude way that she be permitted to talk to your supervisor or someone in charge.
    Which of the following is probably the BEST way to handle this situation?
    A. Inform your supervisor of the demand and ask her to speak to the interviewee
    B. Pay no attention to the demands of the interviewee and continue the interview
    C. Report to your supervisor and tell her to get another interviewer for this interviewee
    D. Tell her you are the one "in charge" and that she should talk to you

15.____

19

16. Suppose that a worker asks a client to answer several required but rather personal questions about the family's health history. The client delays and seems embarrassed about giving the answers.
    Of the following, the MOST reasonable response to the client is one which
    A. shows an awareness of the client's efforts to hide something
    B. demonstrates the worker's qualifications for asking such questions
    C. allows this client to be excused from answering the questions
    D. convinces the client that his uneasiness in the situation is understood

17. A representative from a planned parenthood group comes to see you to get information for a community education program.
    You should
    A. check out this group to make sure it is not promoting zero population growth for minority groups
    B. develop a good relationship with him so as to provide better service to clients
    C. make sure they will not encourage unnecessary abortions
    D. refuse to see him

18. A member of a clerical training program is continually late to classes. He explains to you that he has a hard time getting up and asks that you report him on time because he needs to train for a job.
    What should your response be?
    A. Tell him that you get there on time and so should he
    B. Tell him that you do not lie for anyone
    C. Explain that it is your duty to keep accurate records and refer him to a counselor
    D. Tell him that you will cooperate with him but he has to try to do better

19. In a community meeting to explain a new agency policy, you find that the audience has no questions about the policy or your explanations.
    What would be the MOST appropriate response to the silence?
    A. Leave right away before they think of questions
    B. Thank the audience for their attention and assure them that you will be available if there are any questions later
    C. Ask several members in the audience if they understand the new policy
    D. Explain that the audience could not possibly understand all of the policy and they must have questions

20. Assume that you are confronted by an angry member of the public who has not been able to obtain the information he needs from your office. You do not know the answer to his question.
    The BEST thing for you to do would be to
    A. tell him to come back another time, after you have looked up the information
    B. check with your supervisor to find the correct answer

C. tell him to ask in another office, so that you will not lose time looking for the information
D. make up and answer to keep the man satisfied until the right answer is found

KEY (CORRECT ANSWERS)

1.	C	11.	C
2.	D	12.	C
3.	C	13.	C
4.	C	14.	A
5.	C	15.	A
6.	C	16.	D
7.	C	17.	B
8.	A	18.	C
9.	A	19.	B
10.	B	20.	B

EXAMINATION SECTION
TEST 1

DIRECTIONS: Each question or incomplete statement is followed by several suggested answers or completions. Select the one that BEST answers the question or completes the statement. *PRINT THE LETTER OF THE CORRECT ANSWER IN THE SPACE AT THE RIGHT.*

Questions 1-5.

DIRECTIONS: Questions 1 through 5 consist of a sentence with an underlined word. For each question, select the choice that is CLOSEST in meaning to the underlined word.

    EXAMPLE
This division reviews the fiscal reports of the agency.
In this sentence, the word *fiscal* means MOST NEARLY
    A. financial   B. critical   C. basic   D. personnel
The correct answer is A. "financial" because "financial" is closest to *fiscal*. Therefore, the answer is A.

1. Every good office worker needs basic skills.
   The word *basic* in this sentence means
      A. fundamental   B. advanced   C. unusual   D. outstanding

2. He turned out to be a good instructor.
   The word *instructor* in this sentence means
      A. student   B. worker   C. typist   D. teacher

3. The quantity of work in the office was under study.
   In this sentence, the word *quantity* means
      A. amount   B. flow   C. supervision   D. type

4. The morning was spent examining the time records.
   In this sentence, the word *examining* means
      A. distributing   B. collecting   C. checking   D. filing

5. The candidate filled in the proper spaces on the form.
   In this sentence, the word *proper* means
      A. blank   B. appropriate   C. many   D. remaining

Questions 6-8.

DIRECTIONS: Questions 6 through 8 are to be answered SOLELY on the basis of the information contained in the following paragraph.

The increase in the number of public documents in the last two centuries closely matches the increase in population in the United States. The great number of public documents has become a serious threat to their usefulness. It is necessary to have programs which will reduce the number of public documents that are kept and which will, at the same time, assure keeping those that have value. Such programs need a great deal of thought to have any success.

6. According to the above paragraph, public documents may be less useful if
   A. the files are open to the public
   B. the record room is too small
   C. the copying machine is operated only during normal working hours
   D. too many records are being kept

7. According to the above paragraph, the growth of the population in the United States has matched the growth in the quantity of public documents for a period of MOST NEARLY _____ years.
   A. 50   B. 100   C. 200   D. 300

8. According to the above paragraph, the increased number of public documents has made it necessary to
   A. find out which public documents are worth keeping
   B. reduce the great number of public documents by decreasing government services
   C. eliminate the copying of all original public documents
   D. avoid all new copying devices

Questions 9-10.

DIRECTIONS: Questions 9 and 10 are to be answered SOLELY on the basis of the information contained in the following paragraph.

The work goals of an agency can best be reached if the employees understand and agree with these goals. One way to gain such understanding and agreement is for management to encourage and seriously consider suggestions from employees in the setting of agency goals.

9. On the basis of the above paragraph, the BEST way to achieve the work goals of an agency is to
   A. make certain that employees work as hard as possible
   B. study the organizational structure of the agency
   C. encourage employees to think seriously about the agency's problems
   D. stimulate employee understanding of the work goals

10. On the basis of the above paragraph, understanding and agreement with agency   10._____
    goals can be gained by
    A. allowing the employees to set agency goals
    B. reaching agency goals quickly
    C. legislative review of agency operations
    D. employee participation in setting agency goals

Questions 11-15.

DIRECTIONS: Each of Questions 11 through 15 consists of a group of four words. One word in each group is incorrectly spelled. For each question, print the letter of the correct answer in the space at the right that is the same as the letter next to the word which is INCORRECTLY spelled.

EXAMPLE

A. housing B. certain C. budgit D. money

The word "budgit" is incorrectly spelled, because the correct spelling should be "budget." Therefore, the correct answer is C.

11. A. sentince   B. bulletin   C. notice   D. definition   11._____
12. A. appointment B. exactly   C. typest   D. light   12._____
13. A. penalty   B. suparvise   C. consider   D. division   13._____
14. A. schedule   B. accurate   C. corect   D. simple   14._____
15. A. suggestion B. installed   C. proper   D. agincy   15._____

Questions 16-20.

DIRECTIONS: Each Question 16 through 20 consists of a sentence which may be
   A. incorrect because of bad word usage, or
   B. incorrect because of bad punctuation, or
   C. incorrect because of bad spelling, or
   D. correct
   Read each sentence carefully. Then print in the space at the right A, B, C, or D, according to the answer you choose from the four choices listed above. There is only one type of error in each incorrect sentence. If there is no error, the sentence is correct.

EXAMPLE

George Washington was the father of his contry.
This sentence is incorrect because of bad spelling ("contry" instead of "country").
Therefore, the answer is C.

16. The assignment was completed in record time but the payroll for it has not yet been preparid. 16.____

17. The operator, on the other hand, is willing to learn me how to use the mimeograph. 17.____

18. She is the prettiest of the three sisters. 18.____

19. She doesn't know; if the mail has arrived. 19.____

20. The doorknob of the office door is broke. 20.____

21. A clerk can process a form in 15 minutes.
    How many forms can that clerk process in six hours?
    A. 10   B. 21   C. 24   D. 90 21.____

22. An office staff consists of 120 people. Sixty of them have been assigned to a special project. Of the remaining staff, 20 answer the mail, 10 handle phone calls, and the rest operate the office machines.
    The number of people operating the office machines is
    A. 20   B. 30   C. 40   D. 45 22.____

23. An office worker received 65 applications but on the first day had to return 26 of them for being incomplete and on the second day 25 had to be returned for being incomplete.
    How many applications did NOT have to be returned?
    A. 10   B. 12   C. 14   D. 16 23.____

24. An office worker answered 63 phone calls in one day and 91 phone calls the next day.
    For these 2 days, what was the average number of phone calls he answered per day?
    A. 77   B. 28   C. 82   D. 93 24.____

25. An office worker processed 12 vouchers of $8.50 each, 3 vouchers of $3.68 each, and 2 vouchers of $1.29 each.
    The TOTAL dollar amount of these vouchers is
    A. $116.04   B. $117.52   C. $118.62   D. $119.04 25.____

KEY (CORRECT ANSWERS)

1.	A		11.	A
2.	D		12.	C
3.	A		13.	B
4.	C		14.	C
5.	B		15.	D
6.	D		16.	C
7.	C		17.	A
8.	A		18.	D
9.	D		19.	B
10.	D		20.	A

21.	C
22.	B
23.	C
24.	A
25.	C

TEST 2

DIRECTIONS: Each question or incomplete statement is followed by several suggested answers or completions. Select the one that BEST answers the question or completes the statement. *PRINT THE LETTER OF THE CORRECT ANSWER IN THE SPACE AT THE RIGHT.*

Questions 1-5.

DIRECTIONS: Each Question from 1 through 5 lists four names. The names may not be exactly the same. Compare the names in each question and mark your answer
- A if all the names are different
- B if only two names are exactly the same
- C if only three names are exactly the same
- D if all four names are exactly the same

EXAMPLE
Jensen, Alfred E.
Jensen, Alfred E.
Jensan, Alfred E.
Jensen, Fred E.

Since the name Jensen, Alfred E. appears twice and is exactly the same in both places, the correct answer is B.

1. A. Riviera, Pedro S.   B. Rivers, Pedro S.
   C. Riviera, Pedro N.   D. Riviera, Juan S.   1.____

2. A. Guider, Albert   B. Guidar, Albert
   C. Giuder, Alfred   D. Guider, Albert   2.____

3. A. Blum, Rona   B. Blum, Rona
   C. Blum, Rona   D. Blum, Rona   3.____

4. A. Raugh, John   B. Raugh, James
   C. Raughe, John   D. Raugh, John   4.____

5. A. Katz, Stanley   B. Katz, Stanley
   C. Katze, Stanley   D. Katz, Stanley   5.____

Questions 6-10.

DIRECTIONS: Each Question 6 through 10 consists of numbers or letters in Columns I and II. For each question, compare each line of Column I with its corresponding line in Column II and decide how many lines in Column I are EXACTLY the same as their corresponding lines in Column II. In your answer space, mark your answer
- A if only ONE line in Column I is exactly the same as its corresponding line in Column II
- B if only TWO lines in Column I are exactly the same as their corresponding lines in Column II

C if only THREE lines in Column I are exactly the same as their corresponding lines in Column II
D if all FOUR lines in Column I are exactly the same as their corresponding lines in Column II

EXAMPLE

Column I	Column II
1776	1776
1865	1865
1945	1945
1976	1978

Only three lines in Column I are exactly the same as their corresponding lines in Column II. Therefore, the correct answer is C.

	Column I	Column II	
6.	5653 8727 ZPSS 4952	5653 8728 ZPSS 9453	6.____
7.	PNJP NJPJ JNPN PNJP	PNPJ NJPJ JNPN PNPJ	7.____
8.	effe uWvw KpGj vmnv	eFfe uWvw KpGg vmnv	8.____
9.	5232 PfrC zssz rwwr	5232 PfrN zzss rwww	9.____
10.	czws cecc thrm lwtz	czws cece thrm lwtz	10.____

Questions 11-15.

DIRECTIONS: Questions 11 through 15 have lines of letters and numbers. Each letter should be matched with its number in accordance with the following table.

Letter	F	R	C	A	W	L	E	N	B	T
Matching Number	0	1	2	3	4	5	6	7	8	9

From the table you can determine that the letter F has the matching number 0 below it, the letter R has the matching number 1 below, etc.

For each question, compare each line of letters and numbers carefully to see if each letter has its correct matching number. If all the letters and numbers are matched correctly in

    none of the lines of the question, mark your answer A
    only *one* of the lines of the question, mark your answer B
    only *two* of the lines of the question, mark your answer C
    all three lines of the question, mark your answer D

EXAMPLE

WBCR	4826
TLBF	9580
ATNE	3986

There is a mistake in the first line because the letter R should have its matching number 1 instead of the number 6.

The second line is correct because each letter shown has the correct matching number.

There is a mistake in the third line because the letter N should have the matching number 7 instead of the number 8.

Since all the letters and numbers are correct matched in only one of the lines in the sample, the correct answer is B.

11.   EBCT   6829   11.____
        ATWR   3961
        NLBW   7584

12.   RNCT   1729   12.____
        LNCR   5728
        WAEB   5368

13.   NTWB   7948   13.____
        RABL   1385
        TAEF   9360

14.   LWRB   5417   14.____
        RLWN   1647
        CBWA   2843

15.   ABTC   3792   15.____
        WCER   5261
        AWCN   3417

16.   Your job often brings you into contact with the public.   16.____
        Of the following, it would be MOST desirable to explain the reasons for official actions to people coming into your office for assistance because such explanations
            A. help build greater understanding between the public and your agency
            B. help build greater self-confidence in city employees
            C. convince the public that nothing they do can upset a city employee
            D. show the public that city employees are intelligent

17. Assume that you strongly dislike one of your co-workers.
    You should FIRST
    A. discuss your feeling with the co-worker
    B. demand a transfer to another office
    C. suggest to your supervisor that the co-worker should be observed carefully
    D. try to figure out the reason for this dislike before you say or do anything

18. An office worker who has problems accepting authority is MOST likely to find it difficult to
    A. obey rules
    B. understand people
    C. assist other employees
    D. follow complex instructions

19. The employees in your office have taken a dislike to one person and frequently annoy her.
    Your supervisor should
    A. transfer this person to another unit at the first opportunity
    B. try to find out the reason for the staff's attitude before doing anything about it
    C. threaten to transfer the first person observed bothering this person
    D. ignore the situation

20. Assume that your supervisor has asked a worker in your office to get a copy of a report out of the files. You notice the worker as accidentally pulled out the wrong report.
    Of the following, the BEST way for you to handle this situation is to tell
    A. the worker about all the difficulties that will result from this error
    B. the worker about her mistake in a nice way
    C. the worker to ignore this error
    D. your supervisor that this worker needs more training in how to use the files

21. Filing systems differ in their efficiency.
    Which of the following is the BEST way to evaluate the efficiency of a filing system? A
    A. number of times used per day
    B. amount of material that is received each day for filing
    C. amount of time it takes to locate material
    D. type of locking system used

22. In planning ahead so that a sufficient amount of general office supplies is always available, it would be LEAST important to find out the
    A. current office supply needs of the staff
    B. amount of office supplies used last year
    C. days and times that office supplies can be ordered
    D. agency goals and objectives

23. The MAIN reason for establishing routine office work procedures is that once a routine is established
    A. work need not be checked for accuracy
    B. all steps in the routine will take an equal amount of time to perform
    C. each time the job is repeated, it will take less time to perform
    D. each step in the routine will not have to be planned all over again each time

24. When an office machine centrally located in an agency must be shut down for repairs, the bureaus and divisions using this machine should be informed of the
    A. expected length of time before the machine will be in operation again
    B. estimated cost of repairs
    C. efforts being made to avoid future repairs
    D. type of new equipment which the agency may buy in the future to replace the machine being repaired

25. If the day's work is properly scheduled, the MOST important result would be that the
    A. supervisor will not have to do much supervision
    B. employee will know what to do next
    C. employee will show greater initiative
    D. job will become routine

KEY (CORRECT ANSWERS)

1.	A		11.	C
2.	B		12.	B
3.	D		13.	D
4.	B		14.	B
5.	C		15.	A
6.	B		16.	A
7.	B		17.	D
8.	B		18.	A
9.	A		19.	B
10.	C		20.	B

21.	C
22.	D
23.	D
24.	A
25.	B

EXAMINATION SECTION

TEST 1

DIRECTIONS: Each question or incomplete statement is followed by several suggested answers or completions. Select the one that BEST answers the question or completes the statement. *PRINT THE LETTER OF THE CORRECT ANSWER IN THE SPACE AT THE RIGHT.*

1. Assume that a few co-workers meet near your desk and talk about personal matters during working hours. Lately, this practice has interfered with your work. In order to stop this practice, the BEST action for you to take FIRST is to
   A. ask your supervisor to put a stop to the co-workers' meeting near your desk
   B. discontinue any friendship with this group
   C. ask your co-workers not to meet near your desk
   D. request that your desk be moved to another location

1._____

2. In order to maintain office coverage during working hours, your supervisor has scheduled your lunch hour from 1 P.M. to 2 P.M. and your co-workers' lunch hour from 12 P.M. to 1 P.M. Lately, your co-worker has been returning late from lunch each day. As a result, you don't get a full hour since you must return to the office by 2 P.M.
   Of the following, the BEST action for you to take FIRST is to
   A. explain to your co-worker in a courteous manner that his lateness is interfering with your right to a full hour for lunch
   B. tell your co-worker that his lateness must stop or you will report him to your supervisor
   C. report your co-worker's lateness to your supervisor
   D. leave at 1 P.M. for lunch, whether your co-worker has returned or not

2._____

3. Assume that, as an office worker, one of your jobs is to open mail sent to your unit, read the mail for content, and send the mail to the appropriate person to handle. You accidentally open and begin to read a letter marked *personal* to a co-worker.
   Of the following, the BEST action for you to take is to
   A. report to your supervisor that your co-worker is receiving personal mail at the office
   B. destroy the letter so that your co-worker does not know you saw it
   C. reseal the letter and place it on the co-worker's desk without saying anything
   D. bring the letter to your co-worker and explain that you opened it by accident

3._____

4. Suppose that in evaluating your work, your supervisor gives you an overall rating, but states that you sometimes turn in work with careless errors.
   The BEST action for you to take would be to
   A. ask a co-worker who is good at details to proofread your work
   B. take time to do a careful job, paying more attention to detail
   C. continue working as usual since occasional errors are to be expected
   D. ask your supervisor if she would mind correcting your errors

5. Assume that you are taking a telephone message for a co-worker who is not in the office at the time.
   Of the following, the LEAST important item to write on the message is the
   A. length of the call   B. name of the caller
   C. time of the call   D. telephone number of the caller

Questions 6-13.

DIRECTIONS: Questions 6 through 13 each consist of a sentence which may or may not be an example of good English. The underlined parts of each sentence may be correct or incorrect. Examine each sentence, considering grammar, punctuation, spelling, and capitalization. If the English usage in the underlined parts of the sentence given is better than any of the changes in the underlined words suggested in Options B, C, or D, choose Option A. If the changes in the underlined words suggested in Options B, C, or D would make the sentence correct, choose the correct option. Do not choose an option that will change the meaning of the sentence.

6. This Fall, the office will be closed on Columbus Day, October 9th.
   A. Correct as is   B. fall...Columbus Day, October
   C. Fall...Columbus day, October   D. fall...Columbus Day, october

7. This manual discribes the duties performed by an Office Aide.
   A. Correct as is   B. describe the duties performed
   C. discribe the duties performed   D. describes the duties performed

8. There weren't no paper in the supply closet.
   A. Correct as is   B. weren't any
   C. wasn't any   D. wasn't no

9. The new employees left there office to attend a meeting.
   A. Correct as is   B. they're
   C. their   D. thier

10. The office worker started working at 8:30 a.m.
    A. Correct as is   B. 8:30 a.m.
    C. 8;30 a,m.   D. 8:30 am.

11. The alphabet, or A to Z sequence are the basis of most filing systems.
    A. Correct as is   B. alphabet, or A to Z sequence, is
    C. alphabet, or A to Z sequence are   D. alphabet, or A too Z sequence, is

12. <u>Those</u> file cabinets are five <u>feet</u> tall. 12.____
    A. Correct as is   B. Them…feet
    C. Those…foot   D. Them…foot

13. The Office Aide checked the <u>register and finding</u> the date of the meeting. 13.____
    A. Correct as is   B. regaster and finding
    C. register and found   D. regaster and found

Questions 14-21.

DIRECTIONS: Each of Questions 14 through 21 has two lists of numbers. Each list contains three sets of numbers. Check each of the three sets in the list on the right to see if they are the same as the corresponding set in the list on the left. Mark your answers
   A. if none of the sets in the right list are the same as those in the left list
   B. if only one of the sets in the right list are the same as those in the left list
   C. if only two of the sets in the right list are the same as those in the left list
   D. if all three sets in the right list are the same as those in the left list

14. 7354183476   7354983476   14.____
    4474747744   4474747774
    57914302311   57914302311

15. 7143592185   7143892185   15.____
    8344517699   8344518699
    9178531263   9178531263

16. 2572114731   257214731   16.____
    8806835476   8806835476
    8255831246   8255831246

17. 331476853821   331476858621   17.____
    6976658532996   6976655832996
    3766042113715   3766042113745

18. 8806663315   8806663315   18.____
    74477138449   74477138449
    211756663666   211756663666

19. 990006966996   99000696996   19.____
    53022219743   53022219843
    4171171117717   4171171177717

20. 24400222433004   24400222433004   20.____
    5300030055000355   5300030055500355
    20000075532002022 20000075532002022

35

21. 6111666406600011 16   61116664066001116   21.____
     7111300117001100733   7111300117001100733
     26666446664476518   26666446664476518

Questions 22-25.

DIRECTIONS: Each of Questions 22 through 25 has two lists of names and addresses. Each
             list contains three sets of names and addresses. Check each of the three sets
             in the list on the right to see if they are the same as the corresponding set in
             the list on the left. Mark your answers
                 A. if none of the sets in the right list are the same as those in the left list
                 B. if only one of the sets in the right list are the same as those in the left list
                 C. if only two of the sets in the right list are the same as those in the left list
                 D. if all three sets in the right list are the same as those in the left list

22. Mary T. Berlinger   Mary T. Berlinger   22.____
     2351 Hampton St.   2351 Hampton St.
     Monsey, N.Y. 20117   Monsey, N.Y. 20117

     Eduardo Benes   Eduardo Benes
     473 Kingston Avenue   473 Kingston Avenue
     Central Islip, N.Y. 11734   Central Islip, N.Y. 11734

     Alan Carrington Fuchs   Alan Carrington Fuchs
     17 Gnarled Hollow Road   17 Gnarled Hollow Road
     Los Angeles, CA 91635   Los Angeles, CA 91685

23. David John Jacobson   David John Jacobson   23.____
     178 35 St. Apt. 4C   178 53 St. Apt. 4C
     New York, N.Y. 00927   New York, N.Y. 00927

     Ann-Marie Calonella   Ann-Marie Calonella
     7243 South Ridge Blvd.   7243 South Ridge Blvd.
     Bakersfield, CA 96714   Bakersfield, CA 96714

     Pauline M. Thompson   Pauline M. Thomson
     872 Linden Ave.   872 Linden Ave.
     Houston, Texas 70321   Houston, Texas 70321

24. Chester LeRoy Masterton   Chester LeRoy Masterson   24.____
     152 Lacy Rd.   152 Lacy Rd.
     Kankakee, Ill. 54532   Kankakee, Ill. 54532

     William Maloney   William Maloney
     S. LaCrosse Pla.   S. LaCross Pla.
     Wausau, Wisconsin 52146   Wausau, Wisconsin 52146

5 (#1)

Cynthia V. Barnes
16 Pines Rd.
Greenpoint, Miss. 20376

Cynthia V. Barnes
16 Pines Rd.
Greenpoint, Miss. 20376

25. Marcel Jean Frontenac
6 Burton On The Water
Calender, Me. 01471

Marcel Jean Frontenac
6 Burton On The Water
Calender, Me. 01471

25.____

J. Scott Marsden
174 S. Tipton St.
Cleveland, Ohio

J. Scott Marsden
174 Tipton St.
Cleveland, Ohio

Lawrence T. Haney
171 McDonough St.
Decatur, Ga. 31304

Lawrence T. Haney
171 McDonough St.
Decatur, Ga. 31304

KEY (CORRECT ANSWERS)

1.	C		11.	B
2.	A		12.	A
3.	D		13.	C
4.	B		14.	B
5.	A		15.	B
6.	B		16.	C
7.	D		17.	A
8.	C		18.	D
9.	C		19.	A
10.	B		20.	C

21. C
22. C
23. B
24. B
25. C

TEST 2

DIRECTIONS: Each question or incomplete statement is followed by several suggested answers or completions. Select the one that BEST answers the question or completes the statement. *PRINT THE LETTER OF THE CORRECT ANSWER IN THE SPACE AT THE RIGHT.*

Questions 1-6.

DIRECTIONS: Questions 1 through 6 are to be answered SOLELY on the basis of the information contained in the following passage.

Duplicating is the process of making a number of identical copies of letters, document, etc. from an original. Some duplicating processes make copies directly from the original document. Other duplicating processes require the preparation of a special master, and copies are then made from the master. Four of the most common duplicating processes are stencil, fluid, offset, and xerox.

In the stencil process, the typewriter is used to cut the words into a master called a stencil. Drawings, charts, or graphs can be cut into the stencil using a stylus. As many as 3,500 good-quality copies can be reproduced from one stencil. Various grades of finished paper from inexpensive mimeograph to expensive bond can be used.

The fluid process is a good method of copying from 50 to 125 good-quality copies from a master, which is prepared with a special dye. The master is placed on the duplicator, and special paper with a hard finish is moistened and then passed through the duplicator. Some of the dye on the master is dissolved, creating an impression on the paper. The impression becomes lighter as more copies are made; and once the dye on the master is used up, a new master must be made.

The offset process is the most adaptable office duplicating process because this process can be used for making a few copies or many copies. Masters can be made on paper or plastic for a few hundred copies, or on metal plates for as many as 75,000 copies. By using a special technique called photo-offset, charts, photographs, illustrations, or graphs can be reproduced on the master plate. The offset process is capable of producing large quantities of fine, top-quality copies on all types of finished paper.

The xerox process reproduces an exact duplicate from an original. It is the fastest duplicating method because the original material is placed directly on the duplicator, eliminating the need to make a special master. Any kind of paper can be used. The xerox process is the most expensive duplicating process; however, it is the best method of reproducing small quantities of good-quality copies of reports, letters, official documents, memos, or contracts.

1. Of the following, the MOST efficient method of reproducing 5,000 copies of a graph is 1.____
   A. stencil   B. fluid   C. offset   D. xerox

2. The offset process is the MOST adaptable office duplicating process because
   A. it is the quickest duplicating method
   B. it is the least expensive duplicating method
   C. it can produce a small number or large number of copies
   D. a softer master can be used over and over again

3. Which one of the following duplicating processes uses moistened paper?
   A. Stencil   B. Fluid   C. Offset   D. Xerox

4. The fluid process would be the BEST process to use for reproducing
   A. five copies of a school transcript
   B. fifty copies of a memo
   C. five hundred copies of a form letter
   D. five thousand copies of a chart

5. Which one of the following duplicating processes does NOT require a special master?
   A. Fluid   B. Xerox   C. Offset   D. Stencil

6. Xerox is NOT used for all duplicating jobs because
   A. it produces poor-quality copies
   B. the process is too expensive
   C. preparing the master is too time-consuming
   D. it cannot produce written reports

7. Assume a city agency has 775 office workers.
   If 2 out of 25 office workers were absent on a particular day, how many office workers reported to work on that day?
   A. 713   B. 744   C. 750   D. 773

Questions 8-11,

DIRECTIONS: In Questions 8 through 11, select the choice that is CLOSEST in meaning to the underlined word.

   SAMPLE: This division reviews the fiscal reports of the agency.
              In this sentence, the word *fiscal* means MOST NEARLY
              A. financial   B. critical   C. basic   D. personnel

   The correct answer is A, financial, because financial is closest to *fiscal*.

8. A central file eliminates the need to retain duplicate material.
   The word *retain* means MOST NEARLY
   A. keep   B. change   C. locate   D. process

9. Filing is a routine office task.
   Routine means MOST NEARLY
   A. proper   B. regular   C. simple   D. difficult

10. Sometimes a word, phrase, or sentence must be underlined to correct an error. 10.____
    Deleted means MOST NEARLY
    A. removed   B. added   C. expanded   D. improved

11. Your supervisor will evaluate your work. 11.____
    Evaluate means MOST NEARLY
    A. judge   B. list   C. assign   D. explain

Questions 12-19.

DIRECTIONS: The code table below shows 10 letters with matching numbers. For each Question 12 through 19, there are three sets of letters. Each set of letters is followed by a set of numbers which may or may not match their correct letter according to the code table. For each question, check all three sets of letters and numbers and mark your answer
- A. if no pairs are correctly matched
- B. if only one pair is correctly matched
- C. if only two pairs are correctly matched
- D. if all three pairs are correctly matched

CODE TABLE

T	M	V	D	S	P	R	G	B	H
1	2	3	4	5	6	7	8	9	0

SAMPLE QUESTION: TMVDSP   123456
                   RGBHTM   789011
                   DSPRGB   256789

In the sample question above, the first set of numbers correctly matches its set of letters. But the second and third pairs contain mistakes. In the second pair, M is incorrectly matched with number 1. According to the code table, letter M should be correctly matched with number 2. In the third pair, the letter D is incorrectly matched with number 2. According to the code table, letter D should be correctly matched with number 4. Since only one of the pairs is correctly matched, the answer to this sample question is B.

12. RSBMRM   759262   12.____
     GDSRVH   845730
     VDBRTM   349713

13. TGVSDR   183247   13.____
     SMHRDP   520647
     TRMHSR   172057

14. DSPRGM   456782   14.____
     MVDBHT   234902
     HPMDBT   062491

4 (#2)

15.	BVPTRD	936184	15._____
	GDPHMB	807029	
	GMRHMV	827032	
16.	MGVRSH	283750	16._____
	TRDMBS	174295	
	SPRMGV	567283	
17.	SGBSDM	489542	17._____
	MGHPTM	290612	
	MPBMHT	269301	
18.	TDPBHM	146902	18._____
	VPBMRS	369275	
	GDMBHM	842902	
19.	MVPTBV	236194	19._____
	PDRTMB	647128	
	BGTMSM	981232	

Questions 20-25.

DIRECTIONS: In each of Questions 20 through 25, the names of four people are given. For each question, choose as your answer the one of the four names given which should be filed FIRST according to the usual system of alphabetical filing of names, as described in the following paragraph.

In filing names, you must start with the last name. Names are filed in order of the first letter of the last name, then the second letter, etc. Therefore, BAILY would be filed before BROWN, which would be filed before COLT. A name with fewer letters of the same type comes first; i.e., Smith before Smithe. If the last names are the same, the names are filed alphabetically by the first name. If the first name is an initial, a name with an initial would come before a first name that starts with the same letter as the initial. Therefore, I. BROWN would come before IRA BROWN. Finally, if both last name and first name are the same, the name would be filed alphabetically by the middle name, once again an initial coming before a middle name which starts with the same letter as the initial. If there is no middle name at all, the name would come before those with middle initials or names.

   SAMPLE QUESTION: A. Lester Daniels
   B. William Dancer
   C. Nathan Danzig
   D. Dan Lester

The last names beginning with D are filed before the last name beginning with L. Since DANIELS, DANCER, and DANZIG all begin with the same three letters, you must look at the fourth letter of the last name to determine which name should be filed first. C comes before I or Z in the alphabet, so DANCER is filed before DANIELS or DANZIG. Therefore, the answer to the above sample question is B.

41

5 (#2)

20. A. Scott Biala B. Mary Byala 20.____
    C. Martin Baylor D. Francis Bauer

21. A. Howard J. Black B. Howard Black 21.____
    C. J. Howard Black D. John H. Black

22. A. Theodora Garth Kingston B. Theadore Barth Kingston 22.____
    C. Thomas Kingston D. Thomas T. Kingston

23. A. Paulette Mary Huerta B. Paul M. Huerta 23.____
    C. Paulette L. Huerta D. Peter A. Huerta

24. A. Martha Hunt Morgan B. Martin Hunt Morgan 24.____
    C. Mary H. Morgan D. Martine H. Morgan

25. A. James T. Meerschaum B. James M. Mershum 25.____
    C. James F. Mearshaum D. James N. Meshum

KEY (CORRECT ANSWERS)

1.	C		11.	A
2.	C		12.	B
3.	B		13.	B
4.	B		14.	C
5.	B		15.	A
6.	B		16.	D
7.	A		17.	A
8.	A		18.	D
9.	B		19.	A
10.	A		20.	D

21. B
22. B
23. B
24. A
25. C

TEST 3

DIRECTIONS: Each question or incomplete statement is followed by several suggested answers or completions. Select the one that BEST answers the question or completes the statement. *PRINT THE LETTER OF THE CORRECT ANSWER IN THE SPACE AT THE RIGHT.*

1. Which one of the following statements about proper telephone usage is NOT always correct?
   When answering the telephone, you should
   A. know whom you are speaking to
   B. give the caller your undivided attention
   C. identify yourself to the caller
   D. obtain the information the caller wishes before you do your other work

   1.____

2. Assume that, as a member of a worker's safety committee in your agency, you are responsible for encouraging other employees to follow correct safety practices. While you are working on your regular assignment, you observe an employee violating a safety rule.
   Of the following, the BEST action for you to take FIRST is to
   A. speak to the employee about safety practices and order him to stop violating the safety rule
   B. speak to the employee about safety practices and point out the safety rule he is violating
   C. bring the matter up in the next committee meeting
   D. report this violation of the safety rule to the employee's supervisor

   2.____

3. Assume that you have been temporarily assigned by your supervisor to do a job which you do not want to do.
   The BEST action for you to take is to
   A. discuss the job with your supervisor, explaining why you do not want to do it
   B. discuss the job with your supervisor and tell her that you will not do it
   C. ask a co-worker to take your place on this job
   D. do some other job that you like; your supervisor may give the job you do not like to someone else

   3.____

4. Assume that you keep the confidential personnel files of employees in your unit. A friend asks you to obtain some information from the file of one of your co-workers.
   The BEST action to take is to _____ to your friend.
   A. ask the co-worker if you can give the information
   B. ask your supervisor if you can give the information
   C. give the information
   D. refuse to give the information

   4.____

Questions 5-8.

DIRECTIONS: Questions 5 through 8 are to be answered SOLELY on the basis of the information contained in the following passage.

City government is committed to providing a safe and healthy work environment for all city employees. An effective agency safety program reduces accidents by educating employees about the types of careless acts which can cause accidents. Even in an office, accidents can happen. If each employee is aware of possible safety hazards, the number of accidents on the job can be reduced.

Careless use of office equipment can cause accidents and injuries. For example, file cabinet drawers which are filled with papers can be so heavy that the entire cabinet could tip over from the weight of one open drawer.

The bottom drawers of desks and file cabinets should never be left open since employees can easily trip over open drawers and injure themselves.

When reaching for objects on a high shelf, an employee should use a strong, sturdy object such as a stepstool to stand on. Makeshift platforms made out of books, papers, or boxes can easily collapse. Even chairs can slide out from under foot, causing serious injury.

Even at an employee's desk, safety hazards can occur. Frayed or cut wires should be repaired or replaced immediately. Computers which are not firmly anchored to the desk or table could fall, causing injury.

Smoking is one of the major causes of fires in the office. A lighted match or improperly extinguished cigarette thrown into a wastebasket filled with paper could cause a major fire with possible loss of life. Where smoking is permitted, ashtrays should be used. Smoking is particularly dangerous in offices were flammable chemicals are used.

5. The goal of an effective safety program is to
   A. reduce office accidents
   B. stop employees from smoking on the job
   C. encourage employees to continue their education
   D. eliminate high shelves in offices

6. Desks and file cabinets can become safety hazards when
   A. their drawers are left open
   B. they are used as wastebaskets
   C. they are makeshift
   D. they are not anchored securely to the floor

7. Smoking is especially hazardous when it occurs
   A. near exposed wires
   B. in a crowded office
   C. in an area where flammable chemicals are used
   D. where books and papers are stored

8. Accidents are likely to occur when
   A. employees' desks are cluttered with books and papers
   B. employees are not aware of safety hazards
   C. employees close desk drawers
   D. stepstools are used to reach high objects

9. Assume that part of your job as a worker in the accounting division of a city agency is to answer the telephone.
   When you first answer the telephone, it is LEAST important to tell the caller
   A. your title
   B. your name
   C. the name of your unit
   D. the name of your agency

10. Assume that you are assigned to work as a receptionist, and your duties are to answer phones, greet visitors, and do other general office work. You are busy with a routine job when several visitors approach your desk.
    The BEST action to take is to
    A. ask the visitors to have a seat and assist them after your work is completed
    B. tell the visitors that you are busy and they should return at a more convenient time
    C. stop working long enough to assist the visitors
    D. continue working and wait for the visitors to ask you for assistance

11. Assume that your supervisor has chosen you to take a special course during hours to learn a new payroll procedure. Although you know that you were chosen because of your good work record, a co-worker, who feels that he should have been chosen, has been telling everyone in your unit that the choice was unfair.
    Of the following, the BEST way to handle this situation FIRST is to
    A. suggest to the co-worker that everything in life is unfair
    B. contact your union representative in case your co-worker presents a formal grievance
    C. tell your supervisor about your co-worker's complaints and let her handle the situation
    D. tell the co-worker that you were chosen because of your superior work record

12. Assume that while you are working on an assignment which must be completed quickly, a supervisor from another unit asks you to obtain information for her.
    Of the following, the BEST way to respond to her request is to
    A. tell her to return in an hour since you are busy
    B. give her the names of some people in her own unit who could help her
    C. tell her you are busy and refer her to a co-worker
    D. tell her that you are busy and ask her if she could wait until you finish your assignment

13. A co-worker in your unit is often off from work because of illness. Your supervisor assigns the co-worker's work to you when she is not there. Lately, doing her work has interfered with your own job.
    The BEST action for you to take FIRST is to
    A. discuss the problem with your supervisor
    B. complete your own work before starting your co-worker's work
    C. ask other workers in your unit to assist you
    D. work late in order to get the jobs done

14. During the month of June, 40,587 people attended a city-owned swimming pool. In July, 13,014 more people attended the swimming pool than the number that had attended in June. In August, 39,655 people attended the swimming pool. The TOTAL number of people who attended the swimming pool during the months of June, July, and August was

   A. 80,242   B. 93,256   C. 133,843   D. 210,382

14._____

Questions 15-22.

DIRECTIONS: Questions 15 through 22 test how well you understand what you read. It will be necessary for you to read carefully because your answers to these questions must be based ONLY on the information in the following paragraphs.

The telephone directory is made up of two books. The first book consists of the introductory section and the alphabetical listing of names section. The second book is the classified directory (also known as the yellow pages). Many people who are familiar with one book do not realize how useful the other can be. The efficient office worker should become familiar with both books in order to make the best use of this important source of information.

The introductory section gives general instructions for finding numbers in the alphabetical listing and classified directory. This section also explains how to use the telephone company's many services, including the operator and information services, gives examples of charges for local and long-distance calls, and lists area codes for the entire country. In addition, this section provides a useful zip code map.

The alphabetical listing of names section lists the names, addresses, and telephone numbers of subscribers in an area. Guide names, or *telltales*, are on the top corner of each page. These guide names indicate the first and last name to be found on that page. *Telltales* help locate any particular name quickly. A cross-reference spelling is also given to help locate names which are spelled several different ways. City, state, and federal government agencies are listed under the major government heading. For example, an agency of the federal government would be listed under *United States Government*.

The classified directory, or yellow pages, is a separate book. In this section are advertising services, public transportation line maps, shopping guides, and listings of businesses arranged by the type of product or services they offer. This book is most useful when looking for the name or phone number of a business when all that is known is the type of product offered and the address, or when trying to locate a particular type of business in an area. Businesses listed in the classified directory can usually be found in the alphabetical listing of names section. When the name of the business is known, you will find the address or phone number more quickly in the alphabetical listing of names section.

15. The introductory section provides
    A. shopping guides   B. government listings
    C. business listings   D. information services

15._____

16. Advertising services would be found in the
    A. introductory section   B. alphabetical listing of names section\
    C. classified directory   D. information services

16._____

17. According to the information in the above passage for locating government agencies, the Information Office of the Department of Consumer Affairs of New York City government would be alphabetically listed FIRST under
    A. *I* for Information Offices
    B. *D* for Department of Consumer Affairs
    C. *N* for New York City
    D. *G* for government

18. When the name of a business is known, the QUICKEST way to find the phone number is to look in the
    A. classified directory
    B. introductory section
    C. alphabetical listing of name section
    D. advertising service section

19. The QUICKEST way to find the phone number of a business when the type of service a business offers and its address is known is to look in the
    A. classified directory
    B. alphabetical listing of names section
    C. introductory section
    D. information service

20. What is a *telltale*?
    A. An alphabetical listing
    B. A guide name
    C. A map
    D. A cross-reference listing

21. The BEST way to find a postal zip code is to look in the
    A. classified directory
    B. introductory section
    C. alphabetical listing of names section
    D. government heading

22. To help find names which have several different spellings, the telephone directory provides
    A. cross-reference spelling
    B. *telltales*
    C. spelling guides
    D. advertising services

23. Assume that your agency has been given $2,025 to purchase file cabinets. If each file cabinet costs $135, how many file cabinet can your agency purchase?
    A. 8
    B. 10
    C. 15
    D. 16

24. Assume that your unit ordered 14 staplers at a total cost of $30.20 and each stapler cost the same.
    The cost of one stapler was MOST NEARLY
    A. $1.02
    B. $1.61
    C. $2.16
    D. $2.26

25. Assume that you are responsible for counting and recording licensing fees collected by your department. On a particular day, your department collected in fees 40 checks in the amount of $6 each, 80 checks in the amount of $4 each, 45 twenty dollar bills, 30 ten dollar bills, 42 five dollar bills, and 186 one dollar bills.
The TOTAL amount in fees collected on that day was
A. $1,406   B. $1,706   C. $2,156   D. $2,356

26. Assume that you are responsible for your agency's petty cash fund. During the month of February, you pay out 7 $2.00 subway fares and one taxi fare for $10.85. You pay out nothing else from the fund. At the end of February, you count the money left in the fund and find 3 one dollar bills, 4 quarters, 5 dimes, and 4 nickels.
The amount of money you had available in the petty cash fund at the BEGINNING of February was
A. $4.70   B. $16.35   C. $24.85   D. $29.55

27. You overhear your supervisor criticize a co-worker for handling equipment in an unsafe way. You feel that the criticism may be unfair.
Of the following, it would be BEST for you to
A. take your co-worker aside and tell her how you feel about your supervisor's comments
B. interrupt the discussion and defend your co-worker to your supervisor
C. continue working as if you had not overheard the discussion
D. make a list of other workers who have violated safety rules and give it to your supervisor

28. Assume that you have been assigned to work on a long-term project with an employee who is known for being uncooperative.
In beginning to work with this employee, it would be LEAST desirable for you to
A. understand why the person is uncooperative
B. act in a calm manner rather than an emotional manner
C. be appreciative of the co-worker's work
D. report the co-worker's lack of cooperation to your supervisor

29. Assume that you are assigned to sell tickets at a city-owned ice skating rink. An adult ticket costs $4.50, and a children's ticket costs $2.25. At the end of a day, you find that you have sold 36 adult tickets and 80 children's tickets.
The TOTAL amount of money you collected for that day was
A. $244.80   B. $318.00   C. $342.00   D. $348.00

30. If each office worker files 487 index cards in one hour, how many card can 26 office workers file in one hour?
A. 10,662   B. 12,175   C. 12,662   D. 14,266

KEY (CORRECT ANSWERS)

1.	D	11.	C	21.	B
2.	B	12.	D	22.	A
3.	A	13.	A	23.	C
4.	D	14.	C	24.	C
5.	A	15.	D	25.	C
6.	A	16.	C	26.	D
7.	C	17.	C	27.	C
8.	B	18.	C	28.	D
9.	A	19.	A	29.	C
10.	C	20.	B	30.	C

EXAMINATION SECTION

TEST 1

DIRECTIONS: Each question or incomplete statement is followed by several suggested answers or completions. Select the one that BEST answers the question or completes the statement. *PRINT THE LETTER OF THE CORRECT ANSWER IN THE SPACE AT THE RIGHT.*

1. The one of the following that is MOST advisable to do before transcribing your dictation notes is to
   A. check the syllabification of long words for typing purposes
   B. edit your notes
   C. number the pages of dictation
   D. sort them by the kind of typing format required

2. As a secretary, the one of the following which is LEAST important in writing a letter under your own signature is
   A. the accuracy of the information
   B. the appropriateness of the language
   C. the reason for the letter
   D. your supervisor's approval of the final copy

3. In a typed letter, the reference line is used
   A. for identification purposes on typed pages of more than one page
   B. to indicate under what heading the copy of the letter should be filed
   C. to indicate who dictated the letter and who typed it
   D. to make the subject of the letter prominent by typing it a single space below the salutation

Questions 4-5:

DIRECTIONS: For questions 4 and 5, choose the letter of the sentence that BEST and MOST clearly expresses its meaning.

4.   A. It has always been the practice of this office to effectuate recruitment of prospective employees from other departments.
     B. This office has always made a practice of recruiting prospective employees from other departments.
     C. Recruitment of prospective employees from other departments has always been a practice which has been implemented by this office.
     D. Implementation of the policy of recruitment of prospective employees from other departments has always been a practice of this office.

5.
A. These employees are assigned to the level of work evidenced by their efforts and skills during the training period.
B. The level of work to which these employees is assigned is decided upon on the basis of the efforts and skills evidenced by them during the period in which they were trained.
C. Assignment of these employees is made on the basis of the level of work their efforts and skills during the training period has evidenced.
D. These employees are assigned to a level of work their efforts and skills during the training period have evidenced.

6. An office assistant was asked to mail a duplicated report of 100 pages to a professor in an out-of-town university. The professor sending the report dictated a short letter that he wanted to mail with the report.
Of the following, the MOST inexpensive proper means of sending these two items would be to send the report
   A. and the letter first class
   B. by parcel post and the letter separately by air mail
   C. and the letter by parcel post
   D. by parcel post and attach to the package an envelope with first-class postage in which is enclosed the letter

7. Plans are underway to determine the productivity of the typists who work in a central office. Of the procedures listed, the one generally considered the MOST accurate for finding out the typists' output is to
   A. keep a record of how much typing is done over specified periods of time
   B. ask each typist how fast she types when she is doing a great deal of word processing
   C. give each typist a timed test during a specified period
   D. ask the supervisor to estimate the typing speed of each subordinate

8. Assume that an executive regularly receives the four types of mail listed below.
As a general rule, the executive's secretary should arrange the mail from top to bottom so that the top items are
   A. advertisements
   B. airmail letters
   C. business letters
   D. unopened personal letters

9. An office assistant in transcribing reports and letters from dictation should MOST generally assume that
    A. the transcript should be exactly what was dictated so there is little need to check any details
    B. the dictated material is merely an idea of what the dictator wanted to say so changes should be made to improve any part of the dictation
    C. there may be some slight changes, but essentially the transcription is to be a faithful copy of what was dictated
    D. the transcript is merely a very rough draft and should be typed quickly so that the dictator can review it and make changes preliminary to having the final copy typed

9._____

10. The one of the following which generally is the CHIEF disadvantage of using office machines in place of human workers in office work is that the machines are
    A. slower
    B. less accurate
    C. more costly
    D. less flexible

10._____

11. An office assistant in a New York City college is asked to place a call to a prospective visiting professor in Los Angeles. It is 1 p.m. in New York (EST). The time in Los Angeles is
    A. 9 a.m.   B. 10 a.m.   C. 4 p.m.   D. 5 p.m.

11._____

12. An office assistant is instructed to send a copy of a report to a professor located in a building across campus. The fastest and most efficient way for this report to reach the professor is by
    A. sending a messenger to hand-deliver it to the professor's office
    B. sending it via fax to the main office of the professor's department
    C. e-mailing it to the professor
    D. dictating the contents of the report to the professor over the phone

12._____

13. An office assistant is in the process of typing the forms for recommendation for promotion for a member of the faculty who is away for a week. She notes that two books of which he is the author are listed without dates.
    Of the following, the procedure she should BEST follow at this point generally is to
    A. postpone doing the job until the professor returns to campus the following week
    B. type the material omitting the books
    C. check the professor's office for copies of the books and obtain the correct data
    D. call the professor's wife and ask her when the books were published

13._____

14. An office has introduced work standards for all of the employees.   14._____
    Of the following, it is MOST likely that use of such standards would tend to
    A. make it more difficult to determine numbers of employees needed
    B. lead to a substantial drop in morale among all of the employees
    C. reduce the possibility of planning to meet emergencies
    D. reduce uncertainty about the costs of doing tasks

15. Of the following clerical errors, the one which probably is LEAST   15._____
    important is
    A. adding 543 instead of 548 to a bookkeeping account
    B. putting the wrong code on a data processing card
    C. recording a transaction on the record of Henry Smith instead of on the record of Harry Smith
    D. writing John Murpfy instead of John Murphy when addressing an envelope

16. Of the following errors, the one which probably is MOST important is   16._____
    A. writing "they're" instead of "their" in an office memo
    B. misplacing a decimal point on a sales invoice
    C. forgetting to write the date on a note for a supervisor
    D. sending an e-mail to a misspelled e-mail address

17. The chairman of an academic department tells an office assistant that a   17._____
    meeting of the faculty is to be held four weeks from the current date.
    Of the following responsibilities, the office assistant is MOST frequently held responsible for
    A. planning the agenda of the meeting
    B. presiding over the conduct of the meeting
    C. reserving the meeting room and notifying the members
    D. initiating all formal resolutions

18. Of the following, a centralized filing system is LEAST suitable for filing   18._____
    A. material which is confidential in nature
    B. routine correspondence
    C. periodic reports of the divisions of the department
    D. material used by several divisions of the department

19. A misplaced record is a lost record.   19._____
    Of the following, the MOST valid implication of this statement in regard to office work is that
    A. all records in an office should be filed in strict alphabetical order
    B. accuracy in filing is essential
    C. only one method of filing should be used throughout the office
    D. files should be locked when not in use

20. When typing names or titles on a roll of folder labels, the one of the following which is MOST important to do is to type the caption
    A. as it appears on the papers to be placed in the folder
    B. in capital letters
    C. in exact indexing or filing order
    D. so that it appears near the bottom of the folder tab when the label is attached

20._____

21. A professor at a Boston university asks an office assistant to place a call to a fellow professor in San Francisco. The MOST appropriate local time for the assistant to place the call to the professor in California, given the time difference, would be
    A. 8:30 a.m.   B. 10:00 a.m.   C. 11:30 a.m.   D. 1:30 p.m.

21._____

22. When typing the rough draft of a report, the computer application you would use is
    A. Excel   B. Word
    C. PowerPoint   D. Internet Explorer

22._____

23. Which of the following is the BEST and most appropriate way to proofread and edit a report before submitting it to a supervisor for review?
    A. Scan the report with the program's spell check feature
    B. Proof the report yourself, then ask another office assistant to read the report over as well until it is finished
    C. Give the report to another office assistant who is more skilled at proofreading
    D. Use the spell checker, then scan the report yourself as many times as needed in order to pick up any additional errors

23._____

24. The one of the following situations in which it would be MOST justifiable for an office to use standard or form paragraphs in its business letters is when
    A. a large number of similar letters is to be sent
    B. the letters are to be uniform in length and appearance
    C. it is desired to reduce typing errors in correspondence
    D. the office is to carry on a lengthy correspondence with an individual

24._____

25. Of the following, the MOST important factor in determining whether or not an office filing system is effective is that the
    A. information in the files is legible
    B. records in the files are used frequently
    C. information in the files is accurate
    D. records in the files can be located readily

25._____

KEY (CORRECT ANSWERS)

1. B	11. B	21. D
2. D	12. C	22. B
3. C	13. C	23. D
4. B	14. D	24. A
5. A	15. D	25. D
6. D	16. B	
7. A	17. C	
8. D	18. A	
9. C	19. B	
10. D	20. C	

TEST 2

DIRECTIONS: Each question or incomplete statement is followed by several suggested answers or completions. Select the one that BEST answers the question or completes the statement. *PRINT THE LETTER OF THE CORRECT ANSWER IN THE SPACE AT THE RIGHT.*

1. For the office assistant whose duties include frequent recording and transcription of minutes of formal meetings, the one of the following reference works generally considered to be MOST useful is
   A. *Robert's Rules of Order*
   B. *Bartlett's Familiar Quotations*
   C. *World Almanac and Book of Facts*
   D. *Conway's Reference*

   1._____

2. Of the following statements about the numeric system of filing, the one which is CORRECT is that it
   A. is the least accurate of all methods of filing
   B. eliminates the need for cross-referencing
   C. allows for very limited expansion
   D. requires a separate index

   2._____

3. When more than one name or subject is involved in a piece of correspondence to be filed, the office assistant should GENERALLY
   A. prepare a cross-reference sheet
   B. establish a geographical filing system
   C. prepare out-guides
   D. establish a separate index card file for noting such correspondence

   3._____

4. A tickler file is MOST generally used for
   A. identification of material contained in a numeric file
   B. maintenance of a current listing of telephone numbers
   C. follow-up of matters requiring future attention
   D. control of records borrowed or otherwise removed from the files

   4._____

5. In filing, the name Ms. *Ann Catalana-Moss* should GENERALLY be indexed as
   A. Moss, Catalana, Ann (Ms.)
   B. Catalana-Moss, Ann (Ms.)
   C. Ann Catalana-Moss (Ms.)
   D. Moss-Catalana, Ann (Ms.)

   5._____

6. An office assistant has a set of four cards, each of which contains one of the following names.
   In alphabetic filing, the FIRST of the cards to be filed is
   A. Ms. Alma John
   B. Mrs. John (Patricia) Edwards
   C. John-Edward School Supplies, Inc.
   D. John H. Edwards

7. Generally, of the following, the name to be filed FIRST in an alphabetical filing system is
   A. Diane Maestro
   B. Diana McElroy
   C. James Mackell
   D. James McKell

8. After checking several times, you are unable to locate a student record in its proper file drawer. The file drawer in question is used constantly by many members of the staff.
   In this situation, the NEXT step you should take in locating the missing record is to
   A. ask another worker to look through the file drawer
   B. determine if there is another copy of the record filed in a different place
   C. find out if the record has been removed by another staff member
   D. wait a day or two and see if the record turns up

9. It is MOST important that an enclosure which is to be mailed with a letter should be put in an envelope so that
   A. any printing on the enclosure will not be visible through the address side of the envelope
   B. it is obvious that there is an enclosure inside the envelope
   C. the enclosure takes up less space than the letter
   D. the person who opens the envelope will pull out both the letter and the enclosure

10. Suppose that one of the student aides with whom you work suggests a change in the filing procedure. He is sure the change will result in increased rates of filing among the other employees.
    The one of the following which you should do FIRST is to
    A. ask him to demonstrate his method in order to determine if he files more quickly than the other employees
    B. ask your supervisor if you may make a change in the filing procedure
    C. ignore the aide's suggestion since he is not a filing expert
    D. tell him to show his method to the other employees and to encourage them to use it

11. It is generally advisable to leave at least six inches of working space in a file drawer. This procedure is MOST useful in
    A. decreasing the number of filing errors
    B. facilitating the sorting of documents and folders
    C. maintaining a regular program of removing inactive records
    D. preventing folders and papers from being torn

11._____

12. Assume that a dictator is briefly interrupted because of a telephone call or other similar matter (no more than three minutes).
    Of the following tasks, the person taking the dictation should NORMALLY use the time to
    A. re-read notes already recorded
    B. tidy the dictator's desk
    C. check the accuracy of the dictator's desk files
    D. return to her own desk to type the dictated material

12._____

13. When typing a preliminary draft of a report, the one of the following which you should generally NOT do is
    A. erase typing errors and deletions rather than cross them out
    B. leave plenty of room at the top, bottom and sides of each page
    C. make only the number of copies that you are asked to make
    D. type double or triple space

13._____

14. The BEST way for a receptionist to deal with a situation in which she must leave her desk for a long time is to
    A. ask someone to take her place while she is away
    B. leave a note or sign on her desk which indicates the time she will return
    C. take a chance that no one will arrive while she is gone and leave her desk unattended
    D. tell a coworker to ask any visitors that arrive to wait until she returns

14._____

15. Suppose that two individuals come up to your desk at the same time. One of them asks you for the location of the nearest public phone. After you answer the question, you turn to the second person who asks you the same question.
    The one of the following actions that would be BEST for you to take in this situation is to
    A. ignore the second person since he obviously overheard your first answer
    B. point out that you just answered the same question and quickly repeat the information
    C. politely repeat the information to the second individual
    D. tell the second person to follow the first to the public telephone

15._____

16. Which of the following names should be filed FIRST in an alphabetical filing system?
    A. Anthony Aarvedsen   B. William Aaron
    C. Denise Aron   D. A.J. Arrington

16._____

17. New material added to a file folder should USUALLY be inserted
    A. in the order of importance (the most important in front)
    B. in the order of importance (the most important in back)
    C. chronologically (most recent in front)
    D. chronologically (most recent in back)

17._____

18. An individual is looking for a name in the White Pages of a telephone directory.
    Which of the following BEST describes the system of filing found there?
    A. alphabetic   B. sequential
    C. locator   D. index

18._____

19. The MAIN purpose of a tickler file is to
    A. help prevent overlooking matters that require future attention
    B. check on adequacy of past performance
    C. pinpoint responsibility for recurring daily tasks
    D. reduce the volume of material kept in general files

19._____

20. Which of the following BEST describes the process of *reconciling* a bank statement?
    A. Analyzing the nature of the expenditures made by the office during the preceding month
    B. Comparing the statement of the bank with the banking records maintained in the office
    C. Determining the liquidity position by reading the bank statement carefully
    D. Checking the service charges noted on the bank statement

20._____

21. From the viewpoint of preserving agency or institutional funds, the LEAST acceptable method for making a payment is a check made out to
    A. cash   B. a company
    C. an individual   D. a partnership

21._____

22. Listed below are four of the steps in the process of preparing correspondence for filing.
    If they were to be put in logical sequence, the SECOND step would be
    A. preparing cross-reference sheets or cards
    B. coding the correspondence using a classification system
    C. sorting the correspondence in the order to be filed
    D. checking for follow-up action required and preparing a follow-up slip

22._____

23. The process of *justifying* typed copy involves laying out the copy so that 23._____
    A. each paragraph appears to be approximately the same size
    B. no long words are broken up at the end of a line
    C. the right and left hand margins are even
    D. there is enough room to enter proofreading marks at the end of each line

24. The MOST important reason for a person in charge of a petty cash fund 24._____
    to obtain receipts for payments is that this practice would tend to
    A. decrease robberies by delivery personnel
    B. eliminate the need to keep a record of petty cash expenditures
    C. prove that the fund has been used properly
    D. provide a record of the need for cash in the daily operations of the office

25. You should GENERALLY replenish a petty cash fund 25._____
    A. at regularly established intervals
    B. each time you withdraw a sum
    C. when the amount of cash gets below a certain specified amount
    D. when the fund is completely empty

KEY (CORRECT ANSWERS)

1. A	11. D	21. A
2. D	12. A	22. A
3. A	13. A	23. C
4. C	14. A	24. C
5. B	15. C	25. C
6. D	16. B	
7. C	17. C	
8. C	18. A	
9. D	19. A	
10. A	20. B	

EXAMINATION SECTION
TEST 1

DIRECTIONS: Each question or incomplete statement is followed by several suggested answers or completions. Select the one that BEST answers the question or completes the statement. *PRINT THE LETTER OF THE CORRECT ANSWER IN THE SPACE AT THE RIGHT.*

1. If you open a personal letter by mistake, the one of the following actions which it would generally be BEST for you to take is to

    A. ignore your error, attach the envelope to the letter, and distribute in the usual manner
    B. personally give the addressee the letter without any explanation
    C. place the letter inside the envelope, indicate under your initials that it was opened in error, and give to the addressee
    D. reseal the envelope or place the contents in another envelope and pass on to addressee

    1.____

2. If you receive a telephone call regarding a matter which your office does not handle, you should FIRST

    A. give the caller the telephone number of the proper office so that he can dial again
    B. offer to transfer the caller to the proper office
    C. suggest that the caller re-dial since he probably dialed incorrectly
    D. tell the caller he has reached the wrong office and then hang up

    2.____

3. When you answer the telephone, the MOST important reason for identifying yourself and your organization is to

    A. give the caller time to collect his or her thoughts
    B. impress the caller with your courtesy
    C. inform the caller that he or she has reached the right number
    D. set a business-like tone at the beginning of the conversation

    3.____

4. The one of the following cases in which you would NOT place a special notation in the left margin of a letter that you have typed is when

    A. one of the copies is intended for someone other than the addressee of the letter
    B. you enclose a flyer with the letter
    C. you sign your superior's name to the letter, at his or her request
    D. the letter refers to something being sent under separate cover

    4.____

5. Suppose that you accidentally cut a letter or enclosure as you are opening an envelope with a paper knife.
The one of the following that you should do FIRST is to

    A. determine whether the document is important
    B. clip or staple the pieces together and process as usual
    C. mend the cut document with transparent tape
    D. notify the sender that the communication was damaged and request another copy

    5.____

63

6. As soon as you pick up the phone, a very angry caller begins immediately to complain about city agencies and *red tape*. He says that he has been shifted to two or three different offices. It turns out that he is seeking information which is not immediately available to you. You believe you know, however, where it can be found.
Which of the following actions is the BEST one for you to take?

   A. To eliminate all confusion, suggest that the caller write the mayor stating explicitly what he wants.
   B. Apologize by telling the caller how busy city agencies now are, but also tell him directly that you do not have the information he needs.
   C. Ask for the caller's telephone number, and assure him you will call back after you have checked further.
   D. Give the caller the name and telephone number of the person who might be able to help, but explain that you are not positive he will get results.

7. Suppose that one of your duties is to dictate responses to routine requests from the public for information. A letter writer asks for information which, as expressed in a one-sentence, explicit agency rule, cannot be given out to the public.
Of the following ways of answering the letter, which is the MOST efficient?

   A. Quote verbatim that section of the agency rules which prohibits giving this information to the public.
   B. Without quoting the rule, explain why you cannot accede to the request and suggest alternative sources.
   C. Describe how carefully the request was considered before classifying it as subject to the rule forbidding the issuance of such information.
   D. Acknowledge receipt of the letter and advise that the requested information is not released to the public.

8. Suppose you assist in supervising a staff which has rather high morale, and your own supervisor asks you to poll the staff to find out who will be able to work overtime this particular evening to help complete emergency work.
Which of the following approaches would be MOST likely to win their cooperation while maintaining their morale?

   A. Tell them that the better assignments will be given only to those who work overtime.
   B. Tell them that occasional overtime is a job requirement.
   C. Assure them they'll be doing you a personal favor.
   D. Let them know clearly why the overtime is needed.

9. Suppose that you have been asked to write and to prepare for reproduction new departmental vacation leave regulations.
After you have written the new regulations, all of which fit on two pages, which one of the following would be the BEST method of reproducing 1,000 copies?

   A. An outside private printer because you can best maintain confidentiality using this technique
   B. Photocopying because the copies will have the best possible appearance
   C. Sending the file to all department employees as printable PDFs
   D. Printing and collating on the office high-volume printer

10. You are in charge of verifying employees' qualifications. This involves telephoning previous employers and schools. One of the applications which you are reviewing contains information which you are almost certain is correct on the basis of what the employee has told you.
The BEST thing to do is to

   A. check the information again with the employer
   B. perform the required verification procedures
   C. accept the information as valid
   D. ask a superior to verify the information

11. The practice of immediately identifying oneself and one's place of employment when contacting persons on the telephone is

   A. *good* because the receiver of the call can quickly identify the caller and establish a frame of reference
   B. *good* because it helps to set the caller at ease with the other party
   C. *poor* because it is not necessary to divulge that information when making general calls
   D. *poor* because it takes longer to arrive at the topic to be discussed

12. Which one of the following should be the MOST important overall consideration when preparing a recommendation to automate a large-scale office activity?
The

   A. number of models of automated equipment available
   B. benefits and costs of automation
   C. fears and resistance of affected employees
   D. experience of offices which have automated similar activities

13. A tickler file is MOST appropriate for filing materials

   A. chronologically according to date they were received
   B. alphabetically by name
   C. alphabetically by subject
   D. chronologically according to date they should be followed up

14. Which of the following is the BEST reason for decentralizing rather then centralizing the use of duplicating machines?

   A. Developing and retaining efficient duplicating machine operators
   B. Facilitating supervision of duplicating services
   C. Motivating employees to produce legible duplicated copies
   D. Placing the duplicating machines where they are most convenient and most frequently used

15. Window envelopes are sometimes considered preferable to individually addressed envelopes PRIMARILY because

   A. window envelopes are available in standard sizes for all purposes
   B. window envelopes are more attractive and official-looking
   C. the use of window envelopes eliminates the risk of inserting a letter in the wrong envelope
   D. the use of window envelopes requires neater typing

16. In planning the layout of a new office, the utilization of space and the arrangement of staff, furnishings, and equipment should usually be MOST influenced by the

    A. gross square footage
    B. status differences in the chain of command
    C. framework of informal relationships among employees
    D. activities to be performed

17. Office forms sometimes consist of several copies, each of a different color. The MAIN reason for using different colors is to

    A. make a favorable impression on the users of the form
    B. distinguish each copy from the others
    C. facilitate the preparation of legible carbon copies
    D. reduce cost, since using colored stock permits recycling of paper

18. Which of the following is the BEST justification for obtaining a photocopying machine for the office?

    A. A photocopying machine can produce an unlimited number of copies at a low fixed cost per copy.
    B. Employees need little training in operating a photocopying machine.
    C. Office costs will be reduced and efficiency increased.
    D. The legibility of a photocopy generally is superior to copy produced by any other office duplicating device.

19. An administrative officer in charge of a small fund for buying office supplies has just written a check to Charles Laird, a supplier, and has sent the check by messenger to him. A half-hour later, the messenger telephones the administrative officer. He has lost the check.
    Which of the following is the MOST important action for the administrative officer to take under these circumstances?

    A. Ask the messenger to return and write a report describing the loss of the check.
    B. Make a note on the performance record of the messenger who lost the check.
    C. Take the necessary steps to have payment stopped on the check.
    D. Refrain from doing anything since the check may be found shortly.

20. A petty cash fund is set up PRIMARILY to

    A. take care of small investments that must be made from time to time
    B. take care of small expenses that arise from time to time
    C. provide a fund to be used as the office wants to use it with little need to maintain records
    D. take care of expenses that develop during emergencies such as machine breakdowns and fires

21. Your superior has asked you to send a package from your agency to a government agency in another city. He has written out the message and has indicated the name of the government agency.
    When you prepare the package for mailing, which of the following items that your superior has not mentioned must you be sure to include?

A. Today's date
B. The full address of the government agency
C. A polite opening such as *Dear Sirs*
D. A final sentence such as *We would appreciate hearing from your agency in reply as soon as is convenient for you*

22. In addition to the original piece of correspondence, one should USUALLY also have typed

    A. a single copy
    B. as many copies as can be typed at one time
    C. no more copies than are needed
    D. two copies

22.____

23. The one of the following which is the BEST procedure to follow when making a short insert in a completed dictation is to

    A. label the insert with a letter and indicate the position of the insert in the text by writing the identifying letter in the proper place
    B. squeeze the insert into its proper place within the main text of the dictation
    C. take down the insert and check the placement with the person who dictated when you are ready to transcribe your notes
    D. transcribe the dictation into longhand, including the insert in its proper position

23.____

24. The one of the following procedures which will be MOST efficient in helping you to quickly open your dictation notebook to a clean sheet is to

    A. clip or place a rubberband around the used portion of the notebook
    B. leave the book out and open to a clean page when not in use
    C. transcribe each dictation after it is given and rip out the used pages
    D. use a book marker to indicate which portion of the notebook has been used

24.____

25. The purpose of dating your dictation notebooks is GENERALLY to

    A. enable you to easily refer to your notes at a later date
    B. ensure that you transcribe your notes in the order in which they were dictated
    C. set up a precise record-keeping procedure
    D. show your employer that you pay attention to detail

25.____

KEY (CORRECT ANSWERS)

1. C
2. B
3. C
4. C
5. C

6. C
7. A
8. D
9. D
10. B

11. A
12. B
13. D
14. D
15. C

16. D
17. B
18. C
19. C
20. B

21. B
22. C
23. A
24. A
25. A

TEST 2

DIRECTIONS: Each question or incomplete statement is followed by several suggested answers or completions. Select the one that BEST answers the question or completes the statement. *PRINT THE LETTER OF THE CORRECT ANSWER IN THE SPACE AT THE RIGHT.*

1. With regard to typed correspondence received by most offices, which of the following is the GREATEST problem?

   A. Verbosity
   B. Illegibility
   C. Improper folding
   D. Excessive copies

   1.____

2. Of the following, the GREATEST advantage of flash drives over rewritable CD storage is that they

   A. are portable
   B. are both smaller and lighter
   C. contain more storage space
   D. allow files to be deleted to free space

   2.____

3. Suppose that a large quantity of information is in the files which are located a good distance from your desk. Almost every worker in your office must use these files constantly. Your duties in particular require that you daily refer to about 25 of the same items. They are short, one-page items distributed throughout the files. In this situation, your BEST course would be to

   A. take the items that you use daily from the files and keep them on your desk, inserting *out cards* in their place
   B. go to the files each time you need the information so that the items will be there when other workers need them
   C. make xerox copies of the information you use most frequently and keep them in your desk for ready reference
   D. label the items you use most often with different colored tabs for immediate identification

   3.____

4. Of the following, the MOST important advantage of preparing manuals of office procedures in loose-leaf form is that this form

   A. permits several employees to use different sections simultaneously
   B. facilitates the addition of new material and the removal of obsolete material
   C. is more readily arranged in alphabetical order
   D. reduces the need for cross-references to locate material carried under several headings

   4.____

5. Suppose that you establish a new clerical procedure for the unit you supervise. Your keeping a close check on the time required by your staff to handle the new procedure is WISE mainly because such a check will find out

   A. whether your subordinates know how to handle the new procedure
   B. whether a revision of the unit's work schedule will be necessary as a result of the new procedure
   C. what attitude your employees have toward the new procedure
   D. what alterations in job descriptions will be necessitated by the new procedure

   5.____

6. The numbered statements below relate to the stenographic skill of taking dictation. According to authorities on secretarial practices, which of these are generally recommended guides to development of efficient stenographic skills?

STATEMENTS
1. A stenographer should date her notebook daily to facilitate locating certain notes at a later time.
2. A stenographer should make corrections of grammatical mistakes while her boss is dictating to her.
3. A stenographer should draw a line through the dictated matter in her notebook after she has transcribed it.
4. A stenographer should write in longhand unfamiliar names and addresses dictated to her.

The CORRECT answer is:

   A. Only Statements 1, 2, and 3 are generally recommended guides.
   B. Only Statements 2, 3, and 4 are generally recommended guides.
   C. Only Statements 1, 3, and 4 are generally recommended guides.
   D. All four statements are generally recommended guides.

7. According to generally recognized rules of filing in an alphabetic filing system, the one of the following names which normally should be filed LAST is

   A. Department of Education, New York State
   B. F.B.I.
   C. Police Department of New York City
   D. P.S. 81 of New York City

8. Which one of the following forms for the typed name of the dictator in the closing lines of a letter is generally MOST acceptable in the United States?

   A. (Dr.) James F. Fenton
   B. Dr. James F. Fenton
   C. Mr. James F. Fenton, Ph.D.
   D. James F. Fenton

9. Which of the following is, MOST generally, a rule to be followed when typing a rough draft?

   A. The copy should be single spaced.
   B. The copy should be triple spaced.
   C. There is no need for including footnotes.
   D. Errors must be neatly corrected.

10. An office assistant needs a synonym.
    Of the following, the book which she would find MOST useful is

    A. a world atlas
    B. BARTLETT'S FAMILIAR QUOTATIONS
    C. a manual of style
    D. a thesaurus

11. Of the following examples of footnotes, the one that is expressed in the MOST generally accepted standard form is:

    A. Johnson, T.F. (Dr.), <u>English for Everyone</u>, 3rd or 4th edition; New York City Linton Publishing Company, p. 467
    B. Frank Taylor, <u>English for Today</u> (New York: Rayton Publishing Company, 1971), p. 156
    C. Ralph Wilden, <u>English for Tomorrow,</u> Reynolds Publishing Company, England, p. 451
    D. Quinn, David, Yesterday's English (New York: Baldwin Publishing Company, 1972), p. 431

12. Standard procedures are used in offices PRIMARILY because

    A. an office is a happier place if everyone is doing the tasks in the same manner
    B. particular ways of doing jobs are considered more efficient than other ways
    C. it is good discipline for workers to follow standard procedures approved by the supervisor
    D. supervisors generally don't want workers to be creative in planning their work

13. Assume that an office assistant has the responsibility for compiling, typing, and mailing a preliminary announcement of Spring term course offerings. The announcement will go to approximately 900 currently enrolled students. Assuming that the following equipment is available for use, the MOST EFFECTIVE method for distributing the announcement to all 900 students is to

    A. e-mail it as a text document using the electronic student mailing list
    B. post the announcement as a PDF document for download on the department website
    C. send it by fax
    D. post the announcement and leave copies in buildings around campus

14. *Justified typing* is a term that refers MOST specifically to typewriting copy

    A. that has been edited and for which final copy is being prepared
    B. in a form that allows for an even right-hand margin
    C. with a predetermined vertical placement for each alternate line
    D. that has been approved by the supervisor and his superior

15. Which one of the following is the BEST form for the address in a letter?

    A. Mr. John Jones
       Vice President, The Universal Printing Company
       1220 Fifth Avenue
       New York, 10023 New York
    B. Mr. John Jones, Vice President
       The Universal Printing Company
       1220 Fifth Avenue
       New York, New York 10023
    C. Mr. John Jones, Vice President, The Universal Printing Company
       1220 Fifth Avenue
       New York, New York 10023

D. Mr. John Jones Vice President,
The Universal Printing Company
1220 Fifth Avenue
New York, 10023 New York

16. Of the following, the CHIEF advantage of the use of window envelopes over ordinary envelopes is that window envelopes

    A. eliminate the need for addressing envelopes
    B. protect the confidential nature of enclosed material
    C. cost less to buy than ordinary envelopes
    D. reduce the danger of the address becoming illegible

17. In the complimentary close of a business letter, the FIRST letter of _____ should be capitalized.

    A. all the words
    B. none of the words
    C. only the first word
    D. only the last word

18. Assume that one of your duties is to procure needed office supplies from the supply room. You are permitted to draw supplies every two weeks.
    The one of the following which would be the MOST desirable practice for you to follow in obtaining supplies is to

    A. obtain a quantity of supplies sufficient to last for several months to make certain that enough supplies are always on hand
    B. determine the minimum supply necessary to keep on hand for the various items and obtain an additional quantity as soon as possible after the supply on hand has been reduced to this minimum
    C. review the supplies once a month to determine what items have been exhausted and obtain an additional quantity as soon as possible
    D. obtain a supply of an item as soon after it has been exhausted as is possible

19. Some offices that keep carbon copies of letters use several different colors of carbon paper for making carbon copies.
    Of the following, the CHIEF reason for using different colors of carbon paper is to

    A. facilitate identification of different types of letters in the files
    B. relieve the monotony of typing and filing carbon copies
    C. reduce the costs of preparing carbon copies
    D. utilize both sides of the carbon paper for typing

20. Your supervisor asks you to post an online ad for freelance designers interested in submitting samples for a new company logo. Prospective workers should be proficient in which of the following software?

    A. Microsoft Word
    B. Adobe Acrobat Pro
    C. Adobe Illustrator
    D. Microsoft PowerPoint

21. Gary Thompson is applying for a position with the firm of Gray and Williams.
    Which letter should be filed in top position in the *Application* folder?

    A. A letter of recommendation written on September 18 by Johnson & Smith
    B. Williams' letter of October 8 requesting further details regarding Thompson's experience

C. Thompson's letter of September 8 making application for a position as sales manager
D. Letter of September 20 from Alfred Jackson recommending Thompson for the job

22. The USUAL arrangement in indexing the names of the First National Bank, Toledo, is

    A. First National Bank, Toledo, Ohio
    B. Ohio, First National Bank, Toledo
    C. Toledo, First National Bank, Ohio
    D. Ohio, Toledo, First National Bank

23. A single line through typed text indicating that it's incorrect or invalid is known as a(n)

    A. underline
    B. strikethrough
    C. line font
    D. eraser

24. A typical e-mail with an attachment should contain all of the following for successful transmittal EXCEPT

    A. recipient's address   B. file attachment
    C. body text   D. description of attachment

25. The subject line in a letter is USUALLY typed a _____ space below the _____.

    A. single; inside address   B. single; salutation
    C. double; inside address   D. double; salutation

KEY (CORRECT ANSWERS)

1.	A	11.	B
2.	C	12.	B
3.	C	13.	A
4.	B	14.	B
5.	B	15.	B
6.	C	16.	A
7.	D	17.	C
8.	D	18.	B
9.	B	19.	A
10.	D	20.	C

21.	B
22.	A
23.	B
24.	D
25.	D

EXAMINATION SECTION
TEST 1

DIRECTIONS: Each question or incomplete statement is followed by several suggested answers or completions. Select the one that BEST answers the question or completes the statement. *PRINT THE LETTER OF THE CORRECT ANSWER IN THE SPACE AT THE RIGHT.*

1. In considering a new word processing system for a regional office, which of the following would MOST likely be the MOST important consideration in making a decision?

    A. Ease of operation
    B. Friendliness of service technicians
    C. Availability of service technicians
    D. Capacity of the system to meet the unit's word processing needs

    1.____

2. Your supervisor is out of town for several days and has asked you to act as supervisor in his absence. An employee in the unit comes to you and complains that the supervisor has been dividing the workload unfairly.
   Of the following, the MOST appropriate action for you to take is

    A. defend the actions of your supervisor
    B. encourage the employee to file a grievance
    C. listen to the employee attentively
    D. explain to the employee that you have no authority to handle the situation

    2.____

3. A principal stenographer still on probation is instructed to supervise and coordinate the completion of a large word processing project. Her supervisor asks her how long she thinks the project will take. The principal stenographer gives her supervisor an estimate that is two days longer than she actually thinks the project will take to complete. The project is completed two days earlier, and the principal stenographer is congratulated by her supervisor for her efforts.
   In purposely overestimating the time required to complete the project, the principal stenographer showed

    A. *good* judgment because it helped her appear very efficient
    B. *good* judgment because it helps keep unrealistic supervisors from expecting too much
    C. *poor* judgment because plans and schedules of other components of the project may have been based on her false estimate
    D. *poor* judgment because she should have used the extra time to further check and, proofread the work

    3.____

4. Which of the following would MOST likely be the MOST important in providing support to one's supervisor?

    A. Screening annoying phone calls
    B. Reviewing and forwarding articles and publications that may be of interest to your supervisor
    C. Correctly transmitting instructions from the supervisor to appropriate staff members
    D. Reviewing outgoing correspondence for proper grammatical usage and clarity

    4.____

5. While you are on the telephone answering a question about your agency, a visitor comes to your desk and starts to ask you a question. There is no emergency or urgency in either situation, that of the phone call or that of answering the visitor's question.
   In this case, you should

   A. excuse yourself to the person on the telephone and tell the visitor that you will be with him or her as soon as you have finished on the phone
   B. explain to the person on the phone that you have a visitor and must shorten the conversation
   C. continue to talk with the person on the phone while looking up occasionally at the visitor to let him or her know that you know he or she is there
   D. continue to talk with the person on the telephone until you are finished and then let the visitor know that you're sorry to have kept him or her waiting

6. Your supervisor is out of town on vacation for one week, and asks you to act as supervisor in her absence. The second day she is gone a very important, complex budgetary form, which must be responded to in ten days, arrives in your unit.
   Of the following, it would be BEST if you

   A. filled out the form and submitted it as soon as possible
   B. read the form over, did any time-consuming research that might be needed, and then gave the uncompleted form to your supervisor as soon as she returned
   C. asked for help from your supervisor's supervisor in completing the form
   D. tried to contact your supervisor for advice

7. Of the following, which would MOST likely be of the highest priority?
   The typing of

   A. a grant proposal due next week
   B. new addresses onto a mailing list for a future mailing
   C. a payroll form for a new employee that needs to be submitted immediately
   D. a memorandum from the Commissioner to all employees regarding new procedures

8. Your office is moving to a new location.
   Of the following, it would be MOST important to ensure that

   A. others will know your office's new address and phone number
   B. the new office space is comfortable
   C. your supervisor is happy with his or her new office space
   D. the move itself goes smoothly

9. Of the following, which would generally be considered the LEAST desirable?

   A. Accidentally disconnecting an executive from an important phone call
   B. Ordering the wrong back-up part for a copying machine
   C. Misplacing several hundred dollars worth of personal checks payable to your department
   D. Misplacing a memorandum that needs to be typed

10. Your supervisor has told you not to let anyone disturb her for the rest of the morning unless absolutely necessary because she has some urgent work to complete. The department head telephones and asks to speak to her.
The BEST course of action for you to take is to

   A. ask the department head if he or she can leave a message
   B. ask your supervisor if she can take the call
   C. tell the department head that your supervisor is out
   D. let your supervisor know that her instructions have put you in a difficult position

11. Which of the following would be MOST likely to contribute to efficiency in the operation of an office?

   A. A new computer system is instituted in an office.
   B. The employees are paid well.
   C. Procedures and practices are studied for any redundant operations.
   D. A supervisor delegates work.

12. You are at work at your desk on a special project when a visitor approaches you. You cannot interrupt your work to take care of this person.
Of the following, the BEST and MOST courteous way of handling this situation is to

   A. avoid looking up from your work until you are finished with what you are doing
   B. tell the visitor that you will not be able to assist him or her for quite some time
   C. refer the individual to another employee who can take care of him or her right away
   D. chat with the individual while you continue to work

13. Which of the following would MOST likely be of the highest priority?
A(n)

   A. annual report due next month
   B. irate member of the public who is standing at your desk
   C. important financial report requested by the Commissioner
   D. memorandum to all employees outlining very important new policy needs to be typed and distributed immediately

14. Someone uses *special pull* to obtain the services of your unit at the last minute. You and the four employees you supervise have done everything you could do to provide good service, and you feel things have gone very well. The client is not pleased, however, and enters your office and begins screaming at you and the other employees present.
Of the following, it would be BEST if you

   A. ignored the person
   B. tried to calm the person down
   C. asked the person to leave the office
   D. called your supervisor in to help handle the situation

15. Your supervisor is on vacation for two weeks, and you have been asked to fill in for her. Your office is very busy, and there is a strict procedure for filling requests. Leslie from Unit X wants something completed immediately. You don't feel this is possible or reasonable, and politely explain why to Leslie. Leslie becomes very angry and says that she will complain to your supervisor about your uncooperative behavior as soon as your supervisor returns.
Of the following, it would be BEST if you

   A. filled Leslie's request
   B. reported Leslie to her supervisor
   C. complained to your supervisor about the situation as soon as she returned
   D. stood by your decision once you determined it was correct

15.___

KEY (CORRECT ANSWERS)

1. D	6. B	11. C
2. C	7. C	12. C
3. C	8. A	13. B
4. C	9. C	14. B
5. A	10. B	15. D

CLERICAL ABILITIES
EXAMINATION SECTION
TEST 1

DIRECTIONS: Each question or incomplete statement is followed by several suggested answers or completions. Select the one that BEST answers the question or completes the statement. *PRINT THE LETTER OF THE CORRECT ANSWER IN THE SPACE AT THE RIGHT.*

Questions 1-4.

DIRECTIONS: Questions 1 through 4 are to be answered on the basis of the information given below.

The most commonly used filing system and the one that is easiest to learn is alphabetical filing. This involves putting records in an A to Z order, according to the letters of the alphabet. The name of a person is filed by using the following order: first, the surname or last name; second, the first name; third, the middle name or middle initial. For example, *Henry C. Young* is filed under *Y* and thereafter under *Young, Henry C.* The name of a company is filed in the same way. For example, *Long Cabinet Co.* is filed under *L* while *John T. Long Cabinet Co.* is filed under *L* and thereafter under *Long, John T. Cabinet Co.*

1. The one of the following which lists the names of persons in the CORRECT alphabetical order is:
   A. Mary Carrie, Helen Carrol, James Carson, John Carter
   B. James Carson, Mary Carrie, John Carter, Helen Carrol
   C. Helen Carrol, James Carson, John Carter, Mary Carrie
   D. John Carter, Helen Carrol, Mary Carrie, James Carson

1.____

2. The one of the following which lists the names of persons in the CORRECT alphabetical order is:
   A. Jones, John C.; Jones, John A.; Jones, John P.; Jones, John K.
   B. Jones, John P.; Jones, John K.; Jones, John C.; Jones, John A.
   C. Jones, John A.; Jones, John C.; Jones, John K.; Jones, John P.
   D. Jones, John K.; Jones, John C.; Jones, John A.; Jones, John P.

2.____

3. The one of the following which lists the names of the companies in the CORRECT alphabetical order is:
   A. Blane Co., Blake Co., Block Co., Blear Co.
   B. Blake Co., Blane Co., Blear Co., Block Co.
   C. Block Co., Blear Co., Blane Co., Blake Co.
   D. Blear Co., Blake Co., Blane Co., Block Co.

3.____

4. You are to return to the file an index card on *Barry C. Wayne Materials and Supplies Co.*
Of the following, the CORRECT alphabetical group that you should return the index card to is
   A. A to G   B. H to M   C. N to S   D. T to Z

4._____

Questions 5-10.

DIRECTIONS: In each of Questions 5 through 10, the names of four people are given. For each question, choose as your answer the one of the four names given which should be filed FIRST according to the usual system of alphabetical filing of names, as described in the following paragraph.

In filing names, you must start with the last name. Names are filed in order of the first letter of the last name, then the second letter, etc. Therefore, BAILY would be filed before BROWN, which would be filed before COLT. A name with fewer letters of the same type comes first, i.e., Smith before Smithe. If the last names are the same, the names are filed alphabetically by the first name. If the first name is an initial, a name with an initial would come before a first name that starts with the same letter as the initial. Therefore, I. BROWN would come before IRA BROWN. Finally, if both last name and first name are the same, the name would be filed alphabetically by the middle name, once again an initial coming before a middle name which starts with the same letter as the initial. If there is no middle name at all, the name would come before those with middle initials or names.

SAMPLE QUESTION: A. Lester Daniels
                   B. William Dancer
                   C. Nathan Danzig
                   D. Dan Lester

The last names beginning with D are filed before the last name beginning with L. Since DANIELS, DANCER, and DANZIG all begin with the same three letters, you must look at the fourth letter of the last name to determine which name should be filed first. C comes before I or Z in the alphabet, so DANCER is filed before DANIELS or DANZIG. Therefore, the answer to the above sample question is B.

5. A. Scott Biala
    B. Mary Byala
    C. Martin Baylor
    D. Francis Bauer

5._____

6. A. Howard J. Black
    B. Howard Black
    C. J. Howard Black
    D. John H. Black

6._____

7. A. Theodora Garth Kingston
    B. Theadore Barth Kingston
    C. Thomas Kingston
    D. Thomas T. Kingston

7._____

8.
  A. Paulette Mary Huerta
  B. Paul M. Huerta
  C. Paulette L. Huerta
  D. Peter A. Huerta

9.
  A. Martha Hunt Morgan
  B. Martin Hunt Morgan
  C. Mary H. Morgan
  D. Martine H. Morgan

10.
  A. James T. Meerschaum
  B. James M. Mershum
  C. James F. Mearshaum
  D. James N. Meshum

Questions 11-14.

DIRECTIONS: Questions 11 through 14 are to be answered SOLELY on the basis of the following information.

You are required to file various documents in file drawers which are labeled according to the following pattern:

DOCUMENTS

MEMOS		LETTERS	
File	Subject	File	Subject
84PM1	(A-L)	84PC1	(A-L)
84PM2	(M-Z)	84PC2	(M-Z)

REPORTS		INQUIRIES	
File	Subject	File	Subject
84PR1	(A-L)	84PQ1	(A-L)
84PR2	(M-Z)	84PQ2	(M-Z)

11. A letter dealing with a burglary should be filed in the drawer labeled
    A. 84PM1   B. 84PC1   C. 84PR1   D. 84PQ2

12. A report on Statistics should be found in the drawer labeled
    A. 84PM1   B. 84PC2   C. 84PR2   D. 84PQS

13. An inquiry is received about parade permit procedures. It should be filed in the drawer labeled
    A. 84PM2   B. 84PC1   C. 84PR1   D. 84PQ2

14. A police officer has a question about a robbery report you filed. You should pull this file from the drawer labeled
    A. 84PM1   B. 84PM2   C. 84PR1   D. 84PR2

Questions 15-22.

DIRECTIONS: Each of Questions 15 through 22 consists of four or six numbered names. For each question, choose the option (A, B, C, or D) which indicates the order in which the names should be filed in accordance with the following filing instructions:
- File alphabetically according to last name, then first name, then middle initial.
- File according to each successive letter within a name.
- When comparing two names in which the letters in the longer name are identical to the corresponding letters in the shorter name, the shorter name is filed first.
- When the last names are the same, initials are always filed before names beginning with the same letter.

15. I. Ralph Robinson
    II. Alfred Ross
    III. Luis Robles
    IV. James Roberts

    The CORRECT filing sequence for the above names should be
    A. IV, II, I, III   B. I, IV, III, II   C. III, IV, I, II   D. IV, I, III, II

16. I. Irwin Goodwin
    II. Inez Gonzalez
    III. Irene Goodman
    IV. Ira S. Goodwin
    V. Ruth I. Goldstein
    VI. M.B. Goodman

    The CORRECT filing sequence for the above names should be
    A. V, II, I, IV, III, VI   B. V, II, VI, III, IV, I
    C. V, II, III, VI, IV, I   D. V, II, III, VI, I, IV

17. I. George Allan
    II. Gregory Allen
    III. Gary Allen
    IV. George Allen

    The CORRECT filing sequence for the above names should be
    A. IV, III, I, II   B. I, IV, II, III   C. III, IV, I, II   D. I, III, IV, II

18. I. Simon Kauffman
     II. Leo Kaufman
     III. Robert Kaufmann
     IV. Paul Kauffmann

     The CORRECT filing sequence for the above names should be
     A. I, IV, II, III   B. II, IV, III, I   C. III, II, IV, I   D. I, II, III, IV

19. I. Roberta Williams
     II. Robin Wilson
     III. Roberta Wilson
     IV. Robin Williams

     The CORRECT filing sequence for the above names should be
     A. III, II, IV, I   B. I, IV, III, II   C. I, II, III, IV   D. III, I, II, IV

20. I. Lawrence Shultz
     II. Albert Schultz
     III. Theodore Schwartz
     IV. Thomas Schwarz
     V. Alvin Schultz
     VI. Leonard Shultz

     The CORRECT filing sequence for the above names should be
     A. II, V, III, IV, I, VI   B. IV, III, V, I, II, VI
     C. II, V, I, VI, III, IV   D. I, VI, II, V, III, IV

21. I. McArdle
     II. Mayer
     III. Maletz
     IV. McNiff
     V. Meyer
     VI. MacMahon

     The CORRECT filing sequence for the above names should be
     A. I, IV, VI, III, II, V   B. II, I, IV, VI, III, V
     C. VI, III, II, I, IV, V   D. VI, III, II, V, I, IV

22. I. Jack E. Johnson
     II. R.H. Jackson
     III. Bertha Jackson
     IV. J.T. Johnson
     V. Ann Johns
     VI. John Jacobs

     The CORRECT filing sequence for the above names should be
     A. II, III, VI, V, IV, I   B. III, II, VI, V, IV, I
     C. VI, II, III, I, V, IV   D. III, II, VI, IV, V, I

Questions 23-30.

DIRECTIONS: The code table below shows 10 letters with matching numbers. For each question, there are three sets of letters. Each set of letters is followed by a set of numbers which may or may not match their correct letter according to the code table. For each question, check all three sets of letters and numbers and mark your answer:
- A. if no pairs are correctly matched
- B. if only one pair is correctly matched
- C. if only two pairs are correctly matched
- D. if all three pairs are correctly matched

CODE TABLE

T	M	V	D	S	P	R	G	B	H
1	2	3	4	5	6	7	8	9	0

SAMPLE QUESTION:
TMVDSP – 123456
RGBHTM – 789011
DSPRGB – 256789

In the sample question above, the first set of numbers correctly match its set of letters. But the second and third pairs contain mistakes. In the second pair, M is correctly matched with number 1. According to the code table, letter M should be correctly matched with number 2. In the third pair, the letter D is incorrectly matched with number 2. According to the code table, letter D should be correctly matched with number 4. Since only one of the pairs is correctly matched, the answer to this sample question is B.

23. RSBMRM – 759262
    GDSRVH – 845730
    VDBRTM - 349713

24. TGVSDR – 183247
    SMHRDP – 520647
    TRMHSR - 172057

25. DSPRGM – 456782
    MVDBHT – 234902
    HPMDBT - 062491

26. BVPTRD – 936184
    GDPHMB – 807029
    GMRHMV - 827032

27. MGVRSH – 283750
    TRDMBS – 174295
    SPRMGV - 567283

28. SGBSDM – 489542   28.____
    MGHPTM – 290612
    MPBMHT - 269301

29. TDPBHM – 146902   29.____
    VPBMRS – 369275
    GDMBHM - 842902

30. MVPTBV – 236194   30.____
    PDRTMB – 47128
    BGTMSM - 981232

KEY (CORRECT ANSWERS)

1.	A	11.	B	21.	C
2.	C	12.	C	22.	B
3.	B	13.	D	23.	B
4.	D	14.	D	24.	B
5.	D	15.	D	25.	C
6.	B	16.	C	26.	A
7.	B	17.	D	27.	D
8.	B	18.	A	28.	A
9.	A	19.	B	29.	D
10.	C	20.	A	30.	A

TEST 2

DIRECTIONS: Each question or incomplete statement is followed by several suggested answers or completions. Select the one that BEST answers the question or completes the statement. *PRINT THE LETTER OF THE CORRECT ANSWER IN THE SPACE AT THE RIGHT.*

Questions 1-10.

DIRECTIONS: Questions 1 through 10 each consists of two columns, each containing four lines of names, numbers and/or addresses. For each question, compare the lines in Column I with the lines in Column II to see if they match exactly, and mark your answer A, B, C, or D, according to the following instructions:
    A. all four lines match exactly
    B. only three lines match exactly
    C. only two lines match exactly
    D. only one line matches exactly

<u>COLUMN I</u>　　　　　　　　　　　　　<u>COLUMN II</u>

1.　I.　Earl Hodgson　　　　　　　Earl Hodgson　　　　　　1.____
　　II.　1409870　　　　　　　　　1408970
　　III.　Shore Ave.　　　　　　　　Schore Ave.
　　IV.　Macon Rd.　　　　　　　　Macon Rd.

2.　I.　9671485　　　　　　　　　9671485　　　　　　　　2.____
　　II.　470 Astor Court　　　　　　470 Astor Court
　　III.　Halprin, Phillip　　　　　　Halperin, Phillip
　　IV.　Frank D. Poliseo　　　　　Frank D. Poliseo

3.　I.　Tandem Associates　　　　Tandom Associates　　　3.____
　　II.　144-17 Northern Blvd.　　144-17 Northern Blvd.
　　III.　Alberta Forchi　　　　　　Albert Forchi
　　IV.　Kings Park, NY 10751　　Kings Point, NY 10751

4.　I.　Bertha C. McCormack　　　Bertha C. McCormack　　4.____
　　II.　Clayton, MO　　　　　　　Clayton, MO
　　III.　976-4242　　　　　　　　976-4242
　　IV.　New City, NY 10951　　　New City, NY 10951

5.　I.　George C. Morill　　　　　George C. Morrill　　　　5.____
　　II.　Columbia, SC 29201　　　Columbia, SD 29201
　　III.　Louis Ingham　　　　　　Louis Ingham
　　IV.　3406 Forest Ave.　　　　　3406 Forest Ave.

6.　I.　506 S. Elliott Pl.　　　　　　506 S. Elliott Pl.　　　　　6.____
　　II.　Herbert Hall　　　　　　　Hurbert Hall
　　III.　4712 Rockaway Pkway　　4712 Rockaway Pkway
　　IV.　169 E. 7 St.　　　　　　　169 E. 7 St.

86

7.
  I. 345 Park Ave.   345 Park Pl.
  II. Colman Oven Corp.   Coleman Oven Corp.
  III. Robert Conte   Robert Conti
  IV. 6179846   6179846

7._____

8.
  I. Grigori Schierber   Grigori Schierber
  II. Des Moines, Iowa   Des Moines, Iowa
  III. Gouverneur Hospital   Gouverneur Hospital
  IV. 91-35 Cresskill Pl.   91-35 Cresskill Pl.

8._____

9.
  I. Jeffery Janssen   Jeffrey Janssen
  II. 8041071   8041071
  III. 40 Rockefeller Plaza 40 Rockafeller Plaza
  IV. 407 6 St.   406 7 St.

9._____

10.
  I. 5971996   5871996
  II. 3113 Knickerbocker Ave. 31123 Knickerbocker Ave.
  III. 8434 Boston Post Rd. 8424 Boston Post Rd.
  IV. Penn Station   Penn Station

10._____

Questions 11-14.

DIRECTIONS: Questions 11 through 14 are to be answered by looking at the four groups of names and addresses listed below (I, II, III, and IV), and then finding out the number of groups that have their corresponding numbered lies exactly the same.

	GROUP I	GROUP II
Line 1.	Richmond General Hospital	Richman General Hospital
Line 2.	Geriatric Clinic	Geriatric Clinic
Line 3.	3975 Paerdegat St.	3975 Peardegat St.
Line 4.	Loudonville, New York 11538	Londonville, New York 11538

	GROUP III	GROUP IV
Line 1.	Richmond General Hospital	Richmend General Hospital
Line 2.	Geriatric Clinic	Geriatric Clinic
Line 3.	3795 Paerdegat St.	3975 Paerdegat St.
Line 4.	Loudonville, New York 11358	Loudonville, New York 11538

1. In how many groups is line one exactly the same?
   A. Two   B. Three   C. Four   D. None

11._____

12. In how many groups is line two exactly the same?
    A. Two   B. Three   C. Four   D. None

12._____

13. In how many groups is line three exactly the same?
    A. Two   B. Three   C. Four   D. None

13._____

14. In how many groups is line four exactly the same? 14.____
    A. Two B. Three C. Four D. None

Questions 15-18.

DIRECTIONS: Each of Questions 15 through 18 has two lists of names and addresses. Each list contains three sets of names and addresses. Check each of the three sets in the list on the right to see if they are the same as the corresponding set in the list on the left. Mark your answers:
   A. if none of the sets in the right list are the same as those in the left list
   B. if only one of the sets in the right list is the same as those in the left list
   C. if only two of the sets in the right list are the same as those in the left list
   D. if all three sets in the right list are the same as those in the left list

15. Mary T. Berlinger   Mary T. Berlinger   15.____
    2351 Hampton St.   2351 Hampton St.
    Monsey, N.Y. 20117   Monsey, N.Y. 20117

    Eduardo Benes   Eduardo Benes
    483 Kingston Avenue   473 Kingston Avenue
    Central Islip, N.Y. 11734   Central Islip, N.Y. 11734

    Alan Carrington Fuchs   Alan Carrington Fuchs
    17 Gnarled Hollow Road   17 Gnarled Hollow Road
    Los Angeles, CA 91635   Los Angeles, CA 91685

16. David John Jacobson   David John Jacobson   16.____
    178 34 St. Apt. 4C   178 53 St. Apt. 4C
    New York, N.Y. 00927   New York, N.Y. 00927

    Ann-Marie Calonella   Ann-Marie Calonella
    7243 South Ridge Blvd.   7243 South Ridge Blvd.
    Bakersfield, CA 96714   Bakersfield, CA 96714

    Pauline M. Thompson   Pauline M. Thomson
    872 Linden Ave.   872 Linden Ave.
    Houston, Texas 70321   Houston, Texas 70321

17. Chester LeRoy Masterton   Chester LeRoy Masterson   17.____
    152 Lacy Rd.   152 Lacy Rd.
    Kankakee, Ill. 54532   Kankakee, Ill. 54532

    William Maloney   William Maloney
    S. LaCrosse Pla.   S. LaCross Pla.
    Wausau, Wisconsin 52136   Wausau, Wisconsin 52146

    Cynthia V. Barnes   Cynthia V. Barnes
    16 Pines Rd.   16 Pines Rd.
    Greenpoint, Miss. 20376   Greenpoint,, Miss. 20376

4 (#2)

18. Marcel Jean Frontenac
8 Burton On The Water
Calender, Me. 01471

J. Scott Marsden
174 S. Tipton St.
Cleveland, Ohio

Lawrence T. Haney
171 McDonough St.
Decatur, Ga. 31304

Marcel Jean Frontenac
6 Burton On The Water
Calender, Me. 01471

J. Scott Marsden
174 Tipton St.
Cleveland, Ohio

Lawrence T. Haney
171 McDonough St.
Decatur, Ga. 31304

18._____

Questions 19-26.

DIRECTIONS: Each of Questions 19 through 26 has two lists of numbers. Each list contains three sets of numbers. Check each of the three sets in the list on the right to see if they are the same as the corresponding set in the list on the left. Mark your answers:
- A. if none of the sets in the right list are the same as those in the left list
- B. if only one of the sets in the right list is the same as those in the left list
- C. if only two of the sets in the right list are the same as those in the left list
- D. if all three sets in the right list are the same as those in the left lists

19.	7354183476 4474747744 5791430231	7354983476 4474747774 57914302311	19._____
20.	7143592185 8344517699 9178531263	7143892185 8344518699 9178531263	20._____
21.	2572114731 8806835476 8255831246	257214731 8806835476 8255831246	21._____
22.	331476853821 6976658532996 3766042113715	331476858621 6976655832996 3766042113745	22._____
23.	8806663315 74477138449 211756663666	88066633115 74477138449 211756663666	23._____

89

24. 990006966996   99000696996   24.____
     53022219743   53022219843
     4171171117717   4171171177717

25. 24400222433004   24400222433004   25.____
     5300030055000355   5300030055500355
     20000075532002022   20000075532002022

26. 6111666406600011116   61116664066001116   26.____
     7111300117001100733   7111300117001100733
     26666446664476518   26666446664476518

Questions 27-30.

DIRECTIONS: Questions 27 through 30 are to be answered by picking the answer which is in the correct numerical order, from the lowest number to the highest number, in each question.

27. A. 44533, 44518, 44516, 44547   27.____
     B. 44516, 44518, 44533, 44547
     C. 44547, 44533, 44518, 44516
     D. 44518, 44516, 44547, 44533

28. A. 95587, 95593, 95601, 95620   28.____
     B. 95601, 95620, 95587, 95593
     C. 95593, 95587, 95601. 95620
     D. 95620, 95601, 95593, 95587

29. A. 232212, 232208, 232232, 232223   29.____
     B. 232208, 232223, 232212, 232232
     C. 232208, 232212, 232223, 232232
     D. 232223, 232232, 232208, 232208

30. A. 113419, 113521, 113462, 113462   30.____
     B. 113588, 113462, 113521, 113419
     C. 113521, 113588, 113419, 113462
     D. 113419, 113462, 113521, 113588

KEY (CORRECT ANSWERS)

1.	C	11.	A	21.	C
2.	B	12.	C	22.	A
3.	D	13.	A	23.	D
4.	A	14.	A	24.	A
5.	C	15.	C	25.	C
6.	B	16.	B	26.	C
7.	D	17.	B	27.	B
8.	A	18.	B	28.	A
9.	D	19.	B	29.	C
10.	C	20.	B	30.	D

CODING
EXAMINATION SECTION
TEST 1

COMMENTARY

An ingenious question-type called coding, involving elements of alphabetizing, filing, name and number comparison, and evaluative judgment and application, has currently won wide acceptance in testing circles for measuring clerical aptitude and general ability, particularly on the senior (middle) grades (levels).

While the directions for this question-type usually vary in detail, the candidate is generally asked to consider groups of names, codes, and numbers, and, then, according to a given plan, to arrange codes in alphabetic order; to arrange these in numerical sequence; to rearrange columns of names and numbers in correct order; to espy errors in coding; to choose the correct coding arrangement in consonance with the given directions and examples, etc.

This question-type appears to have few parameters in respect to form, substance, or degree of difficulty.

Accordingly, acquaintance with, and practice in the coding question is recommended for the serious candidate.

DIRECTIONS: Column I consists of serial numbers of dollar bills. Column II shows different ways of arranging the corresponding serial numbers.
The serial numbers of dollar bills in Column I begin and end with a capital letter and have an eight-digit number in between. The serial numbers in Column I are to be arranged according to the following rules:
First: In alphabetical order according to the first letter.
Second: When two or more serial numbers have the same first letter, in alphabetical order according to the last letter.
Third: When two or more serial numbers have the same first and last letters, in numerical order, beginning with the lowest number.

The serial numbers in Column I are numbered (1) through (5) in the order in which they are listed. In Column II, the numbers (1) through (5) are arranged in four different ways to show different arrangements of the corresponding serial numbers. Choose the answer in Column II in which the serial numbers are arranged according to the above rules.

Column I	Column II
1. E75044127B	A. 4, 1, 3, 2, 5
2. B96399104A	B. 4, 1, 2, 3, 5
3. B93939086A	C. 4, 3, 2, 5, 1
4. B47064465H	D. 3, 2, 5, 4, 1

In the simple question, the four serial numbers starting with B should be put before the serial number starting with E. The serial numbers starting with B and ending with A should be put before the serial number starting with B and ending with H. The three serial numbers starting with B and ending with A should be listed in numerical order, beginning with the lowest

number. The correct way to arrange the serial numbers, therefore, is:
    3. B93939086A
    2. B96399104A
    5. B99040922A
    4. B47064465H
    1. E75044127B

Since the order of arrangement is 3, 2, 5, 4, 1, the answer to the sample question is D.

	Column I	Column II	
1.	1. D89143888P 2. D98143838B 3. D89113883B 4. D89148338P 5. D89148388B	A. 3, 5, 2, 1, 4 B. 3, 1, 4, 5, 2 C. 4, 2, 3, 1, 5 D. 4, 1, 3, 5, 2	1._____
2.	1. W62455590E 2. W62455090F 3. W62405099E 4. V62455097F 5. V62405979E	A. 2, 4, 3, 1, 5 B. 3, 1, 5, 2, 4 C. 5, 3, 1, 4, 2 D. 5, 4, 3, 1, 2	2._____
3.	1. N74663826M 2. M74633286M 3. N76633228N 4. M76483686N 5. M74636688M	A. 2, 4, 5, 3, 1 B. 2, 5, 4, 1, 3 C. 1, 2, 5, 3, 4 D. 2, 5, 1, 4, 3	3._____
4.	1. P97560324B 2. R97663024B 3. P97503024E 4. R97563240E 5. P97652304B	A. 1, 5, 2, 3, 4 B. 3, 1, 4, 5, 2 C. 1, 5, 3, 2, 4 D. 1, 5, 2, 3, 4	4._____
5.	1. H92411165G 2. A92141465G 3. H92141165C 4. H92444165C 5. A92411465G	A. 2, 5, 3, 4, 1 B. 3, 4, 2, 5, 1 C. 3, 2, 1, 5, 4 D. 3, 1, 2, 5, 4	5._____
6.	1. X90637799S 2. N90037696S 3. Y90677369B 4. X09677693B 5. M09673699S	A. 4, 3, 5, 2, 1 B. 5, 4, 2, 1, 3 C. 5, 2, 4, 1, 3 D. 5, 2, 3, 4, 1	6._____

3 (#1)

	Column I	Column II	

7.
1. K78425174L
2. K78452714C
3. K78547214N
4. K78442774C
5. K78547724M

A. 4, 2, 1, 3, 5
B. 2, 3, 5, 4, 1
C. 1, 4, 2, 3, 5
D. 4, 2, 1, 5, 3

7._____

8.
1. P18736652U
2. P18766352V
3. T17686532U
4. T17865523U
5. P18675332V

A. 1, 3, 4, 5, 2
B. 1, 5, 2, 3, 4
C. 3, 4, 5, 1, 2
D. 5, 2, 1, 3, 4

8._____

9.
1. L51138101K
2. S51138001R
3. S51188222K
4. S51183110R
5. L51188100R

A. 1, 5, 3, 2, 4
B. 1, 3, 5, 2, 4
C. 1, 5, 1, 4, 3
D. 2, 5, 1, 4, 3

9._____

10.
1. J28475336
2. T28775363D
3. J27843566P
4. T27834563P
5. J2843553D

A. 5, 1, 2, 3, 4
B. 4, 3, 5, 1, 2
C. 1, 5, 2, 4, 3
D. 5, 1, 3, 2, 4

10._____

11.
1. S55126179E
2. R51336177Q
3. P55126177R
4. S55126178R
5. R55126180P

A. 1, 5, 2, 3, 4
B. 3, 4, 1, 5, 2
C. 3, 5, 2, 1, 4
D. 4, 3, 1, 5, 2

11._____

12.
1. T64217813Q
2. I64217817O
3. T64217818O
4. I64217811Q
5. T64217816Q

A. 4, 1, 3, 2, 4
B. 2, 4, 3, 1, 5
C. 4, 1, 5, 2, 3
D. 2, 3, 4, 1, 5

12._____

13.
1. B33886897B
2. B38386882B
3. D33389862B
4. D33336887D
5. B38888697D

A. 5, 1, 3, 4, 2
B. 1, 2, 5, 3, 4
C. 1, 2, 5, 4, 3
D. 2, 1, 4, 5, 3

13._____

14.
1. E11664554M
2. F11164544M
3. F11614455N
4. E11665454M
5. F16161545N

A. 4, 1, 2, 5, 3
B. 2, 4, 1, 5, 3
C. 4, 2, 1, 3, 5
D. 1, 4, 2, 3, 5

14._____

4 (#1)

	Column I	Column II	

15.
1. C86611355W
2. C68631533V
3. G88631533V
4. C68833515V
5. G68833511W

A. 2, 4, 1, 5, 3
B. 1, 2, 4, 3, 5
C. 1, 2, 5, 4, 3
D. 1, 2, 4, 3, 5

15.____

16.
1. R73665312J
2. P73685512J
3. P73968511J
4. R73665321K
5. R63985211K

A. 3, 2, 1, 4, 5
B. 2, 3, 5, 1, 4
C. 2, 3, 1, 5, 4
D. 3, 1, 5, 2, 4

16.____

17.
1. X33661222U
2. Y83961323V
3. Y88991123V
4. X33691233U
5. X38691333U

A. 1, 4, 5, 2, 3
B. 4, 5, 1, 3, 2
C. 4, 5, 1, 2, 3
D. 4, 1, 5, 2, 3

17..____

18.
1. B22838847W
2. B28833874V
3. B22288344X
4. B28238374V
5. B28883347V

A. 4, 5, 2, 3, 1
B. 4, 2, 5, 1, 3
C. 4, 5, 2, 1, 3
D. 4, 1, 5, 2, 3

18.____

19.
1. H44477447G
2. H47444777G
3. H74777477C
4. H44747447G
5. H77747447C

A. 1, 3, 5, 4, 2
B. 3, 1, 5, 2, 4
C. 1, 4, 2, 3, 5
D. 3, 5, 1, 4, 2

19.____

20.
1. G11143447G
2. G15133388C
3. C15134378G
4. G11534477C
5. C15533337C

A. 3, 5, 1, 4, 2
B. 1, 4, 3, 2, 5
C. 5, 3, 4, 2, 1
D. 4, 3, 1, 2, 5

20.____

21.
1. J96693369F
2. J66939339F
3. J96693693E
4. J966T3933E
5. J69639363F

A. 4, 3, 2, 5, 1
B. 2, 5, 4, 1, 3
C. 2, 5, 4, 3, 1
D. 3, 4, 5, 2, 1

21.____

22.
1. L15567834Z
2. P11587638Z
3. M51567688Z
4. O55578784Z
5. N53588783Z

A. 3, 1, 5, 2, 4
B. 1, 3, 5, 4, 2
C. 1, 3, 5, 2, 4
D. 3, 1, 4, 4, 2

22.____

5 (#1)

	Column I	Column II	
23.	1. C83261824G 2. C78361822C 3. G83261732G 4. C88261823C 5. G83261743C	A. 2, 4, 1, 5, 3 B. 4, 2, 1, 3, 5 C. 3, 1, 5, 2, 4 D. , 3, 5, 1, 4	23.____
24.	1. A11710107H 2. H17110017A 3. A11170707A 4. H17170171H 5. A11710177A	A. 2, 1, 4, 3, 5 B. 3, 1, 5, 2, 4 C. 3, 4, 1, 5, 2 D. 3, 5, 1, 2, 4	24.____
25.	1. R26794821S 2. O26794821T 3. M26794821Z 4. Q26794821R 5. S26794821P	A. 3, 2, 4, 1, 5 B. 3, 4, 2, 1, 5 C. 4, 2, 1, 3, 5 D. 5, 4, 1, 2, 3	25.____

KEY (CORRECT ANSWERS)

1.	A		11.	C
2.	D		12.	B
3.	B		13.	B
4.	C		14.	D
5.	A		15.	A
6.	C		16.	C
7.	D		17.	A
8.	B		18.	B
9.	A		19.	D
10.	D		20.	C

21. A
22. B
23. A
24. D
25. A

TEST 2

Questions 1-5.

DIRECTIONS: Questions 1 through 5 consist of a set of letters and numbers located under Column I. For each question, pick the answer (A, B, C, or D) located under Column II which contains ONLY letters and numbers that appear in the question in Column II. *PRINT THE LETTER OF THE CORRECT ANSWER IN THE SPACE AT THE RIGHT.*

SAMPLE QUESTION

Column I

B-9-P-H-2-Z-N-8-4-M

Column II

A. B-4-C-3-R-9
B. 4-H-P-8-6-N
C. P-2-Z-8-M-9
D. 4-B-N-5-E-Z

Choice C is the correct answer because P,2,Z,8,M and 9 all appear in the sample question. All the other choices have at least one letter or number that is not in the question.

Column I

1. 1-7-6-J-L-T-3-S-A-2

2. C-0-Q-5-3-9-H-L-2-7

3. P-3-B-C-5-6-0-E-1-T

4. U-T-Z-2-4-S-8-6-B-3

5. 4-D-F-G-C-6-8-3-J-L

Column II

A. J-3-S-A-7-L
B. T-S-A-2-6-5
C. 3-7-J-L-S-Z
D. A-7-4-J-L-1

A. F-9-T-2-7-Q
B. 3-0-6-9-L-C
C. 9-L-7-Q-C-3
D. H-Q-4-5-9-7

A. B-4-6-1-3-T
B. T-B-P-3-E-0
C. 5-3-0-E-B-G
D. 0-6-P-T-9-B

A. 2-4-S-V-Z-3
B. B-Z-S-8-3-6
C. 4-T-U-8-L-B
D. 9-3-T-Z-1-2

A. T-D-6-8-4-J
B. C-4-3-2-J-F
C. 8-3-C-5-G-6
D. C-8-6-J-G-L

1.____

2.____

3.____

4.____

5.____

Questions 6-12.

DIRECTIONS: Each of the questions numbered 6 through 12 consist of a long series of letters and numbers under Column I and four short series of letters and numbers under Column II. For each question, choose the short series of letters and numbers which is entirely and exactly the same as some part of the long series.

	Column I		Column II	
6.	IE227FE383L4700	A. B. C. D.	E27FE3 EF838L EL4700 83LE70	6.____
7.	77J646G54NPB318	A. B. C. D.	NPB318 J646J5 4G54NP C54NPB	7.____
8.	85887T358W24A93	A. B. C. D.	858887 W24A93 858W24 87T353	8.____
9.	E104RY796B33H14	A. B. C. D.	04RY79 E14RYR 96B3H1 RY7996	9.____
10.	W58NP12141DE07M	A. B. C. D.	8MP121 W58NP1 14DEO7 12141D	10.____
11.	P473R365M442V5W	A. B. C. D.	P47365 73P365 365M44 5X42V5	11.____
12.	865CG441V21SS59	A. B. C. D.	1V12SS V21SS5 5GC441 894CG4	12.____

KEY (CORRECT ANSWERS)

1.	A	7.	A
2.	C	8.	B
3.	B	9.	A
4.	B	10.	D
5.	D	11.	C
6	D	12.	B

TEST 3

DIRECTIONS: Each question from 1 through 8 consists of a set of letters and numbers. For each question, pick as your answer from the column to the right the choice has ONLY numbers and letters that are in the question you are answering.

To help you understand what to do, the following sample question is given:

SAMPLE: B-9-P-H-2-Z-N-8-4-M

A. B-4-C-3-E-9
B. 4-H-P-8-6-N
C. P-2-Z-8-M-9
D. 4-B-N-R-E-A

Choice C is the correct answer because P, 2, Z, 8, M-9 are in the sample question. All the other choices have at least one letter or number that is not in the question.

Questions 1 through 4 are based on Column I.

Column I

1. X-8-3-I-H-9-4-G-P-U
2. 4-1-2-X-U-B-9-H-7-3
3. U-I-G-2-5-4-W-P-3-B
4. 3-H-7-G-4-5-1-U-B

A. I-G-W-8-2-1
B. U-3-G-9-P-8
C. 3-G-I-4-S-U
D. 9-X-4-7-2-H

Questions 5 through 8 are based on Column II.

Column II

5. L-2-9-Z-R-8-Q-Y-5-7
6. J-L-9-N-Y-8-5-Q-Z-2
7. T-Y-3-3-J-Q-2-N-R-Z
8. 8-Z-7-T-N-L-1-E-R-3

A. 8-R-N-3-T-Z
B. 2-L-R-5-7-Q
C. J-2-8-Z-T-5
D. Z-8-9-3-L-5

KEY (CORRECT ANSWERS)

1. B 5. B
2. D 6. C
3. C 7. A
4. C 8. A

TEST 4

DIRECTIONS: Questions 1 through 5 have lines of letters and numbers. Each letter should be matched with its number in accordance with the following table.

Letter:	F	R	C	A	W	L	E	N	B	T
Matching Number:	0	1	2	3	4	5	6	7	8	9

From the table you can determine that the letter F has the matching number 0 below it, the letter R has the matching number 1 below it, etc.

For each question, compare each line of letters and numbers carefully to see if each letter has its correct matching number. If all the letters and numbers are matched correctly in none of the line of the question, mark your answer A; only one of the lines in the question, mark your answer B; only two of the lines of the question, mark your answer C; all three lines of the question, mark your answer D.

```
WBCR    4826
TLBF    9580
ATNE    3986
```

There is a mistake in the first line because the letter R should have its matching number 1 instead of the number 6. The second line is correct because each letter shown has the correct matching number.
There is a mistake in the third line because the letter N should have the matching number 7 instead of the number 8. Since all the letters and numbers are matched correctly in only one of the lines in the sample, the correct answer is B.

1. EBCT   6829   1.____
   ATWR   3962
   NLBW   7584

2. RNCT   1729   2.____
   LNCR   5728
   WAEB   5368

3. STWB   7948   3.____
   RABL   1385
   TAEF   9360

4. LWRB   5417   4.____
   RLWN   1647
   CBWA   2843

5. ABTC   3792   5.____
   WCER   5261
   AWCN   3417

KEY (CORRECT ANSWERS)

1. C
2. B
3. D
4. B
5. A

TEST 5

DIRECTIONS: Assume that each of the capital letters in the table below represents the name of an employee enrolled in the city employees' retirement system. The number directly beneath the letter represents the agency for which the employee works, and the small letter directly beneath represents the code for the employee's account.

Name of Employee:	L	O	T	Q	A	M	R	N	C
Agency:	3	4	5	9	8	7	52	1	6
Account Code:	r	f	b	i	d	t	g	e	n

In each of the following Questions 1 through 10, the agency code numbers and the account code letters in Columns 2 and 3 should correspond to the capital letters in Column 1 and should be in the same consecutive order. For each question, look at each column carefully and mark your answer as follows:
   if there are one or more errors in Column 2 only, mark your answer A;
   if there are one or more errors in Column 3 only, mark your answer B;
   if there are one or more error in Column 2 and one or more errors in Column 3, mark your answer C;
   if there are NO errors in either column, mark your answer D.

The following sample question is given to help you understand the procedure.

Column 1	Column 2	Column 3
TQLMOC	583746	birtfn

In Column 2, the second agency code number (corresponding to letter Q) should be "9," not "8." Column 3 is coded correctly to Column 1. Since there is an error only in Column 2, the correct answer is A.

	Column 1	Column 2	Column 3	
1.	QLNRCA	931268	ifegnd	1.____
2.	NRMOTC	127546	egftbn	2.____
3.	RCTALM	265837	gndbrt	3.____
4.	TAMLON	578341	bdtrfe	4.____
5.	ANTROM	815427	debigt	5.____
6.	MRALON	728341	tgdrfe	6.____
7.	CTNQRO	657924	ndeigf	7.____
8.	QMROTA	972458	itgfbd	8.____

2 (#5)

	Column 1	Column 2	Column 3	
9.	RQMCOL	297463	gitnfr	9.____
10.	NOMRTQ	147259	eftgbi	10.____

KEY (CORRECT ANSWERS)

1. D   6. D
2. C   7. C
3. B   8. D
4. A   9. A
5. B   10. D

TEST 6

DIRECTIONS: Each of Questions 1 through 6 consist of three lines of code letters and numbers. The numbers on each line should correspond to the code letter on the same line in accordance with the table below.

Code Letter:	D	Y	K	L	P	U	S	R	A	E
Corresponding Number:	0	1	2	3	4	5	6	7	8	9

On some of the lines an error exists in the coding. Prepare the letters and numbers in each question carefully. If you find an error or errors on
  only one of the lines in the question, mark your answer A;
  any two lines in the question, mark your answer B;
  all three lines in the question, mark your answer C;
  none of the lines in the question, mark your answer D.

SAMPLE QUESTION
  KSRYELD   2671930
  SAPUEKL   6845913
  RYKADLP   5128034

In the above sample, the first line is correct since each code letter listed has the correct corresponding number. On the second line, an error exists because code letter R should have the number 2 instead of number 1. On the third line, an error exists because the code letter R should have the number 7 instead of the number 5. Since there are errors on two of the three lines, the correct answer is B.

Now answer the following questions using the same procedure.

1. YPUSRLD   1456730   1.____
   UPSAEDY   5648901
   PREYDKS   4791026

2. AERLPUS   8973456   2.____
   DKLYDPA   0231048
   UKLDREP   5230794

3. DAPUSLA   0845683   3.____
   YKLDLPS   1230356
   PUSKYDE   4562101

4. LRPUPDL   3745403   4.____
   SUPLEDR   6543907
   PKEYDLU   4291025

5. KEYDESR   2910967   5.____
   PRSALEY   4678391
   LRAYSK   3687162

107

2 (#6)

6. YESREYL   1967913   6.____
   PLPRAKY   4346821
   YLPSRDU   1346705

   ———

KEY (CORRECT ANSWERS)

1. A   4. A
2. D   5. B
3. C   6. A

———

READING COMPREHENSION
UNDERSTANDING AND INTERPRETING WRITTEN MATERIAL
EXAMINATION SECTION
TEST 1

DIRECTIONS: Each question or incomplete statement is followed by several suggested answers or completions. Select the one that BEST answers the question or completes the statement. *PRINT THE LETTER OF THE CORRECT ANSWER IN THE SPACE AT THE RIGHT.*

Questions 1-4.

DIRECTIONS: Questions 1 through 4 are to be answered SOLELY on the basis of the information contained in the following passage.

After conducting and completing an interview, the interviewer is faced with the responsibility of recording it in some manner. Very considerable amounts of staff time and agency finances are absorbed in recording. Time and cost studies of agency expenditures indicate that, for every dollar spent on interviewing, three dollars are spent on recording. In addition to actual time spent by the worker in recording, such expense involves clerical transcribing time, filing time and space, and time in reading records.

Recording insures a continuity of client-agency contact that transcends the client's contact with any individual social worker. The case record also implements the agency's accountability to the community. It provides a permanent, documented account of services to clients. The interviewer about to record the interview faces the essential question, what should be recorded and how should the recording be organized? Just as purpose guides interview interaction, so it guides selection of material for recording. Traditionally, social work recording has been designed to meet a number of different purposes. We record to achieve more effective practice, to provide material for in-service training and teaching, and for research purposes. There is no consensus on the principal purpose of social work recording. Consequently, recording has served these various purposes with limited effectiveness, and has served no one purpose well.

1. According to the above passage, the relationship between recording and interviewing costs for social work purposes is such that

   A. recording is three times more expensive than interviewing
   B. recording is one-third as expensive as interviewing
   C. recording is four times more expensive than interviewing
   D. interviewing is much more expensive than recording

2. The one of the following that is SPECIFICALLY mentioned as a purpose of case recording is

   A. saving time   B. economy
   C. research   D. convenience

109

3. Of the following, according to the above passage, a MAJOR contributing factor to the expense of case recording is

   A. supervision
   B. in-service training
   C. research
   D. record reading time

4. It can be concluded that the author's opinion regarding the capacity of social work recording to achieve its various purposes is

   A. enthusiastic
   B. guarded
   C. neutral
   D. confused

Questions 5-7.

DIRECTIONS: Questions 5 through 7 are to be answered SOLELY on the basis of the information in the following passage.

It is important that interviewers understand to some degree the manner in which stereotyped thinking operates. Stereotypes are commonly held, but predominantly false, preoccupations about the appearance and traits of individuals of different racial, religious, ethnic, and subcultural groups. Distinct traits, physical and mental, are associated with each group, and membership in a particular group is enough, in the mind of a person holding the stereotype, to assure that these traits will be perceived in individuals who are members of that group. Conversely, possession of the particular stereotyped trait by an individual usually indicates to the holder of the stereotype that the individual is a group member. Linked to the formation of stereotypes is the fact that mental traits, either positive or negative, such as honesty, laziness, avariciousness, and other characteristics are associated with particular stereotypes. Either kind of stereotype, if held by an interviewer, can seriously damage the results of an interview. In general, stereotypes can be particularly dangerous when they are part of the belief patterns of administrators, interviewers, and supervisors, who are in a position to affect the lives of others and to stimulate or retard the development of human potential. The holding of a stereotype by an interviewer, for example, diverts his attention from significant essential facts and information upon which really valid assessments may be made. Unfortunately, it is the rare interviewer who is completely conscious of the real basis upon which he is making his evaluation of the people he is interviewing. The specific reasons given by an interviewer for a negative evaluation, even though apparently logical and based upon what, in the mind of the interviewer, are very good reasons, may not be the truly motivating factors. This is why the careful selection and training of interviewers is such an important responsibility of an agency which is attempting to help a great diversity of human beings.

5. Of the following, the BEST title for the above paragraph is

   A. POSITIVE AND NEGATIVE EFFECTS OF STEREOTYPED THINKING
   B. THE RELATIONSHIP OF STEREOTYPES TO INTERVIEWING
   C. AN AGENCY'S RESPONSIBILITY IN INTERVIEWING
   D. THE IMPACT OF STEREOTYPED THINKING ON PROFESSIONAL FUNCTIONS

6. According to the above passage, MOST interviewers

   A. compensate for stereotyped beliefs to avoid negatively affecting the results of their interviews
   B. are influenced by stereotypes they hold, but put greater stress on factual information developed during the interview
   C. are seldom aware of their real motives when evaluating interviewees
   D. give logical and good reasons for negative evaluations of interviewees

7. According to the above passage, which of the following is NOT a characteristic of stereotypes?

   A. Stereotypes influence estimates of personality traits of people.
   B. Positive stereotypes can damage the results of an interview.
   C. Physical traits associated with stereotypes seldom really exist.
   D. Stereotypes sometimes are a basis upon which valid personality assessments can be made.

Questions 8-12.

DIRECTIONS: Questions 8 through 12 are to be answered SOLELY on the basis of the following passage.

At one time, people thought that in the interview designed primarily to obtain information, the interviewer had to resort to clever and subtle lines of questioning in order to accomplish his ends. Some people still believe that this is necessary, but it is not so. An example of the *tricky* approach may be seen in the work of a recent study. The study deals with materials likely to be buried beneath deep defenses. Interviewers utilized methods of questioning which, in effect, trapped the interviewee and destroyed his defenses. Doubtless, these methods succeeded in bringing out items of information which straightforward questions would have missed. Whether they missed more information than they obtained and whether they obtained the most important facts must remain unanswered questions. In defense of the *clever* approach, it is often said that, in many situations, the interviewee is motivated to conceal information or to distort what he chooses to report.

Technically, it is likely that a highly skilled interviewer can, given the time and the inclination, penetrate the interviewee's defenses and get information which the latter intended to keep hidden. It is unlikely that the interviewer can successfully elicit all of the information that might be relevant. If, for example, he found that an applicant for financial assistance was heavily in debt to gamblers, he might not care about getting any other information. There are situations in which one item, if answered in the *wrong* way, is enough. Ordinarily, this is not true. The usual situation is that there are many considerations and that the plus and minus features must be weighed before a decision may be made. It is, therefore, important to obtain complete information.

8. According to the above passage, it was GENERALLY believed that an interviewer would have difficulty in obtaining the information he sought from a person if he

   A. were tricky in his methods
   B. were open and frank in his approach

C. were clever in his questioning
D. utilized carefully prepared questions

9. The passage does NOT reveal whether the type of questions used

   A. trapped those being interviewed
   B. elicited facts which an open method of questioning might miss
   C. elicited the most important facts that were sought
   D. covered matters which those interviewed were reluctant to talk about openly

10. An argument in favor of the *tricky* or *clever* interviewing technique is that, unless this approach is used, the person interviewed will NOT

    A. offer to furnish all pertinent information
    B. answer questions concerning routine data
    C. clearly understand what is being sought
    D. want to continue the interview

11. According to the above passage, in favorable circumstances, a talented interviewer would be able to obtain from the person interviewed information

    A. which the person regards as irrelevant
    B. which the person intends to conceal
    C. about the person's family background
    D. which the person would normally have forgotten

12. According to the above passage, a highly skilled interviewer should concentrate, in most cases, on getting

    A. one outstanding fact about the interviewee which would do away with the need for prolonged questioning
    B. facts which the interviewee wanted to conceal because these would be the most relevant in making a decision
    C. all the facts so that he can consider their relative values before reaching any conclusion
    D. information about any bad habits of the interviewee, such as gambling, which would make further questioning

Questions 13-14.

DIRECTIONS: Questions 13 and 14 are to be answered SOLELY on the basis of the information given below.

The ability to interview rests not on any single trait, but on a vast complex of them. Habits, skills, techniques, and attitudes are all involved. Competence in interviewing is acquired only after careful and diligent study, prolonged practice (preferably under supervision), and a good bit of trial and error; for interviewing is not an exact science, it is an art. Like many other arts, however, it can and must draw on science in several of its aspects.

There is always a place for individual initiative, for imaginative innovations, and for new combinations of old approaches. The skilled interviewer cannot be bound by a set of rules. Likewise, there is not a set of rules which can guarantee to the novice that his interviewing will be successful. There are, however, some accepted, general guideposts which may help the beginner to avoid mistakes, learn how to conserve his efforts, and establish effective working relationships with interviewees; to accomplish, in short, what he sets out to do.

13. According to the above passage, rules and standard techniques for interviewing are

    A. helpful for the beginner, but useless for the experienced, innovative interviewer
    B. destructive of the innovation and initiative needed for a good interviewer
    C. useful for even the experienced interviewer who may, however, sometimes go beyond them
    D. the means by which nearly anybody can become an effective interviewer

14. According to the above passage, the one of the following which is a prerequisite to competent interviewing is

    A. avoiding mistakes
    B. study and practice
    C. imaginative innovation
    D. natural aptitude

Questions 15-17.

DIRECTIONS: Questions 15 through 17 are to be answered SOLELY on the basis of the following paragraph.

The physical setting of the interview may determine its entire potentiality. Some degree of privacy and a comfortable relaxed atmosphere are important. The interviewee is not encouraged to give much more than his name and address if the interviewer seems busy with other things, if people are rushing about, if there are distracting noises. He has a right to feel that, whether the interview lasts five minutes or an hour, he has, for that time, the undivided attention of the interviewer. If the interviewee has waited in a crowded room for what seems to him an interminably long period, he is naturally in no mood to sit down and discuss what is on his mind. Indeed, by that time the primary thing on his mind may be his irritation at being kept waiting, and he frequently feels it would be impolite to express this. If a wait or interruptions have been unavoidable, it is always helpful to give the client some recognition that these are disturbing and that we can naturally understand that they make it more difficult for him to proceed. At the same time, if he protests that they have not troubled him, the interviewer can best accept his statements at their face value, as further insistence that they must have been disturbing may be interpreted by his as accusing, and he may conclude that the interviewer has been personally hurt by his irritation.

15. Distraction during an interview may tend to limit the client's responses.
    In a case where an interruption has occurred, it would be BEST for the investigator to

    A. terminate this interview and have it rescheduled for another time period
    B. ignore the interruption since it is not continuous
    C. express his understanding that the distraction can cause the client to feel disturbed
    D. accept the client's protests that he has been troubled by the interruption

16. To maximize the rapport that can be established with the client, an appropriate physical setting is necessary. At the very least, some privacy would be necessary.
In addition, the interviewer should

    A. always appear to be busy in order to impress the client
    B. focus his attention only on the client
    C. accept all the client's statements as being valid
    D. stress the importance of the interview to the client

17. Clients who have been waiting quite some time for their interview may, justifiably, become upset.
However, a client may INITIALLY attempt to mask these feelings because he may

    A. personally hurt the interviewer
    B. want to be civil
    C. feel that the wait was unavoidable
    D. fear the consequences of his statement

Questions 18-20.

DIRECTIONS: Questions 18 through 20 are to be answered SOLELY on the basis of information given in the passage below.

A personnel interviewer, selecting job applicants, may find that he reacts badly to some people even on first contact. This reaction cannot usually be explained by things that the interviewee has done or said. Most of us have had the experience of liking or disliking, of feeling comfortable or uncomfortable with people on first acquaintance, long before we have had a chance to make a conscious, rational decision about them. Often, too, our liking or disliking is transmitted to the other person by subtle processes such as gestures, posture, voice intonations, or choice of words. The point to be kept in mind is this: the relations between people are complex and occur at several levels, from the conscious to the unconscious. This is true whether the relationship is brief or long, formal or informal.

Some of the major dynamics of personality which operate on the unconscious level are projection, sublimation, rationalization, and repression. Encountering these for the first time, one is apt to think of them as representing pathological states. In the extreme, they undoubtedly are, but they exist so universally that we must consider them also to be parts of normal personality.

Without necessarily subscribing to any of the numerous theories of personality, it is possible to describe personality in terms of certain important aspects or elements. We are all aware of ourselves as thinking organisms.

This aspect of personality, the conscious part, is important for understanding human behavior, but it is not enough. Many find it hard to accept the notion that each person also has an unconscious. The existence of the unconscious is no longer a matter of debate. It is not possible to estimate at all precisely what proportion of our total psychological life is conscious, what proportion unconscious. Everyone who has studied the problem, however, agrees that consciousness is the smaller part of personality. Most of what we are and do is a result of unconscious processes. To ignore this is to risk mistakes.

18. The above passage suggests that an interviewer can be MOST effective if he

   A. learns how to determine other peoples' unconscious motivations
   B. learns how to repress his own unconsciously motivated mannerisms and behavior
   C. can keep others from feeling that he either likes or dislikes them
   D. gains an understanding of how the unconscious operates in himself and in others

19. It may be inferred from the above passage that the *subtle processes such as gestures, posture, voice intonation, or choice of words* referred to in the first paragraph are USUALLY

   A. in the complete control of an expert investigator
   B. the determining factors in the friendships a person establishes
   C. controlled by a person's unconscious
   D. not capable of being consciously controlled

20. The above passage implies that various different personality theories are USUALLY

   A. so numerous and different as to be valueless to an investigator
   B. in basic agreement about the importance of the unconscious
   C. understood by the investigator who strives to be effective
   D. in agreement that personality factors such as projection and repression are pathological

Questions 21-25.

DIRECTIONS: Questions 21 through 25 are to be answered SOLELY on the basis of the information given in the following paragraph.

   The nature of the interview varies with the aim or the use to which it is put. While these uses vary widely, interviews are basically of three types: fact-finding, informing, and motivating. One of these purposes usually predominates in an interview, but not to the exclusion of the other two. If the main purpose is fact-finding, for example, the interviewer must often motivate the interviewee to cooperate in revealing the facts. A major factor in the interview is the interaction of the personalities of the interviewer and the interviewee. The interviewee may not wish to reveal the facts sought, or even though willing enough to impart them, he may not be able to do so because of a lack of clear understanding as to what is wanted or because of lack of ability to put into words the information he has to give. On the other hand, the interviewer may not be able to grasp and report accurately the facts which the one being interviewed is trying to convey. Also, the interviewer's prejudice may make him not want to get at the real facts or make him unable to recognize the truth.

21. According to the above paragraph, the purpose of an interview

   A. determines the nature of the interview
   B. is usually the same for the three basic types of interviews
   C. is predominantly motivation of the interviewee
   D. is usually to check on the accuracy of facts previously obtained

22. In discussing the use or purpose of an interview, the above paragraph points out that

    A. a good interview should have only one purpose
    B. an interview usually has several uses that are equally important
    C. fact-finding should be the main purpose of an interview
    D. the interview usually has one main purpose

23. According to the above paragraph, an obstacle to the successful interview sometimes attributable to the interviewee is

    A. a lack of understanding of how to conduct an interview
    B. an inability to express himself
    C. prejudice toward the interviewer
    D. too great a desire to please

24. According to the above paragraph, one way in which the interviewer may help the interviewee to reveal the facts sought is to

    A. make him willing to impart the facts by stating clearly the consequences of false information
    B. make sure he understands what information is wanted
    C. motivate him by telling him how important he is in the investigation
    D. tell him what words to use to convey the information wanted

25. According to the above paragraph, bias on the part of the interviewer could

    A. be due to inability to understand the facts being imparted
    B. lead him to report the facts accurately
    C. make the interviewee unwilling to impart the truth
    D. prevent him from determining the facts

KEY (CORRECT ANSWERS)

1.	A	11.	B
2.	C	12.	C
3.	D	13.	C
4.	B	14.	B
5.	B	15.	C
6.	C	16.	B
7.	D	17.	B
8.	B	18.	D
9.	C	19.	C
10.	A	20.	B

21. A
22. D
23. B
24. B
25. D

READING COMPREHENSION
UNDERSTANDING AND INTERPRETING WRITTEN MATERIAL

EXAMINATION SECTION

TEST 1

DIRECTIONS: Each question or incomplete statement is followed by several suggested answers or completions. Select the one that BEST answers the question or completes the statement. *PRINT THE LETTER OF THE CORRECT ANSWER IN THE SPACE AT THE RIGHT.*

Questions 1-5.

DIRECTIONS: Questions 1 through 5 are to be answered SOLELY on the basis of the following passage.

The most effective control mechanism to prevent gross incompetence on the part of public employees is a good personnel program. The personnel officer in the line departments and the central personnel agency should exert positive leadership to raise levels of performance. Although the key factor is the quality of the personnel recruited, staff members other than personnel officers can make important contributions to efficiency. Administrative analysts, now employed in many agencies, make detailed studies of organization and procedures, with the purpose of eliminating delays, waste, and other inefficiencies. Efficiency is, however, more than a question of good organization and procedures; it is also the product of the attitudes and value of the public employees. Personal motivation can provide the will to be efficient. The best management studies will not result in substantial improvement of the performance of those employees who feel no great urge to wok up to their abilities.

1. The above passage indicates that the KEY factor in preventing gross incompetence of public employees is the
   A. hiring of administrative analysts to assist personnel people
   B. utilization of effective management studies
   C. overlapping of responsibility
   D. quality of the employees hired

1.____

2. According to the above passage, the central personnel agency staff SHOULD
   A. work more closely with administrative analysts in the line departments than with personnel officers
   B. make a serious effort to avoid jurisdictional conflicts with personnel officers in line departments
   C. contribute to improving the quality of work of public employees
   D. engage in a comprehensive program to change the public's negative image of public employees

2.____

3. The above passage indicates that efficiency in an organization can BEST be brought about by
   A. eliminating ineffective control mechanisms
   B. instituting sound organizational procedures
   C. promoting competent personnel
   D. recruiting people with desire to do good work

3.____

4. According to the above passage, the purpose of administrative analysts in a public agency is to
   A. prevent injustice to the public employee
   B. promote the efficiency of the agency
   C. protect the interests of the public
   D. ensure the observance of procedural due process

4.____

5. The above passage implies that a considerable rise in the quality of work of public employees can be brought about by
   A. encouraging positive employee attitudes toward work
   B. controlling personnel officers who exceed their powers
   C. creating warm personal associations among public employees in an agency
   D. closing loopholes in personnel organization and procedures

5.____

Questions 6-8.

DIRECTIONS: Questions 6 through 8 are to be answered SOLELY on the basis of the following passage.

EMPLOYEE NEEDS

The greatest waste in industry and in government may be that of human resources. This waste usually derives not from employees' unwillingness or inability, but from management's ineptness to meet the maintenance and motivational needs of employees. Maintenance needs refer to such needs as providing employees with safe places to work, written work rules, job security, adequate salary, employer-sponsored social activities, and with knowledge of their role in the overall framework of the organization. However, of greatest significance to employees are the motivational needs of job growth, achievement, responsibility, and recognition.

Although employee dissatisfaction may stem from either poor maintenance or poor motivation factors, the outward manifestation of the dissatisfaction may be very much like, i.e., negativism, complaints, deterioration of performance, and so forth. The improvement in the lighting of an employee's work area or raising his level of ay won't do much good if the source of the dissatisfaction is the absence of a meaningful assignment. By the same token, if an employee is dissatisfied with what he considers inequitable pay, the introduction of additional challenge in his work may simply make matters worse.

It is relatively easy for an employee to express frustration by complaining about pay, washroom conditions, fringe benefits, and so forth; but most people cannot easily express resentment in terms of the more abstract concepts concerning job growth, responsibility, and achievement.

It would be wrong to assume that there is no interaction between maintenance and motivational needs of employee. For example, conditions of high motivation often overshadow poor maintenance conditions. If an organization is in a period of strong growth and expansion, opportunities for job growth, responsibility, recognition, and achievement are usually abundant, but the rapid growth may have outrun the upkeep of maintenance factors. In this situation, motivation may be high, but only if employees recognize the poor maintenance conditions as unavoidable and temporary. The subordination of maintenance factors cannot go on indefinitely, even with the highest motivation.

Both maintenance and motivation factors influence the behavior of all employees, but employees are not identical and, furthermore, the needs of any individual do not remain orientation toward maintenance factors and those with greater sensitivity toward motivation factors.

A highly maintenance-oriented individual, preoccupied with the factors peripheral to his job rather than the job itself, is more concerned with comfort than challenge. He does not get deeply involved with his work but does with the condition of his work area, toilet facilities, and his time for going to lunch. By contrast, a strongly motivation-oriented employee is usually relatively indifferent to his surroundings and is caught up in the pursuit of work goals.

Fortunately, there are few people who are either exclusively maintenance-oriented or purely motivation-oriented. The former would be deadwood in an organization, while the latter might trample on those around him in his pursuit to achieve his goals.

6. With respect to employee motivational and maintenance needs, the management policies of an organization which is growing rapidly will probably result
    A. more in meeting motivational needs rather than maintenance needs
    B. more in meeting maintenance needs rather than motivational needs
    C. in meeting both of these needs equally
    D. in increased effort to define the motivational and maintenance needs of its employees

7. In accordance with the above passage, which of the following CANNOT be considered as an example of an employee maintenance need for railroad clerks?
    A. Providing more relief periods
    B. Providing fair salary increases at periodic intervals
    C. Increasing job responsibilities
    D. Increasing health insurance benefits

8. Most employees in an organization may be categorized as being interested in
    A. maintenance needs only
    B. motivational needs only
    C. both motivational and maintenance needs
    D. money only, to the exclusion of all other needs

Questions 9-11.

DIRECTIONS: Questions 9 through 11 are to be answered SOLELY on the basis of the following passage.

GOOD EMPLOYEE PRACTICES

As a city employee, you will be expected to take an interest in you work and perform the duties of your job to the best of your ability and in a spirit of cooperation. Nothing shows an interest in your work more than coming to work on time, not only at the start of the day but also when returning from lunch. If it is necessary for you to keep a personal appointment at lunch hour which might cause a delay in getting back to work on time, you should explain the situation to your supervisor and get his approval to come back a little late before you leave for lunch.

You should do everything that is asked of you willingly and consider important even the small jobs that your supervisor gives you. Although these jobs may seem unimportant, if you forget to do them or if you don't do them right, trouble may develop later.

Getting along well with your fellow workers will add much to the enjoyment of your work. You should respect your fellow workers and try to see their side when a disagreement arises. The better you get along with your fellow workers and your supervisor, the better you will like your job and the better you will be able to do it.

9. According to the above passage, in your job as a city employee, you are expected to
   A. show a willingness to cooperate on the job
   B. get your supervisor's approval before keeping any personal appointments at lunch hour
   C. avoid doing small jobs that seem unimportant
   D. do the easier jobs at the start of the day and the more difficult ones later on

10. According to the above passage, getting to work on time shows that you
    A. need the job
    B. have an interest in your work
    C. get along well with your fellow workers
    D. like your supervisor

11. According to the above passage, the one of the following statements that is NOT true is:
    A. If you do a small job wrong, trouble may develop
    B. You should respect your fellow workers
    C. If you disagree with a fellow worker, you should try to see his side of the story
    D. The less you get along with your supervisor, the better you will be able to do your job

Questions 12-15.

DIRECTIONS: Questions 12 through 15 are to be answered SOLELY on the basis of the following passage.

EMPLOYEE SUGGESTIONS

To increase the effectiveness of the city government, the city asks its employees to offer suggestions when they feel an improvement could be made in some government operation. The Employees' Suggestions Program was started to encourage city employees to do this. Through this Program, which is only for city employees, cash awards may be given to those whose suggestions are submitted and approved. Suggestions are looked for not only from supervisors but from all city employees as any city employee may get an idea which might be approved and contribute greatly to the solution of some problem of city government.

Therefore, all suggestions for improvement are welcome, whether they be suggestions on how to improve working conditions, or on how to increase the speed with which work is done, or on how to reduce or eliminate such things as waste, time losses, accidents or fire hazards. There are, however, a few types of suggestions for which cash awards cannot be given. An example of this type would be a suggestion to increase salaries or a suggestion to change the regulations about annual leave or about sick leave. The number of suggestions sent in has increased sharply during the past few years. It is hoped that it will keep increasing in the future in order to meet the city's needs for more ideas for improved ways of doing things.

12. According to the above passage, the MAIN reason why the city asks its employees for suggestions about government operations is to
    A. increase the effectiveness of the city government
    B. show that the Employees' Suggestion Program is working well
    C. show that everybody helps run the city government
    D. have the employee win a prize

13. According to the above passage, the Employees' Suggestion Program can approve awards ONLY for those suggestions that come from
    A. city employees
    B. city employees who are supervisors
    C. city employees who are not supervisors
    D. experienced employee of the city

14. According to the above passage, a cash award cannot be given through the Employees' Suggestion Program for a suggestion about
    A. getting work done faster
    B. helping prevent accidents on the job
    C. increasing the amount of annual leave for city employees
    D. reducing the chance of fire where city employees work

15. According to the above passage, the suggestions sent in during the past few years have
    A. all been approved
    B. generally been well written
    C. been mostly about reducing or eliminating waste
    D. been greater in number than before

Questions 16-18.

DIRECTIONS: Questions 16 through 18 are to be answered SOLELY on the basis of the following passage.

The supervisor will gain the respect of the members of his staff and increase his influence over them by controlling his temper and avoiding criticizing anyone publicly. When a mistake is made, the good supervisor will take it over with the employee quietly and privately. The supervisor will listen to the employee's story, suggest the better way of doing the job, and offer help so the mistake won't happen again. Before closing the discussion, the supervisor should try to find something good to say about other parts of the employee's work. Some praise and appreciation, along with instruction, is more likely to encourage an employee to improve in those areas where he is weakest.

16. A good title that would show the meaning of the above passage would be
    A. How to Correct Employee Errors
    B. How to Praise Employees
    C. Mistakes are Preventable
    D. The Weak Employee

17. According to the above passage, the work of an employee who has made a mistake is more likely to improve if the supervisor
    A. avoids criticizing him
    B. gives him a chance to suggest a better way of doing the work
    C. listens to the employee's excuses to see if he is right
    D. praises good work at the same time he corrects the mistake

18. According to the above passage, when a supervisor needs to correct an employee's mistake, it is important that he
    A. allow some time to go by after the mistake is made
    B. do so when other employee are not present
    C. show his influence with his tone of voice
    D. tell other employee to avoid the same mistake

Questions 19-23.

DIRECTIONS: Questions 19 through 23 are to be answered SOLELY on the basis of the following passage.

In studying the relationships of people to the organizational structure, it is absolutely necessary to identify and recognize the informal organizational structure. These relationships are necessary when coordination of a plan is attempted. They may be with *the boss*, line supervisors, staff personnel, or other representatives of the formal organization's hierarchy, and they may include the *liaison men* who serve as the leaders of the informal organization. An acquaintanceship with the people serving in these roles in the organization, and its formal counterpart, permits a supervisor to recognize sensitive areas in which it is simple to get conflict reaction. Avoidance of such areas, plus conscious efforts to inform other people of his own objectives for various plans, will usually enlist their aid and support. Planning *without* people can lead to disaster because the individuals who must act together to make any plan a success are more important than the plans themselves.

19. Of the following titles, the one that MOST clearly describes the above passage is
    A. Coordination of a Function
    B. Avoidance of Conflict
    C. Planning With People
    D. Planning Objectives

20. According to the above passage, attempts at coordinating plans may fail unless
    A. the plan's objectives are clearly set forth
    B. conflict between groups is resolved
    C. the plans themselves are worthwhile
    D. informal relationships are recognized

21. According to the above passage, conflict
    A. may, in some cases, be desirable to secure results
    B. produces more heat than light
    C. should be avoided at all costs
    D. possibilities can be predicted by a sensitive supervisor

22. The above passage implies that
    A. informal relationships are more important than formal structure
    B. the weakness of a formal structure depends upon informal relationships
    C. liaison men are the key people to consult when taking formal and informal structures into account
    D. individuals in a group are at least as important as the plans for the group

23. The above passage suggests that
    A. some planning can be disastrous
    B. certain people in sensitive areas should be avoided
    C. the supervisor should discourage acquaintanceships in the organization
    D. organizational relationships should be consciously limited

Questions 24-25.

DIRECTIONS: Questions 24 and 25 are to be answered SOLELY on the basis of the following passage.

Good personnel relations of an organization depend upon mutual confidence, trust, and good will. The basis of confidence is understanding. Most troubles start with people who do not understand each other. When the organization's intentions or motives are misunderstood, or when reasons for actions, practices, or policies are misconstrued, complete cooperation from individuals is not forthcoming. If management expects full cooperation from employees, it has a responsibility of sharing with them the information which is the foundation of proper understanding, confidence, and trust. Personnel management has long since outgrown the days when it was the vogue to *treat them rough and tell them nothing.* Up-to-date personnel management provides all possible information about the activities, aims, and purposes of the organization. It seems altogether creditable that a desire should exist among employees for such information which the best-intentioned executive might think would not interest them and which the worst-intentioned would think was none of their business.

24. The above passage implies that one of the causes of the difficulty which an organization might have with its personnel relations is that its employees
    A. have not expressed interest in the activities, aims, and purposes of the organization
    B. do not believe in the good faith of the organization
    C. have not been able to give full cooperation to the organization
    D. do not recommend improvements in the practices and policies of the organization

24.____

25. According to the above passage, in order for an organization to have good personnel relations, it is NOT essential that
    A. employees have confidence in the organization
    B. the purposes of the organization be understood by the employees
    C. employees have a desire for information about the organization
    D. information about the organization be communicated to employees

25.____

KEY (CORRECT ANSWERS)

1.	D		11.	D
2.	C		12.	A
3.	D		13.	A
4.	B		14.	C
5.	A		15.	D
6.	A		16.	A
7.	C		17.	D
8.	C		18.	B
9.	A		19.	C
10.	B		20.	D

21.	D
22.	D
23.	A
24.	B
25.	C

TEST 2

DIRECTIONS: Each question or incomplete statement is followed by several suggested answers or completions. Select the one that BEST answers the question or completes the statement. *PRINT THE LETTER OF THE CORRECT ANSWER IN THE SPACE AT THE RIGHT.*

Questions 1-8.

DIRECTIONS: Questions 1 through 8 are to be answered SOLELY on the basis of the following passage.

    Important figures in education and in public affairs have recommended development of a private organization sponsored in part by various private foundations which would offer installment payment plans to full-time matriculated students in accredited colleges and universities in the United States and Canada. Contracts would be drawn to cover either tuition and fees, or tuition, fees, room and board in college facilities, from one year up to and including six years. A special charge, which would vary with the length of the contract, would be added to the gross repayable amount. This would be in addition to interest at a rate which would vary with the income of the parents. There would be a 3% annual interest charge for families with total income, before income taxes, of $50,000 or less. The rate would increase by 1/10 of 1% for every $1,000 of additional net income in excess of $50,000 up to a maximum of 10% interest. Contracts would carry an insurance provision on the life of the parent or guardian who signs the contract; all contracts must have the signature of a parent or guardian. Payment would be scheduled in equal monthly installments.

1. Which of the following students would be eligible for the payment plan described in the above passage? A
    A. matriculated student taking six semester hours toward a graduate degree
    B. matriculated student taking seventeen semester hours toward an undergraduate degree
    C. graduate matriculated at the University of Mexico taking eighteen semester hours toward a graduate degree
    D. student taking eighteen semester hours in a special pre-matriculation program

1.____

2. According to the above passage, the organization described would be sponsored in part by
    A. private foundations   B. colleges and universities
    C. persons in the field of education   D. persons in public life

2.____

3. Which of the following expenses could NOT be covered by a contract with the organization described in the above passage?
    A. Tuition amounting to $20,000 per year
    B. Registration and laboratory fees
    C. Meals at restaurants near the college
    D. Rent for an apartment in a college dormitory

3.____

4. The total amount to be paid would include ONLY the
   A. principal
   B. principal and interest
   C. principal, interest, and special charge
   D. principal, interest, special charge, and fee

4.____

5. The contract would carry insurance on the
   A. life of the student
   B. life of the student's parents
   C. income of the parents of the student
   D. life of the parent who signed the contract

5.____

6. The interest rate for an annual loan of $25,000 from the organization described in the above passage for a student whose family's net income was $55,000 should be
   A. 3%   B. 3.5%   C. 4%   D. 4.5%

6.____

7. The interest rate for an annual loan of $35,000 from the organization described in the above passage for a student whose family's net income was $100,000 should be
   A. 5%   B. 8%   C. 9%   D. 10%

7.____

8. John Lee has submitted an application for the installment payment plan described in the above passage. John's mother and father have a store which grossed $500,000 last year, but the income which the family received from the store was $90,000 before taxes. They also had $5,000 income from stock dividends. They paid $10,000 in income taxes.
   The amount of income upon which the interest should be based is
   A. $85,000   B. $90,000   C. $95,000   D. $105,000

8.____

Questions 9-13.

DIRECTIONS: Questions 9 through 13 are to be answered SOLELY on the basis of the following passage.

Since the organization chart is pictorial in nature, there is a tendency for it to be drawn in an artistically balanced and appealing fashion, regardless of the realities of actual organizational structure. In addition to being subject to this distortion, there is the difficulty of communicating in any organization chart the relative importance or the relative size of various component parts of an organizational structure. Furthermore, because of the need for simplicity of design, an organization chart can never indicate the full extent of the interrelationships among the component parts of an organization.

These interrelationships are often just as vital as the specifications which an organization chart endeavors to indicate. Yet, if an organization chart were to be drawn with all the wide variety of criss-crossing communication and cooperation networks existent within a typical organization, the chart would probably be much more confusing than informative. It is also obvious that no organization chart as such can prove or disprove that the organizational structure it represents is effective in realizing the objectives of the organization. At best, an organization chart can only illustrate some of the various factors to be taken into consideration in understanding, devising, or altering organizational arrangements.

9. According to the above passage, an organization chart can be expected to portray the
   A. structure of the organization along somewhat ideal lines
   B. relative size of the organizational units quite accurately
   C. channels of information distribution within the organization graphically
   D. extent of the obligation of each unit to meet the organizational objectives

10. According to the above passage, those aspects of internal functioning which are NOT shown on an organization chart
    A. can be considered to have little practical application in the operations of the organization
    B. might well be considered to be as important as the structural relationships which a chart does present
    C. could be the cause of considerable confusion in the operations of an organization which is quite large
    D. would be most likely to provide the information needed to determine the overall effectiveness of an organization

11. In the above passage, the one of the following conditions which is NOT implied as being a defect of an organization chart is that an organization chart may
    A. present a picture of the organizational structure which is different from the structure that actually exists
    B. fail to indicate the comparative size of various organizational units
    C. be limited in its ability to convey some of the meaningful aspects of organizational relationships
    D. become less useful over a period of time during which the organizational facts which it illustrated have changed

12. The one of the following which is the MOST suitable title for the above passage is
    A. The Design and Construction of an Organization Chart
    B. The Informal Aspects of an Organization Chart
    C. The Inherent Deficiencies of an Organization Chart
    D. The Utilization of a Typical Organization Chart

13. It can be inferred from the above passage that the function of an organization chart is to
    A. contribute to the comprehension of the organization form and arrangements
    B. establish the capabilities of the organization to operate effectively
    C. provide a balanced picture of the operations of the organization
    D. eliminate the need for complexity in the organization's structure

Questions 14-16.

DIRECTIONS: Questions 14 through 16 are to be answered SOLELY on the basis of the following passage.

In dealing with visitors to the school office, the school secretary must use initiative, tact, and good judgment. All visitors should be greeted promptly and courteously. The nature of their business should be determined quickly and handled expeditiously. Frequently, the secretary should be able to handle requests, deliveries, or passes herself. Her judgment should determine when a visitor should see members of the staff or the principal. Serious problems or doubtful cases should be referred to a supervisor.

14. In general, visitors should be handled by the
    A. school secretary
    B. principal
    C. appropriate supervisor
    D. person who is free

15. It is wise to obtain the following information from visitors:
    A. Name
    B. Nature of business
    C. Address
    D. Problems they have

16. All visitors who wish to see members of the staff should
    A. be permitted to do so
    B. produce identification
    C. do so for valid reasons only
    D. be processed by a supervisor

Questions 17-19.

DIRECTIONS: Questions 17 through 19 are to be answered SOLELY on the basis of the following passage.

Information regarding payroll status, salary differentials, promotional salary increments, deductions, and pension payments should be given to all members of the staff who have questions regarding these items. On occasion, if the secretary is uncertain regarding the information, the staff member should be referred to the principal or the appropriate agency. No question by a staff member regarding payroll status should be brushed aside as immaterial or irrelevant. The school secretary must always try to handle the question or pass it on to the person who can handle it.

17. If a teacher is dissatisfied with information regarding her salary status, as given by the school secretary, the matter should be
    A. dropped
    B. passed on to the principal
    C. passed on by the secretary to proper agency or the principal
    D. made a basis for grievance procedures

18. The following is an adequate summary of the above passage:
    A. The secretary must handle all payroll matters
    B. The secretary must handle all payroll matter or know who can handle them
    C. The secretary or the principal must handle all payroll matters
    D. Payroll matter too difficult to handle must be followed up until they are solved

19. The above passage implies that
    A. many teachers ask immaterial questions regarding payroll status
    B. few teachers ask irrelevant pension questions
    C. no teachers ask immaterial salary questions
    D. no question regarding salary should be considered irrelevant

19.____

Questions 20-22.

DIRECTIONS: Questions 20 through 22 are to be answered SOLELY on the basis of the following passage.

The necessity for good speech on the part of the school secretary cannot be overstated. The school secretary must deal with the general public, the pupils, the members of the staff, and the school supervisors. In every situation which involves the general public, the secretary serves as a representative of the school. In dealing with pupils, the secretary's speech must serve as a model from which students may guide themselves. Slang, colloquialisms, malapropisms, and local dialects must be avoided.

20. The above passage implies that the speech pattern of the secretary must be
    A. perfect
    B. very good
    C. average
    D. on a level with that of the pupils

20.____

21. The last sentence indicates that slang
    A. is acceptable
    B. occurs in all speech
    C. might be used occasionally
    D. should be shunned

21.____

22. The above passage implies that the speech of pupils
    A. may be influenced
    B. does not change readily
    C. is generally good
    D. is generally poor

22.____

Questions 23-25.

DIRECTIONS: Questions 23 through 25 are to be answered SOLELY on the basis of the following passage.

The school secretary who is engaged in the task of filing records and correspondence should follow a general set of rules. Items which are filed should be available to other secretaries or to supervisors quickly and easily by means of the application of a modicum of common sense and good judgment. Items which, by their nature, may be difficult to find should be cross-indexed. Folders and drawers should be neatly and accurately labeled. There should never be a large accumulation of papers which have not been filed.

23. A good general rule to follow in filing is that materials should be
    A. placed in folders quickly
    B. neatly stored
    C. readily available
    D. cross-indexed

23.____

24. Items that are filed should be available to 24.____
    A. the secretary charged with the task of filing
    B. secretaries and supervisors
    C. school personnel
    D. the principal

25. A modicum of common sense means _____ common sense. 25.____
    A. an average amount of   B. a great deal of
    C. a little   D. no

KEY (CORRECT ANSWERS)

1.	B	11.	D
2.	A	12.	C
3.	C	13.	A
4.	C	14.	A
5.	D	15.	B
6.	B	16.	C
7.	B	17.	C
8.	C	18.	B
9.	A	19.	D
10.	B	20.	B

21. D
22. A
23. C
24. B
25. C

TEST 3

DIRECTIONS: Each question or incomplete statement is followed by several suggested answers or completions. Select the one that BEST answers the question or completes the statement. *PRINT THE LETTER OF THE CORRECT ANSWER IN THE SPACE AT THE RIGHT.*

Questions 1-4.

DIRECTIONS: Questions 1 through 4 are to be answered SOLELY on the basis of the following passage.

The proposition that administrative activity is essentially the same in all organizations appears to underlie some of the practices in the administration of private higher education. Although the practice is unusual in public education, there are numerous instances of industrial, governmental, or military administrators being assigned to private institutions of higher education and, to a lesser extent, of college and university presidents assuming administrative positions in other types of organizations. To test this theory that administrators are interchangeable, there is a need for systematic observation and classification. The myth that an educational administrator must first have experience in the teaching profession is firmly rooted in a long tradition that has historical prestige. The myth is bound up in the expectations of the public and personnel surrounding the administrator. Since administrative success depends significantly on how well an administrator meets the expectations others have of him, the myth may be more powerful than the special experience in helping the administrator attain organizational and educational objectives. Educational administrators who have risen through the teaching profession have often expressed nostalgia for the life of a teacher or scholar, but there is no evidence that this nostalgia contributes to administrative success.

1. Which of the following statements as completed is MOST consistent with the above passage?
   The greatest number of administrators has moved from
   A. industry and the military to government and universities
   B. government and universities to industry and the military
   C. government, the armed forces, and industry to colleges and universities
   D. colleges and universities to government, the armed forces, and industry

   1._____

2. Of the following, the MOST reasonable inference from the above passage is that a specific area requiring further research is the
   A. place of myth in the tradition and history of the educational profession
   B. relative effectiveness of educational administrators from inside and outside the teaching profession
   C. performance of administrators in the administration of public colleges
   D. degree of reality behind the nostalgia for scholarly pursuits often expressed by educational administrators

   2._____

3. According to the above passage, the value to an educational administrator of experience in the teaching profession

    A. lies in the first-hand knowledge he has acquired of immediate educational problems
    B. may lie in the belief of his colleagues, subordinates, and the public that such experience is necessary
    C. has been supported by evidence that the experience contributes to administrative success in educational fields
    D. would be greater if the administrator were able to free himself from nostalgia for his former duties

3.____

4. Of the following, the MOST suitable title for the above passage is

    A. Educational Administration, Its Problems
    B. The Experience Needed For Educational Administration
    C. Administration in Higher Education
    D. Evaluating Administrative Experience

4.____

Questions 5-6.

DIRECTIONS: Questions 5 and 6 are to be answered SOLELY on the basis of the following passage.

Management by objectives (MBO) may be defined as the process by which the superior and the subordinate managers of an organization jointly define its common goals, define each individual's major areas of responsibility in terms of the results expected of him and use these measure as guides for operating the unit and assessing the contribution of each of its members.

The MBO approach requires that after organizational goals are established and communicated, targets must be set for each individual position which are congruent with organizational goals. Periodic performance reviews and a final review using the objectives set as criteria are also basic to this approach.

Recent studies have shown that MBO programs are influenced by attitudes and perceptions of the boss, the company, the reward-punishment system, and the program itself. In addition, the manner in which the MBO program is carried out can influence the success of the program. A study done in the late sixties indicates that the best results are obtained when the manager sets goals which deal with significant problem areas in the organizational unit, or with the subordinate's personal deficiencies. These goals must be clear with regard to what is expected of the subordinate. The frequency of feedback is also important in the success of a management-by-objectives program. Generally, the greater the amount of feedback, the more successful the MBO program.

5. According to the above passage, the expected output for individual employees should be determined

    A. after a number of reviews of work performance
    B. after common organizational goals are defined
    C. before common organizational goals are defined
    D. on the basis of an employee's personal qualities

5.____

6. According to the above passage, the management-by-objectives approach requires
   A. less feedback than other types of management programs
   B. little review of on-the-job performance after the initial setting of goals
   C. general conformance between individual goals and organizational goals
   D. the setting of goals which deal with minor problem areas in the organization

Questions 7-10.

DIRECTIONS: Questions 7 through 10 are to be answered SOLELY on the basis of the following passage.

Management, which is the function of executive leadership, has as its principal phases the planning, organizing, and controlling of the activities of subordinate groups in the accomplishment of organizational objectives. Planning specifies the kind and extent of the factors, forces, and effects, and the relationships among them, that will be required for satisfactory accomplishment. The nature of the objectives and their requirements must be known before determinations can be made as to what must be done, how it must be done and why, where actions should take place, who should be responsible, and similar programs pertaining to the formulation of a plan. Organizing, which creates the conditions that must be present before the execution of the plan can be undertaken successfully, cannot be done intelligently without knowledge of the organizational objectives. Control, which has to do with the constraint and regulation of activities entering into the execution of the plan, must be exercised in accordance with the characteristics and requirements of the activities demanded by the plan.

7. The one of the following which is the MOST suitable title for the above passage is
   A. The Nature of Successful Organization
   B. The Planning of Management Functions
   C. The Importance of Organizational Functions
   D. The Principle Aspects of Management

8. It can be inferred from the above passage that the one of the following functions whose existence is essential to the existence of the other three is the
   A. regulation of the work needed to carry out a plan
   B. understanding of what the organization intends to accomplish
   C. securing of information of the factors necessary for accomplishment of objectives
   D. establishment of the conditions required for successful action

9. The one of the following which would NOT be included within any of the principal phases of the function of executive leadership as defined in the above passage is
   A. determination of manpower requirements
   B. procurement of required material
   C. establishment of organizational objectives
   D. scheduling of production

10. The conclusion which can MOST reasonably be drawn from the above passage is that the control phase of managing is most directly concerned with the
    A. influencing of policy determinations
    B. administering of suggestion systems
    C. acquisition of staff for the organization
    D. implementation of performance standards

10.____

Questions 11-12.

DIRECTIONS: Questions 11 and 12 are to be answered SOLELY on the basis of the following passage.

Under an open-and-above-board policy, it is to be expected that some supervisors will gloss over known shortcomings of subordinates rather than face the task of discussing team face-to-face. It is also to be expected that at least some employees whose job performance is below par will reject the supervisor's appraisal as biased and unfair. Be that as it may, these are inescapable aspects of any performance appraisal system in which human beings are involved. The supervisor who shies away from calling a spade a spade, as well as the employee with a chip on his shoulder, will each in his own way eventually be revealed in his true light—to the benefit of the organization as a whole.

11. The BEST of the following interpretations of the above passage is that
    A. the method of rating employee performance requires immediate revision to improve employee acceptance
    B. substandard performance ratings should be discussed with employees even if satisfactory ratings are not
    C. supervisors run the risk of being called unfair by the subordinates even though their appraisals are accurate
    D. any system of employee performance rating is satisfactory if used properly

11.____

12. The BEST of the following interpretations of the above passage is that
    A. supervisors generally are not open-and-above-board with their subordinates
    B. it is necessary for supervisors to tell employees objectively how they are performing
    C. employees complain when their supervisor does not keep them informed
    D. supervisors are afraid to tell subordinates their weaknesses

12.____

Questions 13-15.

DIRECTIONS: Questions 13 through 15 are to be answered SOLELY on the basis of the following passage.

During the last decade, a great deal of interest has been generated around the phenomenon of *organizational development,* or the process of developing human resources through conscious organization effort. Organizational development (OD) stresses improving interpersonal relationships and organizational skills, such as communication, to a much greater degree than individual training ever did. The kind of training that an organization should emphasize depends upon the present and future structure of the organization. If future organizations are to be unstable, shifting coalitions, then individual skills and abilities, particularly those emphasizing innovativeness, creativity, flexibility, and the latest technological knowledge, are crucial and individual training is most appropriate.

But if there is to be little change in organizational structure, then the main thrust of training should be group-oriented or organizational development. This approach seems better designed for overcoming hierarchical barriers, for developing a degree of interpersonal relationships which make communication along the chain of command possible, and for retaining a modicum of innovation and/or flexibility.

13. According to the above passage, group-oriented training is MOST useful in in
    A. developing a communications system that will facilitate understanding through the chain of command
    B. highly flexible and mobile organizations
    C. preventing the crossing of hierarchical barriers within an organization
    D. saving energy otherwise wasted on developing methods of dealing with rigid hierarchies

14. The one of the following conclusions which can be drawn MOST appropriately from the above passage is that
    A. behavioral research supports the use of organizational development training methods rather than individualized training
    B. it is easier to provide individualized training in specific skills than to set up sensitivity training programs
    C. organizational development eliminates innovative or flexible activity
    D. the nature of an organization greatly influences which training methods will be most effective

15. According to the above passage, the one of the following which is LEAST important for large-scale organizations geared to rapid and abrupt change is
    A. current technological information
    B. development of a high degree of interpersonal relationships
    C. development of individual skills and abilities
    D. emphasis on creativity

Questions 16-18.

DIRECTIONS: Questions 16 through 18 are to be answered SOLELY on the basis of the following passage.

The increase in the extent to which each individual is personally responsible to others is most noticeable in a large bureaucracy. No one person *decides* anything; each decision of any importance, is the product of an intricate process of brokerage involving individuals inside and outside the organization who feel some reason to be affected by the decision, or two have special knowledge to contribute to it. The more varied the organization's constituency, the more inside *veto-groups* will need to be taken into account. But even if no outside consultations were involved, sheer size would produce a complex process of decision. For a large organization is a deliberately created system of tensions into which each individual is expected to bring work-ways, viewpoints, and outside relationships markedly different from those of his colleagues. It is the administrator's task to draw from these disparate forces the elements of wise action from day to day, consistent with the purposes of the organization as a whole.

16. The above passage is essentially a description of decision-making as   16.____
    A. an organization process
    B. the key responsibility of the administrator
    C. the one best position among many
    D. a complex of individual decisions

17. Which one of the following statements BEST describes the responsibilities of   17.____
    an administrator?
    A. He modifies decisions and goals in accordance with pressures from within and outside the organization.
    B. He creates problem-solving mechanisms that rely on the varied interests of his staff and *veto-groups*.
    C. He makes determinations that will lead to attainment of his agency's objectives.
    D. He obtains agreement among varying viewpoints and interests

18. In the context of the operations of a central public personnel agency, a   18.____
    veto-group would LEAST likely consist of
    A. employee organizations
    B. professional personnel societies
    C. using agencies
    D. civil service newspapers

Questions 19-25.

DIRECTIONS: Questions 19 through 25 are to be answered SOLELY on the basis of the following passage, which is an extract from a report prepared for Department X, which outlines the procedure to be followed in the case of transfers of employees.

Every transfer, regardless of the reason therefore, requires completion of the record of transfer, Form DT411. To denote consent to the transfer, DT411 should contain the signatures of the transferee and the personnel officer(s) concerned, except that, in the case of an involuntary transfer, the signatures of the transferee's present and prospective supervisors shall be entered in Boxes 8A and 8B, respectively, since the transferee does not consent. Only a permanent employee may request a transfer; in such cases, the employee's attendance record shall be duly considered with regard to absences, latenesses, and accrued overtime balances. In the case of an inter-district transfer, the employee's attendance record must be included in Section 8A of the transfer request, Form DT410, by the personnel officer of the district from which the transfer is requested. The personnel officer of the district to which the employee requested transfer may refuse to accept accrued overtime balances in excess of ten days.

An employee on probation shall be eligible for transfer. If such employee is involuntarily transferred, he shall be credited for the period of time already served on probation. However, if such transfer is voluntary, the employee shall be required to serve the entire period of his probation in the new position. An employee who has occurred a disability which prevents him from performing his normal duties may be transferred during the period of such disability to other appropriate duties. A disability transfer requires the completion of either DT414 if the disability is job-connected, or Form DT415 if it is not a job-connected disability. In either case, the personnel officer of the district from which the transfer is made signs in Box 6A of the first two copies and the personnel officer of the district to which the transfer is made signs in Box 6B of the last two copies, or, in the case of an intra-district disability transfer, the personnel officer must sign in Box 6A of the first two copies and Box 6B of the last two copies.

19. When a personnel officer consents to an employee's request for transfer from his district, this procedure requires that the personnel officer sign Forms
    A. DT411
    B. DT410 and DT411
    C. DT411 and either Form DT414 or DT415
    D. DT410 and DT411, and either Form DT414 or DT415

20. With respect to the time record of an employee transferred against his wishes during his probationary period, this procedure requires that
    A. he serve the entire period of his probation in his present office
    B. he lose his accrued overtime balance
    C. his attendance record be considered with regard to absences and latenesses
    D. he be given credit for the period of time he has already served on probation

21. Assume you are a supervisor and an employee must be transferred into your office against his wishes.
    According to this procedure, the box you must sign on the record of transfer is
    A. 6A   B. 8A   C. 6B   D. 8B

22. Under this procedure, in the case of a disability transfer, when must Box 6A on Forms DT414 and DT415 be signed by the personnel officer of the district to which the transfer is being made?
    A. In all cases when either Form DT414 or Form DT415 is used
    B. In all cases when Form DT414 is used and only under certain circumstances when Form DT415 is used
    C. In all cases when Form DT415 is used and only under certain circumstances when Form DT414 is used
    D. Only under certain circumstances when either Form DT414 or Form DT415 is used

23. From the above passage, it may be inferred MOST correctly that the number of copies of Form DT414 is
    A. no more than 2
    B. at least 3
    C. at least 5
    D. more than the number of copies of Form DT415

24. A change in punctuation and capitalization only which would change one sentence into two and possibly contribute to somewhat greater ease of reading this report extract would be MOST appropriate in the
    A. 2nd sentence, 1st paragraph
    B. 3rd sentence, 1st paragraph
    C. next to the last sentence, 2nd paragraph
    D. 2nd sentence, 2nd paragraph

25. In the second paragraph, a word that is INCORRECTLY used is
    A. *shall* in the 1st sentence
    B. *voluntary* in the 3rd sentence
    C. *occurred* in the 4th sentence
    D. *intra-district* in the last sentence

KEY (CORRECT ANSWERS)

1.	C	11.	C
2.	B	12.	B
3.	B	13.	A
4.	B	14.	D
5.	B	15.	B
6.	C	16.	A
7.	D	17.	C
8.	B	18.	B
9.	C	19.	A
10.	D	20.	D

21.	D
22.	D
23.	B
24.	B
25.	C

PREPARING WRITTEN MATERIAL
EXAMINATION SECTION
TEST 1

DIRECTIONS: Each question consists of a sentence which may or may not be an example of good English usage. Examine each sentence, considering grammar, punctuation, spelling, capitalization, and awkwardness. Then choose the correct statement about it from the four choices below it. If the English usage in the sentence given is better than any of the changes suggested in choices B, C, or D, pick choice A. (Do not pick a choice that will change the meaning of the sentence.) *PRINT THE LETTER OF THE CORRECT ANSWER IN THE SPACE AT THE RIGHT.*

1. We attended a staff conference on Wednesday the new safety and fire rules were discussed.
   A. This is an example of acceptable writing.
   B. The words "safety," "fire," and "rules" should begin with capital letters.
   C. There should be a comma after the word "Wednesday."
   D. There should be a period after the word "Wednesday" and the word "the" should begin with a capital letter.

2. Neither the dictionary or the telephone directory could be found in the office library.
   A. This is an example of acceptable writing.
   B. The word "or" should be changed to "nor."
   C. The word "library" should be spelled "libery."
   D. The word "neither" should be changed to "either."

3. The report would have been typed correctly if the typist could read the draft.
   A. This is an example of acceptable writing.
   B. The word "would" should be removed.
   C. The word "have" should be inserted after the word "could."
   D. The word "correctly" should be changed to "correct."

4. The supervisor brought the reports and forms to an employees desk.
   A. This is an example of acceptable writing.
   B. The word "brought" should be changed to "took."
   C. There should be a comma after the word "reports" and a comma after the word "forms."
   D. The word "employees" should be spelled "employee's."

5. It's important for all the office personnel to submit their vacation schedules on time.
   A. This is an example of acceptable writing.
   B. The word "It's" should be spelled "Its."
   C. The word "their" should be spelled "they're."
   D. The word "personnel" should be spelled "personal."

6. The report, along with the accompanying documents, were submitted for review.   6.____
   A. This is an example of acceptable writing.
   B. The words "were submitted" should be changed to "was submitted."
   C. The word "accompanying" should be spelled "accompaning."
   D. The comma after the word "report" should be taken out.

7. If others must use your files, be certain that they understand how the system works, but insist that you do all the filing and refiling.   7.____
   A. This is an example of acceptable writing.
   B. There should be a period after the word "works," and the word "but" should start a new sentence.
   C. The words "filing" and "refiling" should be spelled "fileing" and "refileing."
   D. There should be a comma after the word "but."

8. The appeal was not considered because of its late arrival.   8.____
   A. This is an example of acceptable writing.
   B. The word "its" should be changed to "it's."
   C. The word "its" should be changed to "the."
   D. The words "late arrival" should be changed to "arrival late."

9. The letter must be read carefully to determine under which subject it should be filed.   9.____
   A. This is an example of acceptable writing.
   B. The word "under" should be changed to "at."
   C. The word "determine" should be spelled "determin."
   D. The word "carefuly" should be spelled "carefully."

10. He showed potential as an office manager, but he lacked skill in delegating work.   10.____
    A. This is an example of acceptable writing.
    B. The word "delegating" should be spelled "delagating."
    C. The word "potential" should be spelled "potencial."
    D. The words "he lacked" should be changed to "was lacking."

KEY (CORRECT ANSWERS)

1.	D	6.	B
2.	B	7.	A
3.	C	8.	A
4.	D	9.	D
5.	A	10.	A

TEST 2

DIRECTIONS: Each question consists of a sentence which may or may not be an example of good English usage. Examine each sentence, considering grammar, punctuation, spelling, capitalization, and awkwardness. Then choose the correct statement about it from the four choices below it. If the English usage in the sentence given is better than any of the changes suggested in choices B, C, or D, pick choice A. (Do not pick a choice that will change the meaning of the sentence.) *PRINT THE LETTER OF THE CORRECT ANSWER IN THE SPACE AT THE RIGHT.*

1. The supervisor wants that all staff members report to the office at 9:00 A.M. 1.____
    A. This is an example of acceptable writing.
    B. The word "that" should be removed and the word "to" should be inserted after the word "members."
    C. There should be a comma after the word "wants" and a comma after the word "office."
    D. The word "wants" should be changed to "want" and the word "shall" should be inserted after the word "members."

2. Every morning the clerk opens the office mail and distributes it. 2.____
    A. This is an example of acceptable writing.
    B. The word "opens" should be changed to "open."
    C. The word "mail" should be changed to "letters."
    D. The word "it" should be changed to "them."

3. The secretary typed more fast on a desktop computer than on a laptop computer. 3.____
    A. This is an example of acceptable writing.
    B. The words "more fast" should be changed to "faster."
    C. There should be a comma after the words "desktop computer."
    D. The word "than" should be changed to "then."

4. The new stenographer needed a desk a computer, a chair and a blotter. 4.____
    A. This is an example of acceptable writing.
    B. The word "blotter" should be spelled "blodder."
    C. The word "stenographer" should begin with a capital letter.
    D. There should be a comma after the word "desk."

5. The recruiting officer said, "There are many different goverment jobs available." 5.____
    A. This is an example of acceptable writing.
    B. The word "There" should not be capitalized.
    C. The word "government" should be spelled "government."
    D. The comma after the word "said" should be removed.

6. He can recommend a mechanic whose work is reliable. 6.____
    A. This is an example of acceptable writing.
    B. The word "reliable" should be spelled "relyable."
    C. The word "whose" should be spelled "who's."
    D. The word "mechanic should be spelled "mecanic."

141

7. She typed quickly; like someone who had not a moment to lose.   7._____
   A. This is an example of acceptable writing.
   B. The word "not" should be removed.
   C. The semicolon should be changed to a comma.
   D. The word "quickly" should be placed before instead of after the word "typed."

8. She insisted that she had to much work to do.   8._____
   A. This is an example of acceptable writing.
   B. The word "insisted" should be spelled "incisted."
   C. The word "to" used in front of "much" should be spelled "too."
   D. The word "do" should be changed to "be done."

9. He excepted praise from his supervisor for a job well done.   9._____
   A. This is an example of acceptable writing.
   B. The word "excepted" should be spelled "accepted."
   C. The order of the words "well done" should be changed to "done well."
   D. There should be a comma after the word "supervisor."

10. What appears to be intentional errors in grammar occur several times in the   10._____
    passage.
    A. This is an example of acceptable writing.
    B. The word "occur" should be spelled "occurr."
    C. The word "appears" should be changed to "appear."
    D. The phrase "several times" should be changed to "from time to time."

KEY (CORRECT ANSWERS)

1. B   6. A
2. A   7. C
3. B   8. C
4. D   9. B
5. C   10. C

TEST 3

DIRECTIONS: Each question consists of a sentence which may or may not be an example of good English usage. Examine each sentence, considering grammar, punctuation, spelling, capitalization, and awkwardness. Then choose the correct statement about it from the four choices below it. If the English usage in the sentence given is better than any of the changes suggested in choices B, C, or D, pick choice A. (Do not pick a choice that will change the meaning of the sentence.) *PRINT THE LETTER OF THE CORRECT ANSWER IN THE SPACE AT THE RIGHT.*

1. The clerk could have completed the assignment on time if he knows where these materials were located.
    A. This is an example of acceptable writing.
    B. The word "knows" should be replaced by "had known."
    C. The word "were" should be replaced by "had been."
    D. The words "where these materials were located" should be replaced by "the location of these materials."

2. All employees should be given safety training. Not just those who accidents.
    A. This is an example of acceptable writing.
    B. The period after the word "training" should be changed to a colon.
    C. The period after the word "training" should be changed to a semicolon, and the first letter of the word "Not" should be changed to a small "n."
    D. The period after the word "training" should be changed to a comma, and the first letter of the word "Not" should be changed to a small "n."

3. This proposal is designed to promote employee awareness of the suggestion program, to encourage employee participation in the program, and to increase the number of suggestions submitted.
    A. This is an example of acceptable writing.
    B. The word "proposal" should be spelled "proposal."
    C. The words "to increase the number of suggestions submitted" should be changed to "an increase in the number of suggestions is expected."
    D. The word "promote" should be changed to "enhance" and the word "increase" should be changed to "add to."

4. The introduction of inovative managerial techniques should be preceded by careful analysis of the specific circumstances and conditions in each department.
    A. This is an example of acceptable writing.
    B. The word "technique" should be spelled "techneques."
    C. The word "inovative" should be spelled "innovative."
    D. A comma should be placed after the word "circumstances" and after the word "conditions."

5. This occurrence indicates that such criticism embarrasses him.
   A. This is an example of acceptable writing.
   B. The word "occurrence" should be spelled "occurence."
   C. The word "criticism" should be spelled "critisism."
   D. The word "embarrasses" should be spelled "embarasses."

KEY (CORRECT ANSWERS)

1. B
2. D
3. A
4. C
5. A

PREPARING WRITTEN MATERIAL

PARAGRAPH REARRANGEMENT
COMMENTARY

The sentences that follow are in scrambled order. You are to rearrange them in proper order and indicate the letter choice containing the correct answer at the space at the right.

Each group of sentences in this section is actually a paragraph presented in scrambled order. Each sentence in the group has a place in that paragraph; no sentence is to be left out. You are to read each group of sentences and decide upon the best order in which to put the sentences so as to form a well-organized paragraph.

The questions in this section measure the ability to solve a problem when all the facts relevant to its solution are not given.

More specifically, certain positions of responsibility and authority require the employee to discover connection between events sometimes, apparently, unrelated. In order to do this, the employee will find it necessary to correctly infer that unspecified events have probably occurred or are likely to occur. This ability becomes especially important when action must be taken on incomplete information.

Accordingly, these questions require competitors to choose among several suggested alternatives, each of which presents a different sequential arrangement of the events. Competitors must choose the MOST logical of the suggested sequences.

In order to do so, they may be required to draw on general knowledge to infer missing concepts or events that are essential to sequencing the given events. Competitors should be careful to infer only what is essential to the sequence. The plausibility of the wrong alternatives will always require the inclusion of unlikely events or of additional chains of events which are NOT essential to sequencing the given events.

It's very important to remember that you are looking for the best of the four possible choices, and that the best choice of all may not even be one of the answers you're given to choose from.

There is no one right way to solve these problems. Many people have found it helpful to first write out the order of the sentences, as they would have arranged them, on their scrap paper before looking at the possible answers. If their optimum answer is there, this can save them some time. If it isn't, this method can still give insight into solving the problem. Others find it most helpful to just go through each of the possible choices, contrasting each as they go along. You should use whatever method feels comfortable and works for you.

While most of these types of questions are not that difficult, we've added a higher percentage of the difficult type, just to give you more practice. Usually there are only one or two questions on this section that contain such subtle distinctions that you're unable to answer confidently. And you then may find yourself stuck deciding between two possible choices, neither of which you're sure about.

EXAMINATION SECTION
TEST 1

DIRECTIONS: The following groups of sentences need to be arranged in an order that makes sense. Select the letter preceding the sequence that represents the BEST sentence order. *PRINT THE LETTER OF THE CORRECT ANSWER IN THE SPACE AT THE RIGHT.*

1. I. The keyboard was purposely designed to be a little awkward to slow typists down.
    II. The arrangement of letters on the keyboard of a typewriter was not designed for the convenience of the typist.
    III. Fortunately, no one is suggesting that a new keyboard be designed right away.
    IV. If one were, we would have to learn to type all over again.
    V. The reason was that the early machines were slower than the typists and would jam easily.
    The CORRECT answer is:
    A. I, III, IV, II, V
    B. II, V, I, IV, III
    C. V, I, II, III, IV
    D. II, I, V, III, IV

2. I. The majority of the new service jobs are part-time or low-paying.
    II. According to the U.S. Bureau of Labor Statistics, jobs in the service sector constitute 72% of all jobs in this country.
    III. If more and more workers receive less and less money, who will buy the goods and services needed to keep the economy going?
    IV. The service sector is by far the fastest growing part of the United States economy.
    V. Some economists look upon this trend with great concern.
    The CORRECT answer is:
    A. II, IV, I, V, III
    B. II, III, IV, I, V
    C. V, IV, II, III, I
    D. III, I, II, IV, V

3. I. They can also affect one's endurance.
    II. This can stabilize blood sugar levels, and ensure that the brain is receiving a steady, constant, supply of glucose, so that one is *hitting on all cylinders* while taking the test.
    III. By food, we mean real food, not junk food or unhealthy snacks.
    IV. For this reason, it is important not to skip a meal, and to bring food with you to the exam.
    V. One's blood sugar levels can affect how clearly one is able to think and concentrate during an exam.
    The CORRECT answer is:
    A. V, IV, II, III, I
    B. V, II, I, IV, III
    C. V, I, IV, III, II
    D. V, IV, I, III, II

4. I. Those who are the embodiment of desire are absorbed in material quests, and those who are the embodiment of feeling are warriors who value power more than possession.
   II. These qualities are in everyone, but in different degrees.
   III. But those who value understanding yearn not for goods or victory, but for knowledge.
   IV. According to Plato, human behavior flows from three main sources: desire, emotion, and knowledge.
   V. In the perfect state, the industrial forces would produce but not rule, the military would protect but not rule, and the forces of knowledge, the philosopher kings, would reign.
   The CORRECT answer is:
   A. IV, V, I, II, III
   B. V, I, II, III, IV
   C. IV, III, II, I, V
   D. IV, II, I, III, V

5. I. Of the more than 26,000 tons of garbage produced daily in New York City, 12,000 tons arrive daily at Fresh Kills.
   II. In a month, enough garbage accumulates there to fill the Empire State Building.
   III. In 1937, the Supreme Court halted the practice of dumping the trash of New York City into the sea.
   IV. Although the garbage is compacted, in a few years the mounds of garbage at Fresh Kills will be the highest points south of Maine's Mount Desert Island on the Eastern Seaboard.
   V. Instead, tugboats now pull barges of much of the trash to Staten Island and the largest landfill in the world, Fresh Kills.
   The CORRECT answer is:
   A. III, V, IV, I, II
   B. III, V, II, IV, I
   C. III, V, I, II, IV
   D. III, II, V, IV, I

6. I. Communists rank equality very high, but freedom very low.
   II. Unlike communists, conservatives place a high value on freedom and a very low value on equality.
   III. A recent study demonstrated that one way to classify people's political beliefs is to look at the importance placed on two words: freedom and equality.
   IV. Thus, by demonstrating how members of these groups feel about the two words, the study has proved to be useful for political analysts in several European countries.
   V. According to the study, socialists and liberals rank both freedom and equality very high, while fascists rate both very low.
   The CORRECT answer is:
   A. III, V, I, II, IV
   B. V, IV, III, I, II
   C. III, V, IV, II, I
   D. III, I, II, IV, V

7.
   I. "Can there be anything more amazing than this?"
   II. If the riddle is successfully answered, his dead brothers will be brought back to life.
   III. "Even though man sees those around him dying every day," says Dharmaraj, "he still believes and acts as if he were immortal."
   IV. "What is the cause of ceaseless wonder?" asks the Lord of the Lake.
   V. In the ancient epic, The Mahabharata, a riddle is asked of one of the Pandava brothers.

   The CORRECT answer is:
   A. V, II, I, IV, III
   B. V, IV, III, I, II
   C. V, II, IV, III, I
   D. V, II, IV, I, III

8.
   I. On the contrary, the two main theories—the cooperative (neoclassical) theory and the radical (labor theory)—clearly rest on very different assumptions, which have very different ethical overtones.
   II. The distribution of income is the primary factor in determining the relative levels of material well-being that different groups or individuals attain.
   III. Of all issues in economics, the distribution of income is one of the most controversial.
   IV. The neoclassical theory tends to support the existing income distribution (or minor changes), while the labor theory ends to support substantial changes in the way income is distributed.
   V. The intensity of the controversy reflects the fact that different economic theories are not purely neutral, *detached* theories with no ethical or moral implications.

   The CORRECT answer is:
   A. II, I, V, IV, III
   B. III, II, V, I, IV
   C. III, V, II, I, IV
   D. III, V, IV, I, II

9.
   I. The pool acts as a broker and ensures that the cheapest power gets used first.
   II. Every six seconds, the pool's computer monitors all of the generating stations in the state and decides which to ask for more power and which to cut back.
   III. The buying and selling of electrical power is handled by the New York Power Pool in Guilderland, New York.
   IV. This is to the advantage of both the buying and selling utilities.
   V. The pool began operation in 1970, and consists of the state's eight electric utilities.

   The CORRECT answer is:
   A. V, I, II, III, IV
   B. IV, II, I, III, V
   C. III, V, I, IV, II
   D. V, III, IV, II, I

10.
   I. Modern English is much simpler grammatically than Old English.
   II. Finnish grammar is very complicated; there are some fifteen cases, for example.
   III. Chinese, a very old language, may seem to be the exception, but it is the great number of characters/words that must be mastered that makes it so difficult to learn, not its grammar.
   IV. The newest literary language—that is, written as well as spoken—is Finish, whose literary roots go back only to about the middle of the nineteenth century.
   V. Contrary to popular belief, the longer a language is been in use the simpler its grammar—not the reverse.
   The CORRECT answer is:
   A. IV, I, II, III, V
   B. V, I, IV, II, III
   C. I, II, IV, III, V
   D. IV, II, III, I, V

10.____

KEY (CORRECT ANSWERS)

1.	D	6.	A
2.	A	7.	C
3.	C	8.	B
4.	D	9.	C
5.	C	10.	B

TEST 2

DIRECTIONS: This type of question tests your ability to recognize accurate paraphrasing, well-constructed paragraphs, and appropriate style and tone. It is important that the answer you select contains only the facts or concepts given in the original sentences. It is also important that you be aware of incomplete sentences, inappropriate transitions, unsupported opinions, incorrect usage, and illogical sentence order. Paragraphs that do not include all the necessary facts and concepts, that distort them, or that add new ones are not considered correct.

The format for this section may vary. Sometimes, long paragraphs are given, and emphasis is placed on style and organization. Our first five questions are of this type. Other times, the paragraphs are shorter, and there is less emphasis on style and more emphasis on accurate representation of information. Our second group of five questions are of this nature.

For each of Questions 1 through 10, select the paragraph that BEST expresses the ideas contained in the sentences above it. *PRINT THE LETTER OF THE CORRECT ANSWER IN THE SPACE AT THE RIGHT.*

1. I. Listening skills are very important for managers.
    II. Listening skills are not usually emphasized.
    III. Whenever managers are depicted in books, manuals or the media, they are always talking, never listening.
    IV. We'd like you to read the enclosed handout on listening skills and to try to consciously apply them this week.
    V. We guarantee they will improve the quality of your interactions.

    A. Unfortunately, listening skills are not usually emphasized for managers. Managers are always depicted as talking, never listening. We'd like you to read the enclosed handout on listening skills. Please try to apply these principles this week. If you do, we guarantee they will improve the quality of your interactions.
    B. The enclosed handout on listening skills will be important improving the quality of your interactions. We guarantee it. All you have to do is take sometime this week to read and to consciously try to apply the principles. Listening skills are very important for manages, but they are not usually emphasized. Whenever managers are depicted in books, manuals or the media, they are always talking, never listening.
    C. Listening well is one of the most important skills a manager can have, yet it's not usually given much attention. Think about any representation of managers in books, manuals, or in the media that you may have seen. They're always talking, never listening. We'd like you to read the enclosed handout on listening skills and consciously try to apply them the rest of the week. We guarantee you will see a difference in the quality of your interactions.

1.____

D. Effective listening, one very important tool in the effective manager's arsenal, is usually not emphasized enough. The usual depiction of managers in books, manuals or the media is one in which they are always talking, never listening. We'd like you to read the enclosed handout and consciously try to apply the information contained therein throughout the rest of the week. We feel sure that you will see a marked difference in the quality of your interactions.

2. I. Chekhov wrote three dramatic masterpieces which share certain themes and formats: Uncle Vanya, The Cherry Orchard, and The Three Sisters.
   II. They are primarily concerned with the passage of time and how this erodes human aspirations.
   III. The plays are haunted by the ghosts of the wasted life.
   IV. The characters are concerned with life's lesser problems; however, such as the inability to make decisions, loyalty to the wrong cause, and the inability to be clear.
   V. This results in sweet, almost aching, type of a sadness referred to as Chekhovian.

   2.____

   A. Chekhov wrote three dramatic masterpieces: Uncle Vanya, The Cherry Orchard, and The Three Sisters. These masterpieces share certain themes and formats: the passage of time, how time erodes human aspirations, and the ghosts of wasted life. Each masterpiece is characterized by a sweet, almost aching, type of sadness that has become known as Chekhovian. The sweetness of this sadness hinges on the fact that it is not the great tragedies of life which are destroying these characters, but their minor flaws: indecisiveness, misplaced loyalty, unclarity.
   B. The Cherry Orchard, Uncle Vanya, and The Three Sisters are three dramatic masterpieces written by Chekhov that use similar formats to explore a common theme. Each is primarily concerned with the way that passing time wears down human aspirations, and each is haunted by the ghosts of the wasted life. The characters are shown struggling futilely with the lesser problems of life: indecisiveness, loyalty to the wrong cause, and the inability to be clear. These struggles create a mood of sweet, almost aching, sadness that has become known as Chekhovian.
   C. Chekhov's dramatic masterpieces are, along with The Cherry Orchard, Uncle Vanya, and The Three Sisters. These plays share certain thematic and formal similarities. They are concerned most of all with the passage of time and the way in which time erodes human aspirations. Each play is haunted by the specter of the wasted life. Chekhov's characters are caught, however, by life's lesser snares: indecisiveness, loyalty to the wrong cause, and unclarity. The characteristic mood is a sweet, almost aching type of sadness that has come to be known as Chekhovian.
   D. A Chekhovian mood is characterized by sweet, almost aching, sadness. The term comes from three dramatic tragedies by Chekhov which revolve around the sadness of a wasted life. The three masterpieces (Uncle Vanya, The Three Sisters, and The Cherry Orchard) share the same

theme and format. The plays are concerned with how the passage of time erodes human aspirations. They are peopled with characters who are struggling with life's lesser problems. These are people who are indecisive, loyal to the wrong causes, or are unable to make themselves clear.

3.
I. Movie previews have often helped producers decide which parts of movies they should take out or leave in.
II. The first 1933 preview of King Kong was very helpful to the producers because many people ran screaming from the theater and would not return when four men first attacked by Kong were eaten by giant spiders.
III. The 1950 premiere of Sunset Boulevard resulted in the filming of an entirely new beginning, and a delay of six months in the film's release.
IV. In the original opening scene, William Holden was in a morgue talking with thirty-six other "corpses" about the ways some of them had died.
V. When he began to tell them of his life with Gloria Swanson, the audience found this hilarious, instead of taking the scene seriously.

3.____

   A. Movie previews have often helped producers decide what parts of movies they should leave in or take out. For example, the first preview of King Kong in 1933 was very helpful. In one scene, four men were first attacked by Kong and then eaten by giant spiders. Many members of the audience ran screaming from the theater and would not return. The premiere of the 1950 film Sunset Boulevard was also very helpful. In the original opening scene, William Holden was in a morgue with thirty-six other "corpses," discussing the ways some of them had died. When he began to tell them of his life with Gloria Swanson, the audience found this hilarious. They were supposed to take the scene seriously. The result was a delay of six months in the release of the film while a new beginning was added.

   B. Movie previews have often helped producers decide whether they should change various parts of a movie. After the 1933 preview of King Kong, a scene in which four men who had been attacked by Kong were eaten by giant spiders was taken out as many people ran screaming from the theater and would not return. The 1950 premiere of Sunset Boulevard also led to some changes. In the original opening scene, William Holden was in a morgue talking with thirty-six other "corpses" about the ways some of them had died. When he began to tell them of his life with Gloria Swanson, the audience found this hilarious, instead of taking the scene seriously.

   C. What do Sunset Boulevard and King Kong have in common? Both show the value of using movie previews to test audience reaction. The first 1933 preview of King Kong showed that a scene showing four men being eaten by giant spiders after having been attacked by Kong was too frightening for many people. They ran screaming from the theater and couldn't be coaxed back. The 1950 premiere of Sunset Boulevard was also a scream, but not the kind the producers intended. The movie opens with William Holden lying in a morgue discussing the ways they had died with thirty-six other "corpses." When he began to tell them of his life with Gloria Swanson, the audience couldn't take him seriously. Their laughter caused a six-month delay while the beginning was rewritten.

D. Producers very often use movie previews to decide if changes are needed. The premiere of Sunset Boulevard in 1950 led to a new beginning and a six-month delay in film release. At the beginning, William Holden and thirty-six other "corpses" discuss the ways some of them died. Rather than taking this seriously, the audience thought it was hilarious when he began to tell them of his life with Gloria Swanson. The first 1933 preview of King Kong was very helpful for its producers because one scene so terrified the audience that many of them ran screaming from the theater and would not return. In this particular scene, four men who had first been attacked by Kong were eaten by giant spiders.

4.
I. It is common for supervisors to view employees as "things" to be manipulated.
II. This approach does not motivate employees, nor does the carrot-and-stick approach because employees often recognize these behaviors and resent them.
III. Supervisors can change these behaviors by using self-inquiry and persistence.
IV. The best managers genuinely respect those they work with, are supportive and helpful, and are interested in working as a team with those they supervise.
V. They disagree with the Golden Rule that says "he or she who has the gold makes the rules."

4.____

A. Some managers act as if they think the Golden Rule means "he or she who has the gold makes the rules." They show disrespect to employees by seeing them as "things" to be manipulated. Obviously, this approach does not motivate employees any more than the carrot-and-stick approach motivates them. The employees are smart enough to spot these behaviors and resent them. On the other hand, the managers genuinely respect those they work with, are supportive and helpful, and are interested in working as a team. Self-inquiry and persistence can change even the former type of supervisor into the latter.

B. Many supervisors all into the trap of viewing employees as "things" to be manipulated, or try to motivate them by using a carrot-and-stick approach. These methods do not motivate employees, who often recognize the behaviors and resent them. Supervisors can change these behaviors, however, by using self-inquiry and persistence. The best managers are supportive and helpful, and have genuine respect for those with whom they work. They are interested in working as a team with those they supervise. To them, the Golden Rule is not "he or she who has the gold makes the rules."

C. Some supervisors see employees as "things" to be used or manipulated using a carrot-and-stick technique. These methods don't work. Employees often see through them and resent them. A supervisor who wants to change may do so. The techniques of self-inquiry and persistence can be used to turn him or her into the type of supervisor who doesn't think the Golden Rule is "he or she who has the gold makes the rules." They may become like the best managers who treat those with whom they work with respect and give them help and support. These are the manager who know how to build a team.

D. Unfortunately, many supervisors act as if their employees are objects whose movements they can position at will. This mistaken belief has the same result as another popular motivational technique—the carrot-and-stick approach. Both attitudes can lead to the same result—resentment from those employees who recognize the behaviors for what they are. Supervisors who recognize these behaviors can change through the use of persistence and the use of self-inquiry. It's important to remember that the best managers respect their employees. They readily give necessary help and support and are interested in working as a team with those they supervise. To these managers, the Golden Rule is not "he or she who has the gold makes the rules."

5.
I. The first half of the nineteenth century produced a group of pessimistic poets—Byron, De Musset, Heine, Pushkin, and Leopardi.
II. It also produced a group of pessimistic composers—Schubert, Chopin, Schumann, and even the later Beethoven.
III. Above all, in philosophy, there was the profoundly pessimistic philosopher, Schopenhauer.
IV. The Revolution was dead, the Bourbons were restored, the feudal barons were reclaiming their land, and progress everywhere was being suppressed, as the great age was over.
V. "I thank God," said Goethe, "that I am not young in so thoroughly finished a world."

5.____

A. "I thank God," said Goethe, "that I am not young in so thoroughly finished a world." The Revolution was dead, the Bourbons were restored, the feudal barons were reclaiming their land, and progress everywhere was being suppressed. The first half of the nineteenth century produced a group of pessimistic poets: Byron, De Musset, Heine, Pushkin, and Leopardi. It also produced pessimistic composers: Schubert, Chopin, Schumann. Although Beethoven came later, he fits into this group, too. Finally and above all, it also produced a profoundly pessimistic philosopher, Schopenhauer. The great age was over.

B. The first half of the nineteenth century produced a group of pessimistic poets: Byron, De Musset, Heine, Pushkin, and Leopardi. It produced a group of pessimistic composers: Schubert, Chopin, Schumann, and even the later Beethoven. Above all, it produced a profoundly pessimistic philosopher, Schopenhauer. For each of these men, the great age was over. The Revolution was dead, and the Bourbons were restored. The feudal barons were reclaiming their land, and progress everywhere was being suppressed.

C. The great age was over. The Revolution was dead—the Bourbons were restored, and the feudal barons were reclaiming their land. Progress everywhere was being suppressed. Out of this climate came a profound pessimism. Poets, like Byron, De Musset, Heine, Pushkin, and Leopardi; composers, like Schubert, Chopin, Schumann, and even the later Beethoven; and above all, a profoundly pessimistic philosopher, Schopenauer. This pessimism which arose in the first half of the nineteenth century is illustrated by these words of Goethe, "I thank God that I am not young in so thoroughly finished a world."

D. The first half of the nineteenth century produced a group of pessimistic poets, Byron, De Musset, Heine, Pushkin, and Leopardi—and a group of pessimistic composers, Schubert, Chopin, Schumann, and the later Beethoven. Above it all, it produced a profoundly pessimistic philosopher, Schopenhauer. The great age was over. The Revolution was dead, the Bourbons were restored, the feudal barons were reclaiming their land, and progress everywhere was being suppressed. "I thank God," said Goethe, "that I am not young in so thoroughly finished a world."

6. I. A new manager sometimes may feel insecure about his or her competence in the new position.
   II. The new manager may then exhibit defensive or arrogant behavior towards those one supervises, or the new manager may direct overly flattering behavior toward one's new supervisor.

   A. Sometimes, a new manager may feel insecure about his or her ability to perform well in this new position. The insecurity may lead him or her to treat others differently. He or she may display arrogant or defensive behavior towards those he or she supervises, or be overly flattering to his or her new supervisor.
   B. A new manager may sometimes feel insecure about his or her ability to perform well in the new position. He or she may then become arrogant, defensive, or overly flattering towards those he or she works with.
   C. There are times when a new manager may be insecure about how well he or she can perform in the new job. The new manager may also behave defensive or act in an arrogant way towards those he or she supervises, or overly flatter his or her boss.
   D. Sometimes a new manager may feel insecure about his or her ability to perform well in the new position. He or she may then display arrogant or defensive behavior towards those they supervise, or become overly flattering towards their supervisors.

6.____

7. I. It is possible to eliminate unwanted behavior by bringing it under stimulus control—tying the behavior to a cue, and then never, or rarely, giving the cue.
   II. One trainer successfully used this method to keep an energetic young porpoise from coming out of her tank whenever she felt like it, which was potentially dangerous.
   III. Her trainer taught her to do it for a reward, in response to a hand signal, and then rarely gave the signal.

7.____

A. Unwanted behavior can be eliminated by tying the behavior to a cue, and then never, or rarely, giving the cue. This is called stimulus control. One trainer was able to use this method to keep an energetic young porpoise from coming out of her tank by teaching her to come out for a reward in response to a hand signal, and then rarely giving the signal.

B. Stimulus control can be used to eliminate unwanted behavior. In this method, behavior is tied to a cue, and then the cue is rarely, if ever, given. One trainer was able to successfully use stimulus control to keep an energetic young porpoise from coming out of her tank whenever she felt like it—a potentially dangerous practice. She taught the porpoise to come out for a reward when she gave a hand signal, and then rarely gave the signal.

C. It is possible to eliminate behavior that is undesirable by bringing it under stimulus control by tying behavior to a signal, and then rarely giving the signal. One trainer successfully used this method to keep an energetic porpoise from coming out of her tank, a potentially dangerous situation. Her trainer taught the porpoise to do it for a reward, in response to a hand signal, and then would rarely give the signal.

D. By using stimulus control, it is possible to eliminate unwanted behavior by tying the behavior to a cue, and then rarely or never give the cue. One trainer was able to use this method to successfully stop a young porpoise from coming out of her tank whenever she felt like it. To curb this potentially dangerous practice, the porpoise was taught by the trainer to come out of the tank for a reward, in response to a hand signal, and then rarely given the signal.

8. I. There is a great deal of concern over the safety of commercial trucks, caused by their greatly increased role in serious accidents since federal deregulation in 1981.
    II. Recently, 60 percent of trucks in New York and Connecticut and 70 percent of trucks in Maryland randomly stopped by state troopers failed safety inspections.
    III. Sixteen states in the United States require no training at all for truck drivers.

    8.____

    A. Since federal deregulation in 1981, there has been a great deal of concern over the safety of commercial trucks, and their greatly increased role in serious accidents. Recently, 60 percent of trucks in New York and Connecticut, and 70 percent of trucks in Maryland failed safety inspections. Sixteen states in the United States require no training at all for truck drivers.
    B. There is a great deal of concern over the safety of commercial trucks since federal deregulation in 1981. Their role in serious accidents has greatly increased. Recently, 60 percent of trucks randomly stopped in Connecticut and New York and 70 percent in Maryland failed safety inspections conducted by state troopers. Sixteen states in the United States provide no training at all for truck drivers.
    C. Commercial trucks have a greatly increased role in serious accidents since federal deregulation in 1981. This has led to a great deal of concern.

Recently, 70 percent of trucks in Maryland and 60 percent of trucks in New York and Connecticut failed inspection of those that were randomly stopped by state troopers. Sixteen states in the United States require no training for all truck drivers.

D. Since federal deregulation in 1981, the role that commercial trucks have played in serious accidents has greatly increased, and this has led to a great deal of concern. Recently, 60 percent of trucks in New York and Connecticut, and 70 percent of trucks in Maryland randomly stopped by state troopers failed safety inspections. Sixteen states in the U.S. don't require any training for truck drivers.

9.
I. No matter how much some people have, they still feel unsatisfied and want more, or want to keep what they have forever.
II. One recent television documentary showed several people flying from New York to Paris for a one-day shopping spree to buy platinum earrings, because they were bored.
III. In Brazil, some people were ordering coffins that cost a minimum of $45,000 and are equipping them with deluxe stereos, televisions, and other graveyard necessities.

9._____

A. Some people, despite having a great deal, still feel unsatisfied and want more, or think they can keep what they have forever. One recent documentary on television showed several people enroute from Paris to New York for a one day shopping spree to buy platinum earrings, because they were bored. Some people in Brazil are even ordering coffins equipped with such graveyard necessities as deluxe stereos and televisions. The price of the coffins start at $45,000.
B. No matter how much some people have, they may feel unsatisfied. This leads them to want more, or to want to keep what they have forever. Recently, a television documentary depicting several people flying from New York to Paris for a one day shopping spree to buy platinum earrings. They were bored. Some people in Brazil are ordering coffins that cost at least $45,000 and come equipped with deluxe televisions, stereos and other necessary graveyard items.
C. Some people will be dissatisfied no matter how much they have. They may want more, or they may want to keep what they have forever. One recent television documentary showed several people, motivated by boredom, jetting from New York to Paris for a one-day shopping spree to buy platinum earrings. In Brazil, some people are ordering coffins equipped with deluxe stereos, televisions and other graveyard necessities. The minimum price for these coffins—$45,000.
D. Some people are never satisfied. No matter how much they have they still want more, or think they can keep what they have forever. One television documentary recently showed several people flying from New York to Paris for the day to buy platinum earrings because they were bored. In Brazil, some people are ordering coffins that cost $45,000 and are equipped with deluxe stereos, televisions and other graveyard necessities.

10. I. A television signal or video signal has three parts.
    II. Its parts are the black-and-white portion, the color portion, and the synchronizing (sync) pulses, which keep the picture stable.
    III. Each video source, whether it's a camera or a video-cassette recorder contains its own generator of these synchronizing pulses to accompany the picture that it's sending in order to keep it steady and straight.
    IV. In order to produce a clean recording, a video-cassette recorder must "lock-up" to the sync pulses that are part of the video it is trying to record, and this effort may be very noticeable if the device does not have gunlock.

    A. There are three parts to a television or video signal: the black-and-white part, the color part, and the synchronizing (sync) pulses, which keep the picture stable. Whether it's a video-cassette recorder or a camera, each video source contains its own pulse that synchronizes and generates the picture it's sending in order to keep it straight and steady. A video-cassette recorder must "lock up" to the sync pulses that are part of the video it's trying to record. If the device doesn't have gunlock, this effort must be very noticeable.
    B. A video signal or television is comprised of three parts: the black-and-white portion, the color portion, and the sync (synchronizing) pulses, which keep the picture stable. Whether it's a camera or a video-cassette recorder, each video source contains its own generator of these synchronizing pulses. These accompany the picture that it's sending in order to keep it straight and steady. A video-cassette recorder must "lock up" to the sync pulses that are part of the video it is trying to record in order to produce a clean recording. This effort may be very noticeable if the device does not have gunlock.
    C. There are three parts to a television or video signal: the color portion, the black-and-white portion, and the sync (synchronizing pulses). These keep the picture stable. Each video source, whether it's a video-cassette recorder or a camera, generates these synchronizing pulses accompanying the picture it's sending in order to keep it straight and steady. If a clean recording is to be produced, a video-cassette recorder must store the sync pulses that are part of the video it is trying to record. This effort may not be noticeable if the device does not have gunlock.
    D. A television signal or video signal has three parts: the black-and-white portion, the color portion, and the synchronizing (sync) pulses. It's the sync pulses which keep the picture stable, which accompany it and keep it steady and straight. Whether it's a camera or a video-cassette recorder, each video source contains its own generator of these synchronizing pulses. To produce a clean recording, a video-cassette recorder must "lock up" to the sync pulses that are part of the video it is trying to record. If the device does not have gunlock, this effort may be very noticeable.

10._____

KEY (CORRECT ANSWERS)

1. C
2. B
3. A
4. B
5. D

6. A
7. B
8. D
9. C
10. D

ARITHMETICAL REASONING
EXAMINATION SECTION
TEST 1

DIRECTIONS: Each question or incomplete statement is followed by several suggested answers or completions. Select the one that BEST answers the question or completes the statement. *PRINT THE LETTER OF THE CORRECT ANSWER IN THE SPACE AT THE RIGHT.*

1. In 2015, a public agency spent $180 to buy pencils that cost three cents each. In 2017, the agency spent $420 to buy the same number of pencils that it had bought in 2015.
   The price per pencil that the agency paid in 2017 was _____ cents.
   A. 6⅓ B. ⅔ C. 7 D. 7¾

   1.____

2. A stenographer spent her 35 hour work week on taking dictation, transcribing the dictate material, and filing.
   If she spent 20% of the work week on taking dictation and ½ of the remaining time on transcribing the dictated material, the number of hours of the work week that she spent on filing was
   A. 7 B. 10.5 C. 14 D. 17.4

   2.____

3. A typist typed eight pages in two hours.
   If she typed an average of 50 lines per page and an average of 12 words per line, what was her typing speed, in words per minute?
   A. 40 B. 50 C. 60 D. 80

   3.____

4. The daily compensation to be paid to each consultant hired in a certain agency is computed by dividing his professional earnings in the previous year by 250. The maximum daily compensation they can receive is $200 each. Four consultants who were hired to work on a special project had the following professional earnings in the previous year: $37,500, $144,000, $46,500, and $61,100.
   What will be the TOTAL daily cost to the agency for these four consultants?
   A. $932 B. $824 C. $736 D. $712

   4.____

5. In a typing and stenographic pool consisting of 30 employees, 2/5 of them are typists, 1/3 of them are senior typists and senior stenographers, and the rest are stenographers.
   If there are 5 more stenographers than senior stenographers, how many senior stenographers are in the typing and stenographic pool?
   A. 3 B. 5 C. 8 D. 10

   5.____

2 (#1)

6. There are 3,330 copies of a three-page report to be collated. One clerk starts collating at 9:00 A.M. and is joined 15 minutes later by two other clerks. It takes 15 minutes for each of these clerks to collate 90 copies of the report. At what time should the job be completed if all three clerks continue working at the same rate without breaks?
   A. 12:00 Noon   B. 12:15 P.M.   C. 1:00 P.M.   D. 1:15 P.M.

6.____

7. By the end of last year, membership in the blood credit program in a certain agency had increased from the year before by 500, bringing the total to 2,500. If the membership increased by the same percentage this year, the TOTAL number of members in the blood credit program for this agency by the end of this year should be
   A. 2,625   B. 3,000   C. 3,125   D. 3,250

7.____

8. During this year, an agency suggestion program put into practice suggestions from 24 employee, thereby saving the agency 40 times the amount of money it paid in awards.
   If $1/3$ of the employees were awarded $50 each, ½ of the employees were awarded $25 each, and the rest were awarded $10 each, how much money did the agency save by using the suggestions?
   A. $18,760   B. $29,600   C. $32,400   D. $46,740

8.____

9. A senior stenographer earned $20,100 a year and had 4.5% state tax withheld for the year.
   If she was paid every two weeks, the amount of state tax that was taken out of each of her paychecks, based on a 52-week year, was MOST NEARLY
   A. $31.38   B. $32.49   C. $34.77   D. $36.99

9.____

10. Two stenographers have been assigned to address 750 envelopes. One stenographer addresses twice as many envelopes per hour as the other stenographer.
    If it takes five hours for them to complete the job, the rate of the slower stenographer is _____ envelopes per hour.
    A. 35   B. 50   C. 75   D. 100

10.____

11. Suppose that the postage rate for mailing single copies of a magazine to persons not included on a subscription list is 18 cents for the first two ounces of the single copy and 3 cents for each additional ounce.
    Of 19 copies of a magazine, each of which weighs eleven ounces, are mailed to 19 different people, the TOTAL postage cost of these magazines is
    A. $3.42   B. $3.99   C. $6.18   D. $8.55

11.____

12. A senior stenographer spends about 40 hours a month taking dictation. Of that time, 44% is spent taking minutes of meetings, 38% if spent taking dictation of lengthy reports, and the rest of the time is spent taking dictation of letters and memoranda.
    How much more time is spent taking minutes of meetings than n taking dictation of letters and memoranda? 10 hours _____ minutes.
    A. 6   B. 16   C. 24   D. 40

12.____

13. In one week, a stenographer typed 65 letter. Forty letters had 4 copies on colored paper. The rest had 3 copies on colored paper.
    If the stenographer had 50 sheets of colored paper on hand at the beginning of the week when she started typing the letters, how many sheets of colored paper did she have left at the end of the week?
    A. 190   B. 235   C. 265   D. 305

14. An agency is planning to microfilm letters and other correspondence of the last five years. The number of letter-size documents that can be photographed on a 100-foot roll of microfilm is 2,995. The agency estimates that it will need 240 feet of microfilm to do all the pages of all of the letters.
    How many pages of letter-size documents can be photographed on this microfilm?
    A. 5,990   B. 6,785   C. 7,188   D. 7,985

15. In an agency, $2/3$ of the total number of female stenographers and ½ of the total number of male stenographers attended a general staff meeting.
    If there are a total of 56 stenographers in the agency and 25% of them are male, the number of female stenographers who attended the general staff meeting is
    A. 14   B. 28   C. 36   D. 42

16. A worker is currently earning $17,140 a year and pays $350 a month for rent. He expects to get a raise that will enable him to move into an apartment where his rent will be 25% of his new yearly salary.
    If this new apartment is going to cost him $390 a month, what is the TOTAL amount of raise that he expects to get?
    A. $480   B. $980   C. $1,580   D. $1,840

17. The tops of five desks in an office are to be covered with a scratch-resistant material. Each desk top measures 60 inches by 36 inches.
    How many square feet of material will be needed for the five desk tops?
    A. 15   B. 75   C. 96   D. 180

18. Three grades of bond paper are used in a central transcribing unit. The cost per ream of paper is $1.90 for Grade A, $1.70 for Grade B, and $1.60 for Grade C.
    If the central transcribing unit used 6 reams of Grade A paper, 14 reams of Grade B paper, and 20 reams of Grade C paper, the AVERAGE cost, per ream, of the bond paper used by this unit is between
    A. $1.62 and $1.66   B. $1.66 and $1.70
    C. $1.70 and $1.74   D. $1.73 and $1.80

19. The Complaint Bureau of a city agency is composed of an investigation unit, a clerical unit, and a central transcribing unit. The sum of $264,000 has been appropriated for the operation of this bureau. Of this sum, $170,000 is to be allotted to the clerical unit.

Of this bureau's total appropriation, the percentage that is left for the central transcribing unit is MOST NEARLY _____ if 41,200 is allotted for investigations.
   A. 20%   B. 30%   C. 40%   D. 50%

20. Three typists were assigned to address a total of 2,655 postcards. Typist A addressed postcards at the rate of 170 per hour. Typist B addressed the postcards at the rate of 150 per hour. Typist C's rate is not known. After the three typists had addressed postcards for three and a half hours, Typist C was taken off this assignment. It was necessary for Typist A and Typist B to work two and a half hours more to complete this assignment. The rate per hour at which Typist C addressed the postcards was
   A. less than 150
   B. between 150 and 170
   C. more than 170 but less than 200
   D. more than 200

21. In 2015, a city agency bought 12,000 envelopes at $4.00 per hundred. In 2016, the price of envelopes purchased was 40 percent higher than the 2010 price, but only 60 percent as many envelopes were bought.
   The total cost of the envelopes purchased in 2016 was MOST NEARLY
   A. $250   B. $320   C. $400   D. $480

22. A stenographer has been assigned to place entries on 500 forms. She places entries on 25 forms by the end of half an hour, when she is joined by another stenographer. The second stenographer places entries at the rate of 45 an hour.
   Assuming both stenographers continue to work at their respective rates of speed, the TOTAL number of hours required to carry out the entire assignment is
   A. 5   B. 54   C. 64   D. 7

23. On Monday, a stenographer took dictation without interruption for 1½ hours and transcribed all the dictated material in 3½ hours. On Tuesday, she took dictation uninterruptedly for 1¾ hours and transcribed all the material in 3¾ hours. On Wednesday, she took dictation without interruption for 2¼ hours and transcribed all the material in 4½ hours.
   If she took dictation at the average rate of 90 words per minute during these three days, then her average transcription rate, in words per minute, for the same three days was MOST NEARLY
   A. 36   B. 41   C. 54   D. 58

24. In a division of clerks and stenographers, 15 people are currently employed, 20% of whom are stenographers.
   If management plans are to maintain the current number of stenographers, but to increase the clerical staff to the point where 12% of the total staff are stenographers, what is the MAXIMUM number of additional clerks that should be hired to meet these plans?
   A. 3   B. 8   C. 10   D. 12

25. In the first quarter of the year, a certain operator sent out 230 quarterly reports. In the second quarter of that year, he sent out 310 quarterly reports. The percent increase in the number of quarterly reports he sent out in the second quarter of the year compared to the first quarter of the year is MOST NEARLY

    A. 26%   B. 29%   C. 35%   D. 39%

25.____

KEY (CORRECT ANSWERS)

1. C
2. C
3. A
4. C
5. A

6. B
7. C
8. B
9. C
10. B

11. D
12. C
13. C
14. C
15. B

16. C
17. B
18. B
19. A
20. D

21. C
22. B
23. B
24. C
25. C

SOLUTIONS TO PROBLEMS

1. $180 ÷ .03 = 6000$ pencils bought. In 2017, the price per pencil = $420/6000 = .07 = 7 cents

2. Number of hours on filing = $35 - (.20)(35) \cdot (½)(28) = 14$

3. Eight pages contain $(8)(50)(12) = 4800$ words. She thus typed 4800 words in 120 minutes = 40 words per minute

4. $37,500 ÷ 250 = $150; $144,000 ÷ 250 = $576; $46,500 ÷ 250 = $186; $61,100 ÷ 250 = $244.40. Since $200 = maximum compensation for any single consultant, total compensation = $150 + $200 + $186 + $200 = $736

5. Number of typists = $(2/5)(30) = 12$, number of senior typists and senior stenographers = $(1/3)(30) = 10$, number of stenographers = $30 - 12 - 10 = 8$. Finally, number of senior stenographers = $8 - 5 = 3$

6. At 9:15 A.M., 90 copies have been collated. The remaining 3,240 copies are being collated at the rate of $(3)(90) = 270$ every 15 minutes = 1080 per hour. Since $3240 ÷ 1080 = 3$ hours, the clerks will finish at 9:15 A.M. + 3 hours = 12:15 P.M.

7. During the last year, the membership increased from 2000 to 2500, which represents a $(500/2000)(100) = 25\%$ increase. A 25% increase during this year means the membership = $(2500)(1.25) = 3125$

8. Total awards = $(1/3)(24)($50) + (½)(24)($25) + (1/6)(24)($10) = 740. Thus, the savings = $(40)($740) = $29,600$

9. Her pay for 2 weeks = $20,100 ÷ 26 ≈ $773.08. Thus, her state tax for 2 weeks = $($773.08)(.045) ≈ 34.79. (Nearest correct answer is $34.77 in four selections.)

10. $750 ÷ 5$ hours = 150 envelopes per hour for the 2 stenographers combined. Let x = number of envelopes addressed by the slower stenographer. Then, $x + 2x = 150$. Solving, = 50

11. Total cost = $(19)[.18+(.03)(9)] = 8.55

12. $(.44)(40) - (.18)(40) = 10.4$ hours = 10 hrs. 24 min.

13. $500 - (40)(4) - (25)(3) = 265$

14. $2995 ÷ 100 = 29.95$ documents per foot of microfilm roll. Then, $(29.95)(240 \text{ ft}) = 7188$ documents

15. There are $(.75)(56) = 42$ female stenographers. Then, $(2/3)(42) = 28$ of them attended the meeting

16. ($390)(12) = $4679 new rent per year. Then, ($4680)(4) = $18,720 = his new yearly salary. His raise = $18,720 - $17,140 = $1580

17. Number of sq. ft. = (5)(60)(36) ÷ 144 = 75

18. Average cost per ream = [(1.90)(6) + ($1.70)(14) + ($1.60)(20)] /40 = $1.68, which is between $1.66 and $1.77

19. $264,000 - $170,000 - $41,200 = 52,800 = 20%

20. Let x = typist C's rate. Since Typists A and B each worked 6 hrs., while Typist C worked only 3.5 hours, we have (6)(170) + (6)(150) + 3.5x = 2655. Solving, x = 210, which is mre than 200

21. In 2016, the cost per hundred envelopes was ($4.00)(1.40) = $5.60 and (.60)(12,000) = 7200 envelopes were bought. Total cost in 2016 = (72)($5.60) = $403.20, or about $400

22. The first stenographer's rate is 50 forms per hour. After ½ hour, there are 500 – 25 = 475 forms to be done and the combined rate of the 2 stenographers is 95 forms per hr. Thus, total hours required = ½ + (475) ÷ (95) = 5½

23. Total time for dictation = 1¼ + 1¾ + 2¼ = 5¼ hrs. = 315 min. The number of words = (90)(315) = 28,350. The total transcription 3 time = 3¼ + 3¾ + 44 = 11½ hrs. = 690 min. Her average transcription rate = 28,350 ÷ 690 ≈ 41 words per min.

24. Currently, there are (.20)(15) = 3 stenographers, and thus 12 clerks. Let x = additional clerks. Then, $\frac{3}{3+12+x}$ = .12. This simplifies to 3 = (.12)(15+x). Solving, x = 10

25. Percent increase = $(\frac{80}{230})$(100) ≈ 35%

TEST 2

DIRECTIONS: Each question or incomplete statement is followed by several suggested answers or completions. Select the one that BEST answers the question or completes the statement. *PRINT THE LETTER OF THE CORRECT ANSWER IN THE SPACE AT THE RIGHT.*

1. A school has 112 homeroom classes. There were 15 school days in February. The aggregate register of the school for the month of February was 52,920; the aggregate attendance was 43,860.
   The average class size, to the NEAREST tenth, is
      A. 35.3   B. 31.5   C. 29.2   D. 26.9

   1.____

2. As the school secretary in charge of supplies, you are asked to order the following items on a supplementary requisition for general supplies:
       5 gross of red pencils at $8.90 per dozen
       5,000 manila envelopes at $2.35 per C
       36 rulers at $187.20 per gross
       6 boxes of manila paper at $307.20 per carton (24 boxes to a carton)
       180 reams of composition paper at $27.80 per carton (20 reams to a carton)
   The TOTAL amount of the order is
      A. $957.20   B. $1,025.30   C. $916.80   D. $991.30

   2.____

3. In the high school to which you have been assigned as a school secretary, the annual allotment for general supplies, textbooks, repairs, etc. for the school year 2015-16 was $37,500. A special allotment of $10,000 was granted for textbooks ordered from the State Textbook List. The original requisition for general and vocational supplies amounted to $12,514.75; for science supplies, $6,287.75; for textbooks, including the special funds, $13,785.00; monies spent for equipment repairs and science perishables through December 31, 2015, $1,389.68.
   The balance in your supply allotment account on January 1, 2016 will be
      A. $14,913.00   B. $13,523.32   C. $17,308.32   D. $3,523.32

   3.____

4. The teacher of one of the sixth term typing classes in the high school to which you are assigned as a school secretary has agreed to have her students type attendance cards for the incoming students for the new schoolyear, commencing in September, as a work project. There are 24 students in the class; each student can complete 8 cards during a typing period. There will be 4,032 new students in September.
   The number of typing periods required to complete the task is
      A. 31   B. 21   C. 28   D. 24

   4.____

5. As a school secretary assigned to payroll duties, you are required to prepare the extra-curricular payroll report for the coaches teams in your high school. The rate of pay for these activities was increased on November 1 from $148 per session to $174.50 per session. The pay period which you are reporting is for the months of October, November, and December. Mr. Jones, the football coach, conducted 15 practice sessions in October, 20 in November, and 30 in December.

   5.____

His TOTAL gross pay on the December extra-curricular payroll report is
A. $10,547.50   B. $10,415.00   C. $10,945.00   D. $11,342.50

6. The comparative results on a uniform examination given in your school for the last three years follow:

	2014	2015	2016
Number Taking Test	501	496	485
Number Passing Test	441	437	436

The percentage of passing, to the nearest tenth of a percent, for the year in which the HIGHEST percent of students passed is
A. 89.3%   B. 88%   C. 89.9%   D. 90.3%

7. During his first seven terms in high school, a student compiled the following averages:

Term	Numbers of Majors Completed	Average
1	4	81.25%
2	4	83.75%
3	5	86.2%
4	5	85.8%
5	5	87.0%
6	5	83.4%
7	5	82.6%

In his eighth term, the student had the following final marks in major subjects: 90%, 95%, 80%, 90%, 85%. The student's average for all eight terms of high school, correct to the nearest tenth of a percent, is
A. 84.8%   B. 84.7%   C. 84.9%   D. 85.8%

8. A secretary is asked by her employer to order an office machine which lists at a price of $360, less trade discounts of 20% and 10%, terms 2/10, n/30. There is a delivery charge of $8 and an installation charge of $12.
If the machine is paid for in 10 days, the TOTAL cost of the machine will be
A. $264.80   B. $258.40   C. $266.96   D. $274.02

9. The school to which you have been assigned as school secretary has an annual allowance of 5,120 hours for all teacher aides. The principal decides to employ 5 teacher aides from 8:00 A.M. to 12:00 Noon, and 5 other teacher aides from 12:00 Noon to 4:00 P.M. daily for as many days as his allowance permits.
If a teacher aide earns $17.00 an hour, and he is present every day, his TOTAL earnings for the school year will be more than
A. $7,000 but less than $8,000   B. $8,000 but less than $9,000
C. $9,000 but less than $10,000   D. $10,000

10. During examination week in a high school to which you have been assigned as school secretary, teachers are required to be in school at least 6 hours and 20 minutes daily although their arrival and departure times may vary each day. A teacher's time card that you have been asked to check shows the following entries for the week of June 17:

Date	Arrival	Departure
17	7:56 A.M.	2:18 P.M.
18	9:54 A.M.	4:22 P.M.
19	12:54 P.M.	7:03 P.M.
20	9:51 A.M.	4:15 P.M.
21	7:58 A.M.	2:11 P.M.

    During the week of June 17 to June 21, the teacher was in school for AT LEAST the minimum required time on _____ days.
    A. 2 of the 5   B. 3 of the 5   C. 4 of the 5   D. all 5

11. As school secretary, you are asked to find the total of the following bill received in your school:
    750 yellow envelopes at $.22 per C
    2,400 white envelopes at $2.80 per M
    30 rulers at $5.04 per gross
    The TOTAL of the bill is
    A. $69.90   B. $24.27   C. $18.87   D. $9.42

12. A department in the school to which you have been assigned as school secretary has been given a textbook allowance of $5,50 for the school year. The department's textbook order is:
    75 books at $32.50 each
    45 books at $49.50 each
    25 books at $34.50 each
    The TOTAL of the department's order is _____ the allowance.
    A. $27.50 over   B. $27.50 under
    C. $72.50 under   D. $57.50 over

13. The total receipts, including 5% city sales tax, for the G.O. store for the first week of school amounted to $489.09.
    The receipts from the G.O. store for the first week of school, excluding the 5% city sales tax, amounted to
    A. $465.89   B. $364.64   C. $464.63   D. $513.54

14. Class sizes in the school to which you have been assigned as school secretary are as follows:

Number of Classes	Class Size
9	29
12	31
15	32
7	33
11	34

4 (#2)

The average class size in this school, correct to the nearest tenth, is
A. 30.8   B. 31.9   C. 31.8   D. 30.9

15. In 2013, the social security tax was 4.2% for the first $6,600 earned a year. In 2014, the social security tax was 4.4% on the first $6,600 earned a year. For a teacher aide earning $19,200 in 2013 and $20,400 in 2014, the increase in social security tax deduction in 2014 over 2013 was
A. $132.00   B. $13.20   C. $19.20   D. $20.40

15._____

16. A teacher aide earning $23,900 a year will incur automatic deductions of 3.90% for social security and .50% for Medicare, based on the first $6,600 a year earnings.
The TOTAL deduction for these two items will be
A. $274   B. $290.40   C. $525.80   D. $300.40

16._____

17. The school store turns in receipts totaling $131.25 to the school treasurer, including 5% which has been collected for sales tax.
The amount of money which the treasurer MUST set aside for sales tax is
A. $6.56   B. $6.25   C. $5.00   D. $5.25

17._____

18. One of the custodial assistants can wash all the windows in the main office in 3 hours. A second assistant can wash the windows in the main office in 2 hours.
If the two men work together, they should complete the task in _____ hour(s) _____ minutes.
A. 1; 0   B. 1.5; 0   C. 1; 12   D. 1; 15

18._____

19. A school secretary is requested by the principal to order an office machine which lists at a price of $120, less discounts of 10% and 5%.
The net price of the machine to the school will be
A. $100.50   B. $102.00   C. $102.60   D. $103.00

19._____

20. Five students are employed at school under a work-study program through which they are paid $10.00 an hour for work in school offices, but no student may earn more than $450 a month. Three days before the end of the month, you note that the student payroll totals $2,062.50.
The number of hours which each of the students may work during the remainder of the month is _____ hour(s).
A. 4   B. 2   C. 1   D. 3

20._____

21. You are asked to summarize expenditures made by the school within the budget allocation for the school year. You determine that the following expenditures have been made: educational supplies, $2,600; postage, $650; emergency repairs, $225; textbooks, $5,100; instructional equipment, $1,200. Since $10,680 has been allocated to the school, the following sum still remains available for office supplies.
A. $905   B. $1,005   C. $800   D. $755

21._____

22. In preparing the percentage of attendance for the period report, you note that the aggregate attendance is 57,585 and the aggregate register is 62,000.
The percentage of attendance, to the nearest tenth of a percent, is
   A. 91.9%   B. 93.0%   C. 92.8%   D. 92.9%

22._____

23. You borrow $1,200 from your retirement fund which you must repay over a period of three years, with interest of $144, each payment to be divided equally among 36 total payments.
The monthly deduction from your paycheck will be
   A. $37.33   B. $36.00   C. $33.00   D. $37.30

23._____

24. Tickets for a school dance are printed, starting with number 401 and ending with number 1650. They are to be sold for $7.50 each. The tickets remaining unsold should start with number 1569.
The amount of cash which should be collected for the sale of tickets is
   A. $876.75   B. $937.50   C. $876.00   D. $875.25

24._____

25. Stage curtains are purchased by the school and delivered on October 3 under terms of 5/10, 2/30, net/60. The curtains are paid in full by a check for $522.50 on October 12.
The invoice price was
   A. $533.16   B. $522.50   C. $540.00   D. $550.00

25._____

KEY (CORRECT ANSWERS)

1. B
2. B
3. B
4. B
5. C

6. C
7. C
8. D
9. B
10. B

11. D
12. A
13. A
14. C
15. B

16. B
17. B
18. C
19. C
20. D

21. A
22. D
23. A
24. C
25. D

SOLUTIONS TO PROBLEMS

1. Average class size = 52,920 ÷ 15 ÷ 112 = 31.5

2. Total amount = (5)(12)($8.90) + (50)($2.35) + (36)($187.20) ÷ 144 + (6)($307.20) ÷ 24 + (9)($27.80) = $1,025.30

3. Balance = $37,500 + $10,000 - $12,514.75 - $6,287.25 - $13,785 - $1,389.68 = $13,523.32

4. (24)(8) = 192 cards completed in one period. Then, 4032 ÷ 192 = 21 typing periods required

5. Total pay = (15)($148.00) + (20)($174.50) + (30)($174.50) = $10,945.00

6. The passing rates for 2014, 2015, and 2016 were 88.0%, 88.1%, and 89.9%, respectively. So, 89.9% was the highest

7. His 8th term average was 88.0%. His overall average for all 8 terms = [(4)(81.25%) + (4)(83.75%) + (5)(86.2%) + (5)(85.8%) + (5)(87.0%) + (5)(83.4%) + (5)(82.6%) + (5)(88.0%)] ÷ 38 = 84.9%

8. Total cost = ($360)(.80)(.90)(.98) + $8 + $12 ≈ $274.02 (Exact amount = $274.016)

9. 5120 ÷ 4 = 1280 teacher-days. Then, 1280 ÷ 20 = 128 days per teacher. A teacher's earnings for these 128 days = ($17.00)(4)(128) = $8,704, which is more than $8,000 but less than $9,000

10. The number of hours present on each of the 5 days listed was 6 hrs. 22 min., 6 hrs. 29 min., 6 hrs. 9 min., 6 hrs. 24 min., and 6 hrs. 13 min. On 3 days, he met the minimum time.

11. Total cost = (7.5)(.22) + (2.4)($2.80) + (30/144)(5.04) = $9.42

12. Textbook order = (75)($32.50) + (45)($49.50) + (25)($34.50) = $5,527.5, which is $27.50 over the allowance

13. Receipts without the tax = $489.09 ÷ 1.05 = $465.80

14. Average class size = [(9)(29) + (12)(31) + (7)(33) + (15)(32)] ÷ 54 ≈ 31.8

15. ($6,600)(.044-.042) = $13.20

16. ($6,600)(.039+.005) = $290.40

17. $131.25 = 1.05x, x = 125, $131.25 – 125.00 = 6.25

18. Let x = hours needed working together. Then, $(1/3)(x) + (1/2)(x) = 1$
    Simplifying, $2x + 3x = 6$. Solving, $x = 1\frac{1}{5}$ hrs. = 1 hr. 12 min.

19. Net price = 120 – 10% (12) = 108; 108 – 5% (5.40) = 102.60

20. ($225)(5) - $1031.25 = $93.75 remaining in the month. Since the 5 students earn $25 per hour combined, $93.75 ÷ $25 = 3.75, which must be rounded down to 3 hours

21. $10,680 - $2,600 - $650 - $225 - $5,100 - $1,200 = $905 for office supplies

22. 57,585 ÷ 62,000 ≈ .9288 ≈ 92.9%

23. Monthly deduction = $1344 ÷ 36 = $37.33. (Technically, 35 payments of $37.33 and 1 payment of $37.45)

24. (1569-401) = $876.00

25. The invoice price (which reflects the 5% discount) is $522.50 ÷ .95 = $550.00

TEST 3

DIRECTIONS: Each question or incomplete statement is followed by several suggested answers or completions. Select the one that BEST answers the question or completes the statement. *PRINT THE LETTER OF THE CORRECT ANSWER IN THE SPACE AT THE RIGHT.*

1. If an inch on an office layout drawing equals 4 feet of actual floor dimension, then a room which actually measures 9 feet by 14 feet is represented on the drawing by measurements equaling _____ inches × _____ inches.
   A. 2¼; 3½   B. 2½; 3½   C. 2¼; 3¼   D. 2½; 3¼

   1._____

2. A cooperative education intern works from 1:30 P.M. to 5 P.M. on Mondays, Wednesdays, and Fridays, and from 10 A.M. to 2:30 P.M. with no lunch hour on Tuesdays and Thursdays. He earns $13.50 an hour on this job. In addition, he has a Saturday job paying $16.00 an hour at which he works from 9 A.M. to 3 P.M. with a half hour off for lunch.
   The gross amount that the student earns each week is MOST NEARLY
   A. $321.90   B. $355.62   C. $364.02   D. $396.30

   2._____

3. Thirty-five percent of the College Discovery students who entered community college earned an associate degree. Of these students, 89% entered senior college, of which 67% went on to earn baccalaureate degrees.
   If there were 529 College Discovery students who entered community college, then the number of those who went on to finally receive a baccalaureate degree is MOST NEARLY
   A. 354   B. 315   C. 124   D. 110

   3._____

4. It takes 5 office assistants two days to type 125 letters. Each of the assistants works at an equal rate of speed.
   How many days will it take 10 office assistants to type 200 letters?
   A. 1   B. 1³⁄₅   C. 2   D. 2¹⁄₅

   4._____

5. The following are the grades and credits earned by Student X during the first two years in college.

Grade	Credits	Weight	Quality Points
A	10 ½	×4	
B	24	×3	
C	12	×2	
D	4 ½	×1	
F, FW	5	×0	

   5._____

   To compute an index number:
   I. Multiply the number of credits of each grade by the weight to get the number of quality points
   II. Add the credits
   III. Add the quality points
   IV. Divide the total quality point by the total credits and carry the division to two decimal places

175

On the basis of the given information, the index number for Student X is
A. 2.55 B. 2.59 C. 2.63 D. 2.68

6. Typist X can type 20 forms per hour, and Typist Y can type 30 forms per hour. If there are 30 forms to be typed and both typists are put to work on the job, how son should they be expected to finish the work? _____ minutes.
A. 32 B. 34 C. 36 D. 38

7. Assume that there were 18 working days in February and that the six clerks in your unit had the following number of absences:

Clerk	Absences
F	3
G	2
H	8
I	1
J	0
K	5

The average percentage attendance for the six clerks in your unit in February was MOST NEARLY
A. 80% B. 82% C. 84% D. 86%

8. A certain employee is paid at the rate of $7.50 per hour, with time and a half for overtime. Hours in excess of 40 hours a week count as overtime. During the past week, the employee put in 48 working hours.
The employee's gross wages for the week are MOST NEARLY
A. $330 B. $350 C. $370 D. $390

9. You are making a report on the number of inside and outside calls handled by a particular switchboard. Over a 15-day period, the total number of all inside and outside calls handled by the switchboard was 5,760. The average number of inside calls per day was 234. You cannot find one day's tally of outside calls, but the total number of outside calls for the other fourteen days was 2,065.
From this information, how many outside calls must have been reported on the missing tally?
A. 175 B. 185 C. 195 D. 205

10. A floor plan has been prepared for a new building, drawn to a scale of ¾ inch = 1 foot. A certain area is drawn 1 and ½ feet long and 6 inches wide on the floor plan.
What are the ACTUAL dimensions of this area in the new building?
_____ feet long and _____ feet wide
A. 21; 8 B. 24; 8 C. 27; 9 D. 30; 9

11. You are preparing a package of six books to mail to a professor who is on sabbatical. They weigh, respectively, 1 pound 11 ounces, 1 pound 6 ounces, 2 pounds 1 ounce, 2 pounds 2 ounces, 1 pound 7 ounces, and 1 pound 8 ounces. The packaging material weighs 6 ounces.
    The TOTAL weight of the package will be _____ pounds _____ ounces.
    A. 10; 3   B. 10; 9   C. 11; 5   D. 12; 5

12. Part-time students are charged $70 per credit for courses at a particular college. In addition, they musts pay a $24.00 student activity fee if they take six credits or more and $14.00 lab fee for each laboratory course.
    If a person takes one 3-credit course and one 4-credit course and his 4-credit course is a laboratory course, the TOTAL cost to him will be
    A. $504   B. $528   C. $542   D. $552

13. The graduating course of a certain community college consisted of 378 majors in secretarial science, 265 majors in engineering science, 57 majors in nursing, 513 majors in accounting, and 865 majors in liberal arts.
    The percent of students who major in liberal arts at this college was MOST NEARLY
    A. 24.0%   B. 41.6%   C. 52.3%   D. 71.6%

14. Donald Smith earns $12.80 an hour for forty hours a week, with time and a half for all hours over forty. Last week, his total earnings amounted to $627.20.
    He worked _____ hours.
    A. 46   B. 47   C. 48   D. 49

15. Mr. Jones desires to sell an article costing $28 at a gross profit of 30% of the selling price, and to allow a trade discount of 20% of the list price.
    The list price of the article should be
    A. $43.68   B. $45.50   C. $48.00   D. $50.00

16. The gauge of an oil storage tank in an elementary school indicates 1/5 full. After a truck delivers 945 gallons of oil, the gauge indicates 4/5 full.
    The capacity of the tank is _____ gallons.
    A. 1,260   B. 1,575   C. 1,625   D. 1,890

17. An invoice dated April 3, terms 3/10, 2/30, net/60, was paid in full with a check for $787.92 on May 1.
    The amount of the invoice was
    A. $772.16   B. $787.92   C. $804.00   D. $812.29

18. Two pipes supply the water for the swimming pool at Blenheim High School. One pipe can fill the pool in 9 hours. The second pipe can fill the pool in 6 hours.
    If both pipes were opened simultaneously, the pool could be filled in _____ hours _____ minutes.
    A. 3; 36   B. 4; 30   C. 5; 15   D. 7; 30

4 (#3)

19. John's father spent $24,000, which was one-fourth of his savings. He bought a car with three-eighths of the remainder of his savings.
His bank balance now amounts to
   A. $30,000   B. $32,000   C. $45,000   D. $50,000

19.____

20. A clock that loses 4 minutes every 24 hours was set at 6 A.M. on October 1 What time was indicated by the clock when the CORRECT time was 12:00 Noon on October 6th?
   A. 11:36   B. 11:38   C. $11:39   D. 11:40

20.____

21. Unit S's production fluctuated substantially from one year to another. In 2009, Unit s's production was 100% greater than in 2008. In 2010, production decreased by 25% from 2009. In 2011, Unit S's production was 10% greater than in 2010.
On the basis of this information, it is CORRECT to conclude that Unit S's production in 2011 exceeded Unit S's production in 2008 by
   A. 65%   B. 85%   C. 95%   D. 135%

21.____

22. Agency X is moving into a new building. It has 1,500 employees presently on its staff and does not contemplate much variance from this level. The new building contains 100 available offices, each with a maximum capacity of 30 employees. It has been decided that only 2/3 of the maximum capacity of each office will be utilized.
The TOTAL number of office that will be occupied by Agency X is
   A. 30   B. 65   C. 75   D. 90

22.____

23. One typist completes a form letter every 5 minutes and another typist completes one every 6 minutes.
If the two typists start together, how many minutes later will they again start typing new letters simultaneously and how many letters will they have completed by that time?
   A. 11; 30   B. 12; 24   C. 24; 12   D. 30; 1

23.____

24. During one week, a machine operator produces 10 fewer pages per hour of work than he usually does.
If it ordinarily takes him six hours to produce a 300-page report, how many hour LONGER will that same 300-page report take him during the week when he produces more slowly?
   A. 1½   B. 1$^2/_3$ C. 2   D. 2¾

24.____

25. A study reveals that Miss Brown files N cards in M hours, and Miss Smith files the same number of cards in T hours.
If the two employees work together, the number of hours it will take them to file N cards is
   A. $\dfrac{N}{\frac{N}{M}+\frac{N}{N}}$ B. $\dfrac{N}{T+M}+\dfrac{2N}{MT}$ C. $N(\dfrac{M}{N}+\dfrac{N}{T})$ D. $\dfrac{N}{NT+MN}$

25.____

KEY (CORRECT ANSWERS)

1. A
2. B
3. D
4. B
5. A

6. C
7. B
8. D
9. B
10. B

11. B
12. B
13. B
14. A
15. D

16. B
17. C
18. A
19. C
20. C

21. A
22. C
23. D
24. A
25. A

SOLUTIONS TO PROBLEMS

1. 9/4 = 2¼" and 14/4 = 3½"

2. Gross amount = (3)($6.75)(3.5) + (2)($6.75)(4.5) + ($8.00)(5.5) = $174.624, which is closest to selection B ($177.81)

3. (529)(.35)(.89)(.67) ≈ 110

4. 10 worker-days are needed to type 125 letters, so (200)(10) ÷ 125 = 16 worker-days are needed to type 200 letters. Finally, 16 ÷ 10 workers = 1 3/5 days

5. Index number = [(14)(10½) + (3)(24) + (2)(12) + (1)(4½) + (0)(5)] ÷ 56 ≈ 2,54

6. Typist X could do 30 forms in 30/20 = 1½ hours. Let x = number of hour needed when working together with Typist Y.
   Then, $(\frac{1}{1\frac{1}{2}})(x) + (\frac{1}{1})x = 1$. Simplifying, 2x + 3x = 3, so x = $\frac{3}{5}$ hr. = 36 min.

7. (3+2+8+1+0+5) ÷ 6 = 3.16. Then, 18 − 3.$\overline{6}$ = 14.$\overline{83}$.

   Finally, 14.$\overline{83}$ ÷ 18 ≈ 82%

8. Wages = ($7.50)(40) + ($11.25)(8) = $390

9. (234)(15) = 3510 inside calls. Then, 5760 − 3510 = 2259 outside calls. Finally, 2250 − 2065 = 185 outside calls on the missing day.

10. 18 ÷ ¾ - 24 feet long and 6 ÷ ¾ = 8 feet wide

11. Total weight = 1 lb. 11 oz. + 1 lb. 6 oz. + 2 lbs. 1 oz. + 2 lbs. 2 oz. + 1 lb. 7 oz. + 1 lb. 8 oz. + 6 oz = 8 lbs. 41 oz. 10 lbs. 9 oz.

12. Total cost = ($70)(7) + $24 + $14 = $528

13. 865 ÷ 2078 ≈ 41.6% liberal arts majors

14. ($12.80)(40) = $512, so he made $627.20 - $512 = $115.20 in overtime. His overtime rate = ($12.80)(1.5) = $19.20 per hour. Thus, he worked $115.20 ÷ $19.20 = 6 overtime hours. Total hours worked = 46

15. Let x = list price. Selling price = .80x. Then, .80x − (.30)(.80x) = $28. Simplifying, .56x = $28. Solving, x = $50.00

7 (#3)

16. 945 gallons represents $\frac{4}{5} \cdot \frac{1}{5} = \frac{3}{5}$ of the tank's capacity.

    Then, the capacity = $945 \div \frac{3}{5}$ = 1575 gallons

17. $787.92 ÷ .98 = $804.00

18. Let x = number of required hours. Then, (1/9)(x) + (1/6)(x) = 1
    Simplifying, 2x + 3x = 18. Solving, x = 3.6 hours = 3 hours 36 minutes

19. Bank balance = $96,000 - $24,000 – (3/8)($72,000) = $45,000

20. From Oct. 1, 6 A.M. to Oct. 6, Noon = 5½ days. The clock would show a loss of (4 min.)(5½) = 21 min. Thus, the clock's time would incorrectly) show 12:00 Noon – 21 min. = 11:39 A.M.

21. 2008 = x, 2009 = 200x, 2010 = 150x, 2011 = 165x
    65% more

22. (2/3)(30) = 20 employees in each office. Then, 1500 ÷ 20 = 75 offices

23. After 30 minutes, the typists will have finished a total of 6 + 5 = 11 letters

24. When he works more slowly, he will only produce 300 – (6)(10) = 240 pages in 6 hrs. His new slower rate is 40 pages per hour, so he will need 60/40 = 1½ more hours to do the remaining 60 pages.

25. Let x = required hours. Then $(\frac{1}{M})(x) + (\frac{1}{10})(x) = 1$.

    Simplifying, x(T+M) = MT. Solving, x = MT/(T+M)

    Note: The N value is immaterial. Also, choice A reduces to MT/(T+M)

GLOSSARY OF PERSONNEL TERMS

CONTENTS

	Page
Abandonment of Positions………………………. Appointment, Noncompetitive	1
Appointment, Superior Qualifications…………………………Bargaining Unit	2
Basic Workweek……. …………………….Certification, Top of the Register	3
Change in Duty Station………………………………………………..Consultant	4
Consultation……………………………………………... Employee Development	5
Employee, Exempt………………………………….......Expected Service	6
Exclusive Recognition…………………………………….General Schedule	7
Grade…………………………………………………….. Injury, Work Related	8
Injury, Traumatic…………………………………………….Leave, Military	9
Leave, Sick…………………………………….National Consultation Rights	10
Negotiability………………………………………………….Pass Over	11
Pay Retention………………………………………….....Position "PL 313 Type"	12
Preference, Compensable Disability ("CP")………..Promotion, Competitive	13
Promotion Certificate…………………………………………... Reinstatement	14
Removal…………………………………………………………….Retirement	15
Review, Classification………………………….. Steward (Union Steward)	16
Strike……………………………………………………….....Tenure Groups	17
Tenure Subgroups……………………………………………….Voucher	18
Wage Employees………………………………… .. Within-Grade Increase	19

GLOSSARY OF PERSONNEL TERMS

A

Abandonment of Position—When an employee quits work without resigning. (715)

Absence Without Leave (AWOL) Absence — without prior approval, therefore without pay, that may be subject to disciplinary action. See also, *Leave Without Pay,* which is an approved absence. (630)

Administrative Workweek— A period of seven consecutive calendar days designated in advance by the head of the agency. Usually an administrative workweek coincides with a calendar week. (610)

Admonishment— Informal reproval of an employee by a supervisor; usually oral, but some agencies require written notice. (751)

Adverse Action— A removal, suspension, furlough without pay for 30 days or less, or reduction-in-grade or pay. An adverse action may be taken against an employee for disciplinary or non-disciplinary reasons. However, if the employee is covered by FPM part 752, the action must be in accordance with those procedures. Removals or reductions-in-grade based solely on unacceptable performance are covered by Part 432. Actions taken for reductions-in-force reasons are covered by Part 351. (752)

Affirmative Action — A policy followed closely by the Federal civil service that requires agencies to take positive steps to insure equal opportunity in employment, development, advancement, and treatment of all employees and applicants for employment regardless of race, color, sex, religion, national origin, or physical or mental handicap. Affirmative action also requires that specific actions be directed at the special problems and unique concerns in assuring equal employment opportunity for minorities, women and other disadvantaged groups.

Agreement—See *Collective Bargaining*.

Annuitant—A retired Federal civil service employee or a survivor (spouse or children) being paid an annuity from the Retirement Fund. (831)

Annuity—Payments to a former employee who retired, or to the surviving spouse or children. It is computed as an annual rate but paid monthly. (831)

Appeal—A request by an employee for review of an agency action by an outside agency: The right to such review-is provided by law or regulation and may include an adversary-type hearing and a written decision in which a finding of facts is made and applicable law, Executive order and regulations are applied.

Appointing Officer—A person having power by law or lawfully delegated authority to make appointments. (210, 311)

Appointment, Noncompetitive— Employment without competing with others, in the sense that it is done without regard to civil service registers, etc. Includes reinstatements, transfers, reassignments, demotions, and promotion. (335)

Appointment, Superior Qualifications—Appointment of a candidate to a position in grade 11 or above of the General Schedule at a rate above the minimum because of the candidate's superior qualifications. A rate above the minimum for the grade must be justified by the applicant's unusually high or unique qualifications, a special need of the Government for the candidate's services, or because the candidate's current pay is higher than the minimum for the grade which he or she is offered. (338, 531)

Appointment, TAPER—Abbreviation for "temporary appointment pending establishment of a register." Employment made under an OPM authority granted to an agency when there are insufficient eligibles on a register appropriate to fill the position involved. (316)

Appointment, Temporary Limited—Nonpermanent appointment of an employee hired for a specified time of one year or less, or for seasonal or intermittent positions. (316)

Appointment, Term—Nonpermanent appointment of an employee hired to work on a project expected to last over one year, but less than four years. (316)

Appropriate Unit—A group of employees which a labor organization seeks to represent for the purpose of negotiating agreements; an aggregation of employees which has a clear and identifiable community of interest and which promotes effective dealings and efficiency of operations. It may be established on a plant or installation, craft, functional or other basis. (Also known as bargaining unit, appropriate bargaining unit.) (711)

Arbitration—Final step of the negotiated grievance procedure which may be invoked by the agency or the union (not the employee) if the grievance has not been resolved. Involves use of an impartial arbitrator selected by the agency and union to render a binding award to resolve the grievance. (711)

Arbitrator—An impartial third party to whom disputing parties submit their differences for decision (award). An *ad hoc* arbitrator is one selected to act in a specific case or a limited group of cases. A permanent arbitrator is one selected to serve for the life of the agreement or a stipulated term, hearing all disputes that arise during this period. (711)

Area Office (OPM)—Focal point for administering and implementing all OPM programs, except investigations, in the geographic area assigned. Provides personnel management advice and assistance to agencies, and personnel evaluation, recruiting and examining and special program leadership. Principal source of employment information for agencies and the public.

Audit, Work—Visit to an employee or his supervisor to verify or gather information about a position. Sometimes called "desk audit."

B

Bargaining Rights—Legally recognized right of the labor organization to represent employees in negotiations with employers. (711)

Bargaining Unit—An appropriate grouping of employees represented on an exclusive basis by a labor organization. "Appropriate" for this purpose means that it is a grouping of employees who share a community of interest and which promotes effective union and agency dealings and efficient agency operations. (711)

Basic Workweek—For a full-time employee, the 40-hour non overtime work schedule within an administrative workweek. The usual workweek consists of five 8-hour days, Monday through Friday. (610)

Break in Service—The time between separation and reemployment that may cause a loss of rights or privileges. For transfer purposes, it means not being on an agency payroll for one working day or more. For the three-year career conditional period or for reinstatement purposes, it means not being on an agency payroll for over 30 calendar days. (315)

Bumping—During reduction-in-force, the displacement of one employee by another employee in a higher group or subgroup. (351)

C

Career—Tenure of a permanent employee in the competitive service who has completed three years of substantially continuous creditable Federal service. (315)

Career-Conditional—Tenure of a permanent employee in the competitive service who *has not* completed three years of substantially continuous creditable Federal service. (315)

Career Counseling—Service available to employees to assist them in: (1) assessing their skills, abilities, interests, and aptitudes; (2) determining qualifications required for occupations within the career system and how the requirements relate to their individual capabilities; (3) defining their career goals and developing plans for reaching the goals; (4) identifying and assessing education and training opportunities and enrollment procedures; (5) identifying factors which may impair career development; and (6) learning about resources, inside or outside the agency, where additional help is available. (250)

Career Development—Systematic development designed to increase an employee's potential for advancement and career change. It may include classroom training, reading, work experience, etc. (410)

Career Ladder—A career ladder is a series of developmental positions of increasing difficulty in the same line of work, through which an employee may progress to a journeyman level on his or her personal development and performance in that series.

Career Reserved Position—A position within SES that has a specific requirement for impartiality. May be filled" only by career appointment. (920)

Ceiling, Personnel—The maximum number of employees authorized at a given time. (312)

Certification—The process by which eligibles are ranked, according to regulations, for appointment or promotion consideration. (332, 335)

Certification, Selective—Certifying only the names of eligibles who have special qualifications required to fill particular vacant positions. (332)

Certification, Top of the Register—Certifying in regular order, beginning with the eligibles at the top of the register. (332)

Change in Duty Station—A personnel action that changes an employee from one geographical location to another in the same agency. (296)

Change to Lower Grade—Downgrading a position or reducing an employee's grade. See *Demotion*. (296)

Class of Positions—All positions sufficiently similar in: (1) kind or subject matter of work; (2) level of difficulty and responsibility; and (3) qualification requirements, so as to warrant similar treatment in personnel and pay administration. For example, all Grade GS-3 Clerk-Typist positions. (511)

Classified Service—See *Competitive Service* (212)

Collective Bargaining—Performance of the mutual obligation of the employer and the exclusive (employee) representative to meet at reasonable times, to confer and negotiate in good faith, and to execute a written agreement with respect to conditions of employment, except that by any such obligation neither party shall be compelled to agree to proposals, or be required to make concessions. (Also known as collective negotiations, negotiations, and negotiation of agreement.) (711)

Collective Bargaining Agreement—A written agreement between management and a labor-organization which is usually for a definite term, and usually defines conditions of employment, and includes grievance and arbitration procedures. The terms "collective bargaining agreement" and "contract" are synonymous. (711)

Collective Bargaining Unit—A group of employees recognized as appropriate for representation by a labor organization for collective bargaining. (See *Appropriate Unit*) (711)

Compensatory Time Off—Time off (hour-for-hour) granted an employee in lieu of overtime pay. (550)

Competitive Area—For reduction-in-force, that part of an agency within which employees are in competition for retention. Generally, it is that part of an agency covered by a single appointing office. (351)

Competitive Service—Federal positions normally filled through open competitive examination (hence the term "competitive service") under civil service rules and regulations. About 86 percent of all Federal positions are in the competitive service. (212)

Competitive Status—Basic eligibility of a person to be selected to fill a position in the competitive service without open competitive examination. Competitive status may be acquired by career-conditional or career appointment through open competitive examination, or may be granted by statute, executive order, or civil service rules without competitive examination. A person with competitive status may be promoted, transferred, reassigned, reinstated, or demoted subject to the conditions prescribed by civil service rules and regulations. (212)

Consultant—An advisor to an officer or instrumentality of the Government, as distinguished from an officer or employee who carries out the agency's duties and responsibilities. (304)

Consultation—The obligation of an agency to consult the labor organization on particular personnel issues. The process of consultation lies between notification to the labor organization, which may amount simply to providing information, and negotiation, which implies agreement on the part of the labor organization. (711)

Conversion—The process of changing a person's tenure from one type of appointment to another (e.g., conversion from temporary to career-conditional). (315)

D

Demotion—A change of an employee, while serving continuously with the same agency:
(a) To a lower grade when both the old and the new positions are in the General Schedule or under the same type graded wage schedule; or
(b) To a position with a lower rate of pay when both the old and the new positions are under the same type ungraded wage schedule, or are in different pay method categories. (335, 752)

Detail—A temporary assignment of an employee to different duties or to a different position for a specified time, with the employee returning to his/her regular duties at the end of the detail. (300)

Differentials—Recruiting incentives in the form of compensation adjustments justified by: (1) extraordinarily difficult living conditions; (2) excessive physical hardship; or (3) notably unhealthful conditions. (591)

Disciplinary Action—Action taken to correct the conduct of an employee; may range from an admonishment through reprimand, suspension, reduction in grade or pay, to removal from the service. (751, 752)

Displaced Employee Program—(DEP)— A system to help find jobs for career and career-conditional employees displaced either through reduction-in-force or by an inability to accept assignment to another commuting area. (330)

Downgrading—Change of a position to a lower grade. (511, 532)

Dual Compensation—When an employee receives compensation for more than one Federal position if he/she worked more than 40 hours during the week. The term is also used in connection with compensation from a full-time Federal position as well as a retirement annuity for prior military service. (550)

Duty Station—The specific geographical area in which an employee is permanently assigned. (296)

E

Eligible—Any applicant for appointment or promotion who meets the minimum qualification requirements. (337)

Employee Development—A term which may include *career development* and *upward mobility*. It may be oriented toward development for better performance on an employee's current job, for learning a new policy or procedure, or for enhancing an employee's potential for advancement. (410, 412)

Employee, Exempt—An employee exempt from the overtime provisions of the Fair Labor Standards Act. (551)

Employee, Nonexempt—An employee subject to the overtime provision of the Fair Labor Standards Act. (551)

Employee Organization— See *Labor Organization.*

Employee Relations—The personnel function which centers upon the relationship between the supervisor and individual employees. (711)

Entrance Level Position—A position in an occupation at the beginning level grade. (511)

Environmental Differential—Additional pay authorized for a duty involving unusually severe hazards or working conditions. (532, 550)

Equal Employment Opportunity—Federal policy to provide equal employment opportunity for all; to prohibit discrimination on the grounds of age, race, color, religion, sex, national origin, or physical or mental handicap; and to promote the full realization of employees' potential through a continuing affirmative action program in each executive department and agency. (713)

Equal Employment Opportunity Commission—Regulates and enforces the Federal program for insuring equal employment opportunity, and oversees the development and implementation of Federal agencies' affirmative action programs.

Equal Pay for Substantially Equal Work—An underlying principle that provides the same pay level for work at the same level of difficulty and responsibility. (271)

Examination, Assembled—An examination which includes as one of its parts a written or performance test for which applicants are required to assemble at appointed times and places. (337)

Examination— A means of measuring, in a practical and suitable manner, qualifications of applicants for employment in specific positions. (337)

Examination, Fitness-For-Duty—An agency directed examination given by a Federal medical officer or an employee-designated, agency-approved physician to determine the employee's physical, mental, or emotional ability to perform assigned duties safely and efficiently. (339, 831)

Examination, Unassembled—An examination in which applicants are rated on their education, experience, and other qualifications as shown in the formal application and any supportive evidence that may be required, without assembling for a written or performance test. (337)

Excepted Service—Positions in the Federal civil service not subject to the appointment requirements of the competitive service. Exceptions to the normal, competitive requirements are authorized by law, executive order, or regulation. (213, 302)

Exclusive Recognition—The status conferred on a labor organization which receives a majority of votes cast in a representation election, entitling it to act for and negotiate agreements covering all employees included in an appropriate bargaining unit. The labor organization enjoying this status is known as the exclusive representative, exclusive bargaining representative, bargaining agent, or exclusive bargaining agent. (711)

Executive Inventory—An OPM computerized file which contains background information on all members of the Senior Executive Service and persons in positions at GS-16 through GS-18 or the equivalent, and individuals at lower grades who have been certified as meeting the managerial criteria for SES. It is used as an aid to agencies in executive recruiting and as a planning and management tool. (920)

Executive Resources Board—Panel of top agency executives responsible under the law for conducting the merit staffing process for career appointment to Senior Executive Service (SES) positions in the agency. Most Boards are also responsible for setting policy on and overseeing such areas as SES position planning and executive development. (920)

F

Federal Labor Relations Authority (FLRA)—Administers the Federal service labor-management relations program. It resolves questions of union representation of employees; prosecutes and adjudicates allegations of unfair labor practices; decides questions of what is or is not negotiable; and on appeal, reviews decisions of arbitrators. (5 USC 7104)

Federal Personnel Manual (FPM)—The official publication containing Federal personnel regulations and guidance. Also contains the code of Federal civil service law, selected Executive orders pertaining to Federal employment, and civil service rules. (171)

Federal Service Impasses Panel (FSIP)—Administrative body created to resolve bargaining impasses in the Federal service. The Panel may recommend procedures, including arbitration, for settling impasses, or may settle the impasse itself. Considered the legal alternative to strike in the Federal sector. (711)

Federal Wage System (FWS)—A body of laws and regulations governing the administrative processes related to trades and laboring occupations in the Federal service. (532)

Full Field Investigation—Personal investigation of an applicant's background to determine whether he/she meets fitness standards for a critical-sensitive Federal position. (736)

Function—All, or a clearly identifiable segment, of an agency's mission, including all the parts of the mission (e.g. procurement), regardless of how performed. (351)

G

General Position—A position within the Senior Executive Service that may be filled by a career, noncareer, or limited appointment. (920)

General Schedule—(GS)The graded pay system as presented by Chapter 51 of Title 5, United States Code, for classifying positions. **(511)**

Grade—All classes of positions which, although different with respect to kind or subject matter of work, are sufficiently equivalent as to (1) level of difficulty and responsibility, and (2) level of qualification requirements of the work to warrant the inclusion of such classes of positions within one range of rates of basic compensation. (511, 532)

Grade Retention—The right of a General Schedule or prevailing rate employee, when demoted for certain reasons, to retain the higher grade for most purposes for two years. (536)

Grievance, (Negotiated Procedure)—Any complaint or expressed dissatisfaction by an employee against an action by management in connection with his job, pay or other aspects of employment. Whether such complaint or expressed dissatisfaction is formally recognized and handled as a "grievance" under a negotiated procedure depends on the scope of that procedure. (711)

Grievance (Under Agency Administrative Procedure)—A request by an employee or by a group of employees acting as individuals, for personal relief in a matter of concern or dissatisfaction to the employee, subject to the control of agency management.

Grievance Procedure—A procedure, either administrative or negotiated, by which employees may seek redress of any matter subject to the control of agency management. (711, 771)

H

Handbook X-118— The official qualification standard a manual for General Schedule Positions. (338)

Handbook X-118C—The official qualification standards manual for Wage System positions. (338)

Hearing—The opportunity for contending parties under a grievance, complaint, or other remedial process, to introduce testimony and evidence and to confront and examine or cross examine witnesses. (713, 771, 772)

I

Impasse Procedures—Procedures for resolving deadlocks between agencies and union in collective bargaining. (711)

Incentive Awards—An all-inclusive term covering awards granted under Part 451 or OPM regulations. Includes an award for a suggestion submitted by an employee and adopted by management; a special achievement award for performance exceeding job requirements, or an honorary award in the form of a certificate, emblem, pin or other item. (451)

Indefinite—Tenure of a nonpermanent employee hired for an unlimited time. (316)

Injury, Work Related—For compensation under the Federal Employees' Compensation Act, a personal injury sustained while in the performance of duty. The term "injury" includes diseases proximately caused by the employment. (810)

Injury, Traumatic—Under the Federal Employees' Compensation Act, for continuation of pay purposes, a wound or other condition of the body caused by external force, including stress or strain. The injury must be identifiable by time and place of occurrence and member or function of the body affected, and be caused by a specific event or incident or series of events or incidents within a single day or work shift. (810)

Intergovernmental Personnel Assignment—Assignments of personnel to and from the Executive Branch of the Federal Government, state and local government agencies, and institutions of higher education up to two years, although a two-year extension may be permitted. The purpose is to provide technical assistance or expertise where needed for short periods of time. (334)

Intermittent—Less than full-time employment requiring irregular work hours which cannot be prescheduled. (610)

J

Job Analysis—Technical review and evaluation of a position's duties, responsibilities, and level of work and of the skills, abilities, and knowledge needed to do the work. (511, 532)

Job Enrichment—Carefully planned work assignments and/or training to use and upgrade employee skills, abilities, and interests; and to provide opportunity for growth, and encourage self-improvement. (312)

Job Freeze—A restriction on hiring and/or promotion by administrative or legislative action. (330)

Job Title— The formal name of a position as determined by official classification standards. (511, 532)

Journeyman Level—(Full Performance Level)The lowest level of a career ladder position at which an employee has learned the full range of duties in a specific occupation. All jobs below full performance level are developmental levels, through which each employee in the occupation may progress to full performance. (511)

L

Labor-Management Relations—Relationships and dealings between employee unions and management. (711)

Labor Organization—An organization composed in whole or in part of employees, in which employees participate and pay dues, and which has as a purpose dealing with an agency concerning grievances and working conditions of employment. (711)

Lead Agency—Under the Federal Wage-System, the Federal agency with the largest number of Federal wage workers in a geographical area; consequently, it has the primary role for determining wage rates for all Federal employees who work in that area and are covered by the System. (532)

Leave, Annual—Time allowed to employees for vacation and other absences for personal reasons. (630)

Leave, Court—Time allowed to employees for jury and certain types of witness service. (630)

Leave, Military—Time allowed to employees for certain types of military service. (630)

Leave, Sick—Time allowed to employees for physical incapacity, to prevent the spread of contagious diseases, or to obtain medical, dental or eye examination or treatment. (630)

Leave Without Pay (LWOP)—A temporary nonpay status and absence from duty, requested by an employee. The permissive nature of "leave without pay" distinguishes it from "absence without leave." (630)

Level of Difficulty—A classification term used to indicate the relative ranking of duties and responsibilities. (511, 532)

M

Maintenance Review—A formal, periodic review (usually annual) of all positions in an organization, or portion of an organization, to insure that classifications are correct and position descriptions are current. (511)

Major Duty—Any duty or responsibility, or group of closely related tasks, of a position which (1) determines qualification requirements for the position, (2) occupies a significant amount of the employee's time, and (3) is a regular or recurring duty. (511)

Management Official—An individual employed by an agency in a position whose duties and responsibilities require or authorize the individual to formulate, determine or influence the policies of the agency. (711)

Management Rights—The right of management to make day-today personnel decisions and to direct the work force without mandatory negotiation with the exclusive representative. (See "Reserved Rights Doctrine.") Usually a specific list of management authorities not subject to the obligation to bargain. (117)

Mediation—Procedure using a third-party to facilitate the reaching of an agreement voluntarily. (711)

Merit Promotion Program—The system under which agencies consider an employee for internal personnel actions on the basis of personal merit. (335)

Merit Systems Protection Board (MSPB)—An independent agency which monitors the administration of the Federal civil service system, prosecutes and adjudicates allegations of merit principle abuses, and hears and decides other civil service appeals. (5 USC 1205)

N

National Agency Check and Inquiry (NACI)—The Investigation of applicants for nonsensitive Federal positions by means of a name check through national investigative files and voucher inquiries. (731)

National Consultation Rights—A relationship established between the headquarters of a Federal agency and the national office of a union under criteria of the Federal Labor Relations Authority. When a union holds national consultation rights, the agency must give the union notice of proposed new substantive personnel policies, and of proposed changes in personnel policies, and an opportunity to comment on such proposals. The union has a right to: (1) suggest changes in personnel policies and have those suggestions carefully considered; (2) consult at reasonable times with appropriate officials about personnel policy matters; and (3) submit its views in writing on personnel policy matters at any time. The agency must provide the union with a written statement (which need not be detailed) of reasons for taking its final action on a policy. (711)

Negotiability—A determination as to whether a matter is within the obligation to bargain. (711)

Negotiated Grievance Procedure—A procedure applicable to members of a bargaining unit for considering grievances. Coverage and scope are negotiated by the parties to the agreement, except that the procedures may not cover certain matters designated in Title VII of the CSRA as excluded from the scope of negotiated grievance procedures. (711)

Negotiations—The bargaining process used to reach a settlement between labor and management over conditions of employment. (711)

Nominating Officer—A subordinate officer of an agency to whom authority has been delegated by the head of the agency to nominate for appointment but not actually appoint employees. (311)

O

Objection—A written statement by an agency of the reasons why it believes an eligible whose name is on a certificate is not qualified for the position to which referred. If the Examining Office sustains the objection, the agency may eliminate the person from consideration. (332)

Occupational Group—Positions of differing kinds but within the same field of work. For example, the GS-500 Accounting and Budget Occupational Group includes: General Accounting Clerical and Administrative Series; Financial Management; Internal Revenue Agent Accounting Technician; Payroll; etc. (511, 532)

Office of Personnel Management (OPM)—Regulates, administers, and evaluates the civil service program according to merit principles. (5 USC 1103)

Office of Workers Compensation Programs (OWCP)—In the Department of Labor, administers statutes that allow compensation to employees and their survivors for work-related injuries and illnesses. Decides and pays claims. (810)

Official Personnel Folder (OPF)—The official repository of employment records and documents affecting personnel actions during an employee's Federal civilian service. (293)

Overtime Work—Under Title 5, U.S. Code, officially ordered or approved work performed in excess of eight hours in a day or 40 hours in a week. Under the Fair Labor Standards Act, work in excess of 40 hours in a week by a nonexempt employee. (550, 551)

P

Pass Over—Elimination from appointment consideration of a veteran preference eligible on a certificate (candidate list), to appoint a lower ranking nonveteran, when the agency submits reasons which OPM finds sufficient. (332)

Pay Retention—The right of a General Schedule or prevailing rate employee (following a grade retention period or at other specified times when the rate of basic pay would otherwise be reduced) to continue to receive the higher rate. Pay is retained indefinitely. (536)

Pay, Severance—Money paid to employees separated by reduction-in-force and not eligible for retirement. The following formula is used, but the amount cannot be more than one year's pay:
Basic Severance Pay— One week's pay for each year of civilian service up to 10 years, and two weeks' pay for each year served over 10 years, plus
Age Adjustment Allowance —10 percent of the basic severance pay for each year over age 40. (550)

Performance Appraisal—The comparison, under a performance appraisal system, of an employee's actual performance against the performance standards previously established for the position. (430)

Personal Action— The process necessary to appoint, separate, reinstate, or make other changes affecting an employee (e.g., change in position assignment, tenure, etc.). (296)

Personnel Management—Management of human resources to accomplish a mission and provide individual job satisfaction. It is the line responsibility of the operating supervisor and the staff responsibility of the personnel office. (250)

Position—A specific job consisting of all the current major duties and responsibilities assigned or delegated by management. (312)

Position Change—A promotion, demotion, or reassignment. (335)

Position Classification—Analyzing and categorizing jobs by occupational group, series, class, and grade according to like duties, responsibilities, and qualification requirements. (511, 532)

Position Classifier—A specialist in job analysis who determines the titles, occupational groups, series, and grades of positions. (312)

Position Description—An official written statement of the major duties, responsibilities and supervisory relationships of a position. (312)

Position Management—The process of designing positions to combine logical and consistent duties and responsibilities into an orderly, efficient, and productive organization to accomplish agency mission. (312)

Position Survey—Agency review of positions to determine whether the positions are still needed and, if so, whether the classification and position description are correct. (312)

Position, "PL 313 Type"—Positions established under Public Law 80-313 of August 1, 1947, or similar authorities. A small group of high level professional and scientific positions generally in the competitive service, but not filled through competitive examinations. Salaries are set between GS-12 and GS-18. (534)

Preference, Compensable Disability ("CP")—Ten-point preference awarded to a veteran separated under honorable conditions from active duty, who receives compensation of 10 percent or more for a service-connected disability. Eligible "CP" veterans are placed at the top of civil service lists of eligibles for positions at GS-9 or higher. (211)

Preference, 30 Percent or More, Disabled ("CPS")—A disabled veteran whose disability is rated at 30 percent or more, entitled to special preference in appointment and during reduction in force.

Preference, Disability ("XP")—Ten-point preference in hiring for a veteran separated under honorable conditions from active duty and who has a service-connected disability or receives compensation, pension, or disability retirement from the VA or a uniformed service. (211)

Preference, Mother ("XP")—Ten-point preference to which the mother of a deceased or disabled military veteran may be entitled. (211)

Preference, Spouse ("XP")—Ten-point preference to which a disabled military veteran's spouse may be entitled. (211)

Preference, Tentative ("TP")— Five-point veteran preference tentatively awarded an eligible who served on active duty during specified periods and was separated from military service under honorable conditions. It must be verified by the appointing officer. (211)

Preference, Veteran—The statutory right to special advantage in appointments or separations; based on a person's discharge under honorable conditions from the armed forces, for a service-connected disability. *Not* applicable to the Senior Executive Service. (211)

Preference, Widow or Widower ("XP")—Ten-point preference to which a military veteran's widow or widower may be entitled. (211)

Premium Pay—Additional pay for overtime, night, Sunday and holiday work. (550)

Prevailing Rate System—A subsystem of the Federal Wage System used to determine the employee's pay in a particular wage area. The determination requires, comparing. the_. rate of pay with the private sector for similar duties and responsibilities. (532)

Probationary Period—A trial period which is a condition of the initial competitive appointment. Provides the final indispensable test of ability, that of actual performance on the job. (315)

Promotion—A change of an employee to a higher grade when both the old and new positions are under the same job classification system and pay schedule, or to a position with higher pay in a different job classification system and pay schedule. (335)

Promotion, Career—Promotion of an employee without current competition when: (1) he/ she had earlier been competitively selected from a register or under competitive promotion procedures for an assignment intended as a matter of record to be preparation for the position being filled; or (2) the position is reconstituted at a higher grade because of additional duties and responsibilities. (335)

Promotion, Competitive—Selection of a current or former Federal civil service employee for a higher grade position, using procedures that compare the candidates on merit. (335)

Promotion Certificate—A list of best qualified candidates to be considered to fill a position under competitive promotion procedures. (335)

Q

Qualifications Review Board—A panel attached to OPM that determines whether a candidate for career appointment in the Senior Executive Service meets the managerial criteria established by law.

Qualification Requirements—Education, experience, and other prerequisites to employment or placement in a position. (338)

Quality Graduate—College graduate who was a superior student and can be hired at a higher grade than the one to which he/she would otherwise be entitled '(338)

Quality Increase—An additional within-grade increase granted to General Schedule employees for high quality performance above that ordinarily found in the type of position concerned (531).

R

Reassignment—The change of an employee, while serving continuously within the same agency, from one position to another, without promotion or demotion. (210)

Recognition—Employer acceptance of a labor organization as authorized to negotiate, usually for all members of a bargaining unit. (711) Also, used to refer to incentive awards granted under provisions of Parts 451 and 541 of OPM Regulations, and Quality Increases granted under Part 531.

Recruitment—Process of attracting a supply of qualified eligibles for employment consideration. (332)

Reduction-in-Force (RIF)—A personnel action that may be required due to lack of work or funds, changes resulting from reorganization, downward reclassification of a position, or the need to make room for an employee with reemployment or restoration rights. Involves separating an employee from his/her present position, but does not necessarily result in separation or downgrading. (351) (See also *Tenure Groups.*)

Reemployment Priority List—Career and career-conditional employees, separated by reduction-in-force, who are identified, in priority order, for reemployment to competitive positions in the agency in the commuting area where the separations occurred. (330)

Reemployment Rights—Right of an employee to return to an agency after detail, transfer, or appointment to: (1) another Executive agency during an emergency; (2) an international organization; or (3) other statutorily covered employment, e.g., the Peace Corps. (352)

Register—A list of eligible applicants compiled in the order of their relative standing for referral to Federal jobs, after competitive civil service examination. (332, 210)

Reinstatement— Noncompetitive reemployment in the competitive service based on previous service under a career or career-conditional appointment. (315)

Removal—Separation of an employee for cause or because of continual unacceptable performance. (432, 752)

Representation—Actions and rights of the labor organization to consult and negotiate with management on behalf of the bargaining unit and represent employees in the unit. (711)

Representation Election—Election conducted to determine whether the employees in an appropriate unit (See *Bargaining Unit*) desire a labor organization to act as their exclusive representative. (711)

Reprimand—An official rebuke of an employee. Normally in writing and placed in the temporary side of an employee's OPF-(751)

"Reserved Rights Doctrine"—Specific functions delegated to management by Title VII of CSRA that protect management's ability to perform its necessary functions and duties. (See Management Rights.) Delegates to management specific functions not subject to negotiation except as to procedures and impact. (711)

Resignation—A separation, prior to retirement, in response to an employee's request for the action. It is a voluntary expression of the employee's desire to leave the organization and must not be demanded as an alternative to some other action to be taken or withheld. (715)

Restoration Rights—Employees who enter military service or sustain a compensable job-related injury or disability are entitled to be restored to the same or higher employment status held prior to their absence. (353)

Retention Preference—The relative standing of employees competing in a reduction-inforce. Their standing is determined by veteran's preference, tenure group, length of service, and performance appraisal. (351)

Retention Register—A list of all employees, arranged by competitive level, describing their retention preference during reductions-in-force. (351)

Retirement—Payment of an annuity after separation from a position under the Civil Service Retirement System and based on meeting age and length of service requirements. The types of retirement are:
> *Deferred* - An employee with five years civilian service who separates or transfers to a position not under the Retirement Act, may receive an annuity, does not withdraw from the Retirement Fund. (.83:1)
> *Disability* - An immediate annuity paid to an employee under the retirement system who has completed five years of civilian service and has suffered a mental, emotional, or physical disability not the result of the employee's vicious habits, intemperance, or willful misconduct, (831)
> *Discontinued Service* - An immediate annuity paid to an employee who is involuntarily separated, through no personal fault of the employee, after age 50 and 20 years of service, or at any age with 25 years of service. This annuity is reduced by 1/6 of one percent for each full month under age 55 (two percent per year). (831)
> *Optional* - The minimum combinations of age and service for this kind of immediate annuity are: age 62 with five years of service; age 60 with 20 years of service; age 55 with 30 years of service. (831)

Review, Classification—An official written request for reclassification of a position. Previously called a classification appeal.

S

Schedules A, B, and C—Categories of positions excepted from the competitive service by regulation. (213)
> *Schedule A*—Positions other than confidential or policy determining, for which it is not practical to examine.
> *Schedule B*— Positions other than confidential or policy determining for which it is not practical to hold a competitive examination.
> *Schedule C*—Positions of a confidential or policy determining character.

Senior Executive Service—A separate personnel system for persons who set policy and administer programs at the top levels of the Government (equivalent to GS-16 through Executive Level IV). (920)

Service Computation Date-Leave—The date, either actual or adjusted, from which service credit is accumulated for determining the rate of leave accrual; it may be different from the service computation date, which determines relative standing in a subgroup for reduction-in-force, or service computation date for retirement. (296)

Service Record Card (Standard Form 7)—A brief of the employee's service history. It is kept on file in accordance with agency disposition instructions. (295)

Special Salary Rates—Salary rates higher than regular statutory schedule; established for occupations in which private enterprise pays substantially more than the regular Federal Schedule. (530)

Spoils System—The personnel system characterized by the political appointment and removal of employees without regard to merit. (212)

Staffing—Use of available and projected personnel through recruitment, appointment, reassignment, promotion, reduction-in-force, etc., to provide the work force required to fulfill the agency's mission. (250)

Standard Form—171 ("Personal Qualification Statement") Used in applying for a Federal position through a competitive examination. (295)

Standards of Conduct For Labor Organization—In the Federal sector, a code governing internal democratic practices and fiscal responsibility, and procedures to which a labor organization must adhere to be eligible to receive any recognition. (711)

Steward (Union Steward)—A local union's representative in a plant or department, appointed by the union to carry out union duties, adjust grievances, collect dues and solicit new members. Stewards are employees trained by the union to carry out their duties.

Strike—Temporary stoppage of work by a group of employees to express a grievance, enforce a demand for changes in conditions of employment, obtain recognition, or resolve a dispute with management. *Wildcat strike-* a strike not sanctioned by union and which may violate a collective agreement. *Quickie strike-* a spontaneous or unannounced strike of short duration. *Slowdown-a* deliberate reduction of output without an actual strike in order to force concessions from *an* employer. *Walkout* -same as strike. Strikes are illegal for Federal employees. (711)

Suitability—An applicant's or employee's fitness for Federal employment as indicated by character and conduct. (731)

Supervisor—An individual employed by an agency having authority, in the interest of the agency, to hire, direct, assign, promote, reward, transfer, furlough, lay off, recall, suspend, discipline-or remove employees, to adjust their grievances, or to effectively recommend such action-if the exercise of the authority is not merely routine or clerical in nature but requires the consistent exercise of independent judgment. With respect to any unit which includes firefighters or nurses, the term "supervisor" includes only those individuals who devote a preponderance of their employment time to exercising such authority. (711).

Survey, Classification—An intensive study of all positions in an organization or organizational segment to insure their correct classification.

Suspension—Placing an employee, for disciplinary reasons, in a temporary status without duties and pay. (751, 752)

T

Tenure—The time an employee may reasonably expect to serve under a current appointment. It is governed by the type of appointment, without regard to whether the employee has competitive status. (210)

Tenure Groups—Categories of employees ranked in priority order for retention during reduction in force . Within each group, veterans are ranked above nonveterans. For the competitive service, the tenure groups are, in descending order:
    Group I—Employees under career appointments and not serving probation.
    Group II—Employees serving probation, career-conditional employees, and career employees in obligated positions.
    Group III—Employees with indefinite appointments, status quo employees under any other nonstatus, nontemporary appointment. (351)
    For the *excepted service,* they are in descending order:
    Group I—*Permanent* employees, not serving a trial period, whose appointments carry no restriction or condition, such as "indefinite" or "time-limited".
    Group II—Employees serving trial periods, those whose tenure is indefinite because they occupy obligated positions, and those whose tenure is equivalent to career-conditional in the competitive service.
    Group III—Employees whose tenure is indefinite, but not potentially permanent, and temporary employees who have completed one year of current continuous employment. (351)

Tenure Subgroups—The ranking of veterans above nonveterans in each tenure group, as follows:
>*Subgroup AD*—Veterans with service-connected disability of 30% or more.
>*Subgroup A*— All other veterans
>*Subgroup B*—Nonveterans

Time-in-Grade Restriction—A requirement intended to prevent excessively rapid promotions in the General Schedule. Generally, an employee may not be promoted more than two grades within one year to positions up to GS-5. At GS-5 and above, an employee must serve a minimum of one year in grade, and cannot be promoted more than one grade, or two grades if that is the normal progression. (300)

Tour of Duty—The hours of a day (a daily tour of duty) and the day of an administrative workweek (weekly tour of duty) scheduled in advance and during which an employee is required to work regularly. (610)

Training—Formal instruction or controlled and planned exposure to learning. (410)

Transfer—A change of an employee, without a break in service of one full workday, from a position in one agency to a position in another agency. (315)

Transfer of Function—For reduction-in-force, the transfer of a continuing function from one agency or competitive area to another, or when the competitive area in which work is performed is moved to another commuting area. (315)

U

Unemployment Compensation—Income maintenance payments to former Federal employees who: (1) are unemployed; (2) file a claim at a local employment office for unemployment compensation; and (3) register for work assignment. The program is administered through state and D.C. employment service offices, which determine eligibility and make the payments. (850)

Unfair Labor Practices—Prohibited actions by agency management and labor organizations. (711)

Union—See *Labor Organization.*

Upward Mobility—Systematic career development requiring competitive selection in positions that provide experience and training leading to future assignments in other, more responsible positions.(410)

V

Veteran—A person entitled to preference under 5 USC 2108, including a spouse, widow, widower, or mother entitled to preference under the law. (211)

Voucher—In staffing terms, a formal inquiry to employers, references, professors, and others who presumably know a job applicant well enough to describe job qualifications and personal character. (337)

W

Wage Employees—Those employees-in trades, crafts, or labor occupations covered by the Federal Wage System, whose pay is fixed and adjusted periodically in accordance with prevailing rates. (532)

Within-Grade Increase—A salary increase provided in certain Government pay plans based upon time-in-grade and acceptable or satisfactory work performance. Also known as "periodic increase" or "step increase." (531)

NOTE:

Numbers in parentheses after the definitions refer to the appropriate FEDERAL PERSONNEL MANUAL (FPM) Chapter indicated.

www.ingramcontent.com/pod-product-compliance
Lightning Source LLC
Chambersburg PA
CBHW060327240426
43665CB00047B/2691